# the
# confident
# indie

A Simple Guide to
Deductions, Income and Taxes
For The Creatively Self-employed

By
JUNE WALKER

*Publisher:*
*Indie Power Media*
*Santa Fe, New Mexico*
*editor@indie-power-media.com*
*877.666.5144*

*ISBN 978-1-939470-01-0 paper*
*ISBN 978-1-939470-02-7 ePub*
*ISBN 978-1-939470-00-3 Kindle*

*Cover Design: Frances White*
*Book Design: June Walker*
*Editor: Warren Sloat*
*Technical Advisor: Mindshare Studios*
*Production Coordinator: Mindshare Studios*

*June Walker*
*Santa Fe, New Mexico*
*http://junewalkeronline.com/*
*indie@junewalkeronline.com*
*505.466.8317*

To my guy, Warren Sloat

# TABLE OF CONTENTS

# ABOUT THE CONFIDENT INDIE

Since my first book was published in 2005, the indie scene has changed.

Back then hardly anyone knew what an app was. Now apps are reaching tens of millions of users within weeks. In 2006 smartphones accounted for 6% of mobile phone sales. Now, according to Technology Review[1], "smartphones represent more than two-thirds of all US mobile phone sales."

All across the country smartphones and tablets are replacing televisions, computers, CD and DVD players, and are being used for driving directions, appointment reminders and just about everything else. The binder notebook will eventually be to the techno-home-office what candles are to electricity.

Digital devices have changed the culture of work, especially for those who work at home. Working at home is no longer a stigma, technologically it's easier, and we indies like it much better than the corporate cubicle.

In 2009, when my second edition was published, there were 33 million self-employed Americans, or about 23 percent of the workforce. Now there are 41 million, or about 29 percent. These are federal statistics from the Small Business and Self-employed Operating Division of the IRS[2], as such they lag a couple of years behind the times. That means there are even more of us than the numbers show.

What's happening? Some analysts attribute the trend to the amazing new technology. Others contend that the chief cause is the unfavorable job market – that it's easier to freelance than to find employment. However, a survey of 900 self-employed people by Kelly Services, Inc.[3], found that nine out of ten said they were not forced by circumstances but voluntarily chose self-employment. Well, it's clear to anyone who works with indies (as I do every day) that the driving force is independence and an urge to develop creativity to the maximum. And that ***creativity inheres in, guides and drives not only independent artists but every indie***. Anyone who works as a solo must be creative, must wear many hats, must be able to work out situations ranging from marketing to office furniture arrangement, to hardware purchase and set-up, to recordkeeping and taxes. Just fitting them all in, regardless of the indie profession, takes a mastermind in creativity.

But the urge to stay independent and develop one's creativity is not enough. In order to succeed in the 21st century business milieu of self-employment, indies have to enter it well-prepared for a work culture that differs drastically from the corporate life that they may have come from, or that surrounds them – although perhaps not for long – and that continues to determine the tax and financial regulations that indies must follow. That's right. While the technology is advancing and the economy changes, the US tax system is still mired in the last century. The IRS still behaves as though almost all of the working population consists of employees.

Having worked with independent professionals for more than 25 years, I know how much help they need with the business side of their ventures. I know how to guide them so they can make a tax system – that isn't constructed or administered with them in mind – work for them. My publications, my website and blog are aimed at providing that help. You may visit my website at http://junewalkeronline.com/.

Since I first began in the 1980s to lead workshops and then later to write a column for an online magazine for indies, I have received thousands of comments, many applauding the clarity and simplicity of my information and advice. Highly gratifying to me because this is my goal as a writer and as a speaker. And although I hadn't intended to write or speak inspirational prose, many indies have let me know that my work has not just informed and guided them, but has also instilled in them the unexpected extra of confidence. It has enabled them to approach self-employment issues with poise, ready with the knowledge to ask the right questions and able to judge the accuracy of the answers they get. Here's what some indies have said about my earlier books and seminars.

"She is passionate about providing reliable and understandable information (to the self-employed) about taxes and the IRS." (Southwest Book Views)

"All the tax myths I had heard about being an individual in business were suddenly cleared up by June Walker using lots of easy to understand, real life examples." (Paul D. Gregg from Palo Alto, California)

"I find it to be just the resource I was looking for. Your writing style makes it down-to-earth and easy to understand." (Jason Kuchnicki, rock climber and ski descent guidebook writer from Carson City, Nevada)

"I own your book and found that it brought me hope about continuing to stay self-employed. It made taxes seem more approachable as I face them with increasing dread each year. Thank you." (Trista Hill, Professional musician, teacher ... Delaware, Ohio)

"For someone like myself who just left his W2 position with a lot in his savings account and a dream, your book gave me the confidence to trust that I had made the right decision." (Morgan Moore, employee turned indie, Rancho Cordova, California)

And so the birth of "The Confident Indie."

**THE CONFIDENT INDIE** contains much of the information, updated, revised and added to, that appeared in my previous books and blogs.

Some indies found my earlier book "entertaining" and "fun" – unusual appraisals of a book on taxes. I was surprised by some who said the book "reads like a novel" and is "funny." I thought of it instead as a group of very-short stories; the humor, when it comes up, springs from my well-founded skepticism about and irreverence toward the supposed wisdom of the mahogany-office accountants.

So, too, with **THE CONFIDENT INDIE**. Upon reading it you will be armed with an understanding of the basics of self-employment and will develop the confidence to move forward with assurance in your independent endeavor. You will walk a clear path toward becoming a "confident indie."

I wish you much success in your self-employed venture.

*June Walker*

June Walker
Santa Fe, New Mexico

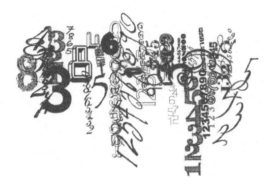

# INTRODUCTION

Whether you are an ...

Artist

Antiques Dealer

Systems Analyst

Landscape Architect

Personal Trainer

Musician

Midwife

Writer

Blogger

Oil and Gas Landman

Design Engineer

Graphic Designer

Psychologist

Yacht Broker

Investment Counselor

Multimedia Producer

Carpenter

Website Developer

Exotic Dancer

Solo performer on the stage or in the business world ...

*... each of you is unique.*

Yet despite your uniqueness you all have one thing in common –

*you are all self-employed!*

You may call yourself by another name – sole proprietor, freelancer, indie, subcontractor, free agent, independent professional – but to the taxing authorities all these descriptions mean the same thing. And the taxing authorities require all of you, no matter what you call yourselves, to follow the same rules.

Self-employment has grown to about 30 percent of the workforce. The biggest factor in the vast increase is the one-person show, the independent professional – the indie.

Despite your growing numbers, the tax laws are written without you in mind. And as for your needs, the mahogany-office accountants don't have a clue. So often an indie staggers out of a tax meeting, eyes glazed and mind a jumble of irrelevant and often incorrect advice.

You deserve better. You are (with a few exceptions) talented and spirited people, motivated and deeply interested in your work – bright, intuitive people whose talents probably outweigh your practical sense. But where do you find that practical know-how on business deductions, business losses, hobby versus business, what's income and what is not, reimbursements, recordkeeping requirements, estimated taxes. *Where do you go for the basics?*

You can not succeed as a solo in business if you don't understand tax fundamentals. That's why I never cease to be puzzled by the huge volume of advice for indies offered as webinars or at conferences, in books or as private consultation, on marketing, time-management, work-space wellness, pricing, and social media for business. You are exhorted by motivational speakers to get that entrepreneurial spirit and master self-discipline. But when it comes to taxes they tell you to "keep good business records" and they provide a list of tax payment due dates. Instead of telling you how to keep your tax bill low or even whether you can deduct your trip to Grandma's as a business expense, they make hostile remarks about the IRS, and then go on to the next subject – like the importance of ergonomically correct desk chairs or how to pace your day.

Let's face the hard facts. You can choose the wrong office furniture and survive. An uncultivated phone manner may lose a customer, but it's not the difference between life and death for a freelancer. An episode of fear and loss of confidence may do some harm, but you'll get another chance. Taxes are different. If you don't understand them and you gum up the works, you will find that getting the gum out is expensive, time-consuming, and worrisome. The remedies include paying interest and penalties to Uncle Sam, hiring a professional, going through the anxiety of an audit – and time away from your business. Such complications could prove fatal to your enterprise. It's a lot more serious than not knowing how to use your iPad at a product presentation.

I'm not saying that the offerings of information about self-employment are trivial. Many are important. Most are useful. But they ignore an essential: Tax know-how. And when tax information is offered it is either too highly technical or presented in a Taxes-Lite style that never gets beyond surface information.

**THE CONFIDENT INDIE** is written for smart solos who don't know much about the tax rules and even less about how to make the rules work for them – but want to learn because they know that understanding taxes and learning the foundations of recordkeeping are indispensable to making it in the unforgiving world of self-employment. In a career based on advising self-employed people I have found that ***you've got to know the basics***.

With **THE CONFIDENT INDIE** you will learn the basics.


## I AM SELF-EMPLOYED, TOO

For more than twenty-five years I've been an accountant and tax advisor with an unusual clientele made up entirely of self-employed people. Many of them are in the arts and creativity runs like an electric current through almost all my clients regardless of profession. Each made a conscious choice for self-employment in order to express that creativity. Some of them can't earn enough as inventors, or musicians, to support themselves and their family, so augment their income with other indie ventures – like a dog-walking business or selling health care products.

At one time I had offices in New York and New Jersey. Now I live in glorious Santa Fe, New Mexico, while my clients are scattered all over the States, in Europe and the Middle East. Most have been with me for many years. And although it is a rarity there are a few I've never actually met face to face – a former **New York Times** staff reporter who still works for the paper on special assignment; or those I seldom see – a South African opera singer who now performs in Europe. We communicate electronically.

I'm in Santa Fe and so have tried telepathic communication but I think the subject of taxes can't get through the spiritual shield.

My style suits the kinds of people that I advise. I have written for many publications about finances and taxes with an emphasis on self-employment and on the tax problems of people in the arts.

In my writing and seminars I focus on fostering in the self-employed the same mastery in business matters that they possess in their creative and professional pursuits.

I maintain a deep respect for the talent, intelligence and creativity of those who have struck out on their own. My responsibility to my clients has always been to be clear and coherent in steering them past the obstacles that lie on the financial path of their chosen professions. Dealing with an atypical and spirited clientele has forced me to innovate with approaches centered on their particular needs.

In that way my perspective differs from that of other accountants – I don't expect the creative mind to think linearly even in its approach to business and taxes. I can't play the banjo, build furniture, analyze a security system, teach yoga or create an app. I don't expect a poet to do accounting and I hope she doesn't expect me to write a sonnet.

Each time that I meet with a client I want him to understand more about his finances than he did the meeting before. Whether plotting tax strategy, gathering information for tax return preparation or budgeting for irregular income, I guide my client so that he can do as much of the preliminary work as possible himself. The client who does the preliminary work on his own not only saves accountant fees but also enhances his own financial awareness.

By adjusting a financial procedure to fit my client's preferred method of recordkeeping, I get orthodox results via an unorthodox route. My role is part accountant, part guide and part teacher. I neither talk down to my clients nor confuse them. I make complicated things simple and understandable.

In **THE CONFIDENT INDIE** I will teach you how to develop an indie power mindset, a deeply ingrained way of thinking about your business life as a self-employed.

## IS THE CONFIDENT INDIE FOR YOU?

*Yes,* if you are:
- self-employed.
- not sure whether you're self-employed.
- just starting out.
- juggling both a regular job and a self-employed venture.
- planning to freelance in the future.
- already the sole proprietor of an established business.

Or if you:
- are confused about business expenses.
- are not satisfied with your recordkeeping method.
- already have an accountant.
- have never met with an accountant.
- have never met with an accountant you understood.
- have never met with an accountant who understood you.

Or simply if:
- you avoid even thinking about taxes or recordkeeping.
- you want to overcome your tax-time terror.
- you just happen to enjoy reading about taxes and money.

*Yes,* if you earn:
- $5,000 a year
- $50,000 a year
- $500,000 a year

Amount of income, even absence of income, does not limit the beneficial impact of **THE CONFIDENT INDIE.**

*Yes*, if you're full-time self-employed, just starting out, been at it for a decade, moonlighting, making a big profit, or losing money by the basketful.

*Yes*, if you're single, married, with kids, or supporting your parents.

*Yes*, if your time is limited. When you're in your own business and holding down another job or beset with family responsibilities, time is at a premium. You want to put all your energies into getting customers, making your product, or marketing your service. You do not want to lose productive time struggling with understanding income, expenses and taxes.

If you're reading this book there's a good chance you are teetering on a weak foundation due to a lack of understanding of the business side of your indie venture. Perhaps you're paying too much in taxes or hiding your income to avoid taxes. Maybe you're not keeping records, or you're keeping the wrong ones, or you don't know what to do with the records you do keep. If you need to build that basic foundation, and develop your indie confidence so that you can easily keep your tax bill as low as legitimately possible, **THE CONFIDENT INDIE** is for you.

## WHAT CAN *THE CONFIDENT INDIE* DO FOR YOU?

- It will simplify your business life.
- The blurry boundary between what is personal and what is business will become clearer.
- You will begin to understand the tax consequences of your business decisions.
- You will know what is (and what is not) a business deduction.
- No matter what your level of tax and recordkeeping sophistication **THE CONFIDENT INDIE** will benefit you. It will provide the *basic* foundation for *all* your tax transactions.

### This Is A Guide Book

In these pages I will show you, in the most simple way, how to miss not one single business deduction and, therefore, how to pay the least tax legitimately possible.

In **PART V** you will get a full explanation of taxes. You will learn how your estimated tax payments can be calculated, when to pay which taxes and what happens if you don't or can't pay a tax when it is due.

This is *not* a handbook on starting a business.

This is *not* a tax preparation manual.

This is *not* a recordkeeping instruction book.

This is *not* everything you need to know about indie finances.

It is a book of basics – understanding self-employed status, income, expenses, how to make timely tax payments, and the foundation of recordkeeping. Just as you shouldn't attempt the high dive before you know how to swim, neither should you attempt to hire employees or establish a pension or decide on which bookkeeping method will work for you until you understand the basics.

**THE CONFIDENT INDIE** provides you with a foundation in recordkeeping. It is not a recordkeeping how-to instruction guide. That instruction, for either manual or digital recordkeeping, is given in my companion publication, the revised **Five Easy Steps**. In it you will learn the **Most Simple System**, a quick, easy, accurate and foolproof method of recordkeeping of my own devising. If you adopt it, you will never miss a tax deduction and you will be armed with solid backup in case you are ever audited. Here, in **THE CONFIDENT INDIE**, you will get the basics you need to make **Five Easy Steps** work smoothly, quickly and to your tax advantage. Please note that any worksheets mentioned in this book are among those available in **Five Easy Steps**.

If you have a tax professional who prepares your tax return you still need the guidance and how-to instruction of **THE CONFIDENT INDIE** which will give you the sure-footedness to stride into your accountant's or tax practitioner's office confident that you understand your business finances.

I have presented the information in **THE CONFIDENT INDIE** to many people. When it's one-on-one to a client I'm invariably told that "no one has ever before made it so easy to understand." And, when I've presented it to groups at seminars I've often drawn applause at the end of the workshop – no small feat when you're talking taxes. The applause conveyed to me that the audiences – for the first time – realized that they could make the tax laws work for them without devoting a big chunk of their waking hours to the effort. One writer in attendance said, "I knew there had to be some way to save taxes but nobody before had ever told me how to do it without a whole lot of time, sweat and accountant fees." He said he didn't know anything about money but he understood every word I said. So will you.

You, too, will find the explanations simple and easy to understand. You will have the confidence of firm footing as you find your way through the tax maze.

## How to Use This Book

If I know my readers you will not start at page one and read straight through to the end of this book but will skip around looking for what interests you. I'm sure if you're really curious or baffled by, let's say, OFFICE-IN-THE-HOME, then you'll jump to that section of the book. So here are some hints to help you get the most out of your hopping, skipping and jumping:

In order to know what it takes to be regarded as a self-employed in the eyes of the IRS (and to have the confidence of regarding yourself as one) read straight through to the end of CHAPTER 3. HOBBY OR BUSINESS? FOR FUN OR PROFIT? Then, if you like, start skipping.

Subjects may be covered more than once at different places, for different reasons.

This is a reference book. Refer to it often.

---

### WHATTA CONCEPT!

From time to time throughout the book it will be necessary to explain some tax concept to you so that the material that follows makes sense. Each will be noted this way.

---

### REALITY √ CHECK

There are lots of examples, some fictional – such as, Caitlin Caterer and Lily Legal – and some actual IRS cases. Both provide concrete examples of abstract theories and principles. Some of these examples are **REALITY √ CHECKS**.

---

About the fictional names: Yes, I know that they are often corny. But many of them are based on actual situations of real indies, and I don't have to explain why I can't use their real names. So I use names that indicate their professions. There are lots of them, and the names – like Syd System (the tech consultant and information architect) and Billy Bridesnapper (the wedding photographer) are a mnemonic device to help you understand and remember a complex tax situation. Some are alliterative and some more referential, like P.R. Bernays (the public relations guy) and Miles Mingus (the musician). Sammy Segar is my depiction of the clueless CPA who doesn't understand the first thing about the indie business world.

---

### THE IRS SAYS ABOUT ...

In these boxes I present the exact IRS wording on the topic under discussion.

---

---

**ALERT!**

In here I'll place a warning that there's something out of the ordinary that you need to store in your memory bank.

---

If an idea initially seems weird to you, please be patient, read on. Many of you will have read or been told other ways to view a tax situation or given other procedures for determining the business merits of a deduction. Those ways haven't worked or you wouldn't be reading this book. This is not the method that the mahogany-office accountants will tell you about. It is not the approach to understanding indie taxes and recordkeeping that any book I've read or lecture I've attended has ever suggested. ***But it works!***

### And of Course The Caveat

Things change. Tax law modifications were in the works as I wrote these pages and are ongoing as you read this. Before you make a major decision ask questions; check with your tax advisor; be aware.

I welcome all comments, questions and suggestions. Please send them to editor@indie-power-media.com or indie@junewalkeronline.com or go directly to **THE CONFIDENT INDIE** on my website at http://junewalkeronline.com/confidence-comments/.

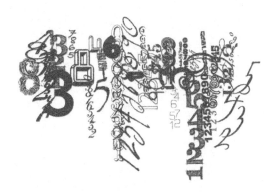

# PART I: SELF-EMPLOYED - WHAT DOES THAT MEAN?

*You* say you're self-employed. But will the IRS?

The journey through the maze of tax rules governing the self-employed must be sure-footed; you've got to have the confident stride of someone who not only considers himself self-employed but can prove his self-employed status to the IRS. In the introduction I noted that the self-employed go by various names – freelancers, sole proprietors, free agents, indies, solos, subs. The IRS, however, classifies all of us by one official title: **independent contractor**.

To determine independent contractor status the IRS looks at two conditions:

1. Are you really self-employed or are you an employee?

   and

2. Are you running a business or is it a hobby?

You need to establish that you are *both* self-employed *and* engaged in a business in order to qualify as an independent contractor for tax purposes.

The IRS has set down a number of guidelines and requirements for being classified as a self-employed in business. But before looking at those guidelines and requirements, I want to go over with you the difference between pay received by an employee and that received by a self-employed, and the tax consequences of each kind of payment.

## CHAPTER 1: W-2 OR 1099: IT'S A MATTER OF FORM

### What is the difference between pay received by an employee and that received by a self-employed?

A new client of mine said upon our first meeting that he hadn't yet decided how he would treat the income he had earned for the year so far – as self-employed income or not. I had to tell him, sorry, but if the income has already been earned then it's too late – most likely that decision has already been made for you!

Often those who work part-time or fill in for staff shortages aren't sure under which basis they are working – as employees or independent contractors. There are times when a person gets called to a job, gets paid, and never thinks about whether he's self-employed or not. Income is income, right? Not so when tax-time rolls around. The amount you have to hand over to Uncle Sam will depend upon whether you were paid as an employee or as a self-employed.

---

**WHATTA CONCEPT!**

**A View of Income**

You sold your car; won the lottery; the boss gave you a raise; the stock Dad gave you just hit the roof and you sold it. There are all kinds of income – some of it taxable, some not. In tax jargon there's a classification for every kind of income. Problem is, the classification may change depending upon the circumstances. For instance, grants and scholarships are sometimes considered earned income, but sometimes not. Tax-free interest and dividends although not taxable may be included as income for certain calculations.

---

For our purposes let's use the following income definition: **Earned income is payment for services performed.** It is money or goods that you receive in the form of salary, wages, professional fees, tips, etc. for work that you do. Earned income is not money or things you receive for reasons other than work. For instance, earned income is not a gift from Grandma, nor unemployment compensation, nor dividend income, nor insurance proceeds.

THE CONFIDENT INDIE
PART I: SELF-EMPLOYED - WHAT DOES THAT MEAN?

3

There are only two types of earned income:
1. W-2 earnings

and

2. Self-employed income

Let's see how to tell the difference between the two.

Rick Reporter writes a feature story not assigned by his editor about sailing and contaminated waterways. The editor thinks it's a good take on the environment and publishes it in the newspaper's Sunday supplement. Rick is paid $1,000 for this feature. In his next paycheck the $1,000 payment is added to his regular weekly salary. Taxes were withheld. *That $1,000 is W-2 earnings.*

Rick then decides to send the same piece to the Better Bayou Blog funded by an environmental philanthropist. The blog accepts Rick's piece virtually unchanged and will also pay him $1,000. A month after publication Rick receives a $1,000 check from the blog. No taxes were withheld. *That $1,000 is self-employed income.*

Simply stated: *If taxes are withheld it's W-2 income; and if no taxes are withheld it's self-employed income.*

From the two publications, Rick earned the same amount of money for the same piece of work; however, he generated two different types of earned income.

It is important to understand the distinction and to keep them separate in your records. Why? Because they are treated differently on your tax return and the tax you pay on each is not the same.

**W-2 income** is referred to as salary, wages, paycheck, take-home pay, or regular income. Those who earn W-2 income are called employees. I call them "W-2 people." At the end of the year W-2 people receive a Form W-2[4] from their employers stating income and withholdings for the year. The government also receives a copy of the W-2.

**Self-employed income** can be called anything from commissions, fees, royalties, stipends, or freelance income. Self-employed people are dubbed freelancers, consultants, sole proprietors, indies, sub-contractors, or just gutsy. Self-employed income is not under-the-table, off-the-books, or paid-in-the-parking-lot income. (More on that later.)

THE CONFIDENT INDIE
PART I: SELF-EMPLOYED - WHAT DOES THAT MEAN?

4

If a self-employed is paid $600 or more in one year by an individual or corporation then that individual or corporation should send the self-employed a federal Form 1099-MISC[5] at the end of the year stating "nonemployee compensation" paid. The government is also sent a copy of the form. Even if the self-employed receives no 1099 – because his earnings were less than $600 or the payer neglected to send it – the income is still taxable and must be claimed on his tax return.

## HOW DO W-2 EARNINGS COMPARE TO SELF-EMPLOYED INCOME?

Astrid Astrologer's *gross income is $20,000* a year as a self-employed. She has a neighbor whose *total wages are $20,000* a year as a supermarket employee.

Let's look at how the *same* income amounts compare from the perspective of **take-home pay** for the employee and **net income** for the self-employed. They are not alike!

### Take-home Pay

W-2 people often refer to the money they receive on payday as take-home pay. Take-home pay is important because it's what the W-2 person lives on until his next paycheck. The amount he takes home is considerably less than his gross wages or actual salary.

From gross wages some of the following payroll deductions must and others may be withheld by the employer:

- Federal income tax
- FICA (Social Security Tax)
- Medicare tax
- State income tax
- City or local income tax
- State unemployment insurance
- State disability insurance
- United Way Contributions
- Pension Contributions
- Savings Plan Deductions
- Medical Insurance
- Pre-tax Childcare Costs

THE CONFIDENT INDIE
PART I: SELF-EMPLOYED - WHAT DOES THAT MEAN?

5

### *For W-2 people:*
**Gross Wages** minus **Deductions** equals **Take-Home Pay**

Rick Reporter, who made $1,000 extra for the piece in his paper's Sunday supplement, did not take home an additional $1,000. Deductions probably reduced it to about $600 in take-home pay.

Keep in mind:
- A W-2 person's income tax is calculated on gross wages.
- With his take-home pay he buys food, pays the rent, plays the slots at the casinos. But he doesn't make the tax payments on it: his employer has already withheld the tax and sent it on its way to Uncle Sam and the state tax folks.
- When a bank loan officer asks a W-2 person to state his income, the banker is asking about ***gross wages.***

### Net Income
Net income is the amount a self-employed has left after subtracting his business expenses from his gross self-employed income.

Rick Reporter did receive a check for the full amount of $1,000 from the Better Bayou Blog. His only expense was a $20 express mail fee. Look at it this way:

|  | | |
|---:|---:|:---|
| | $1,000 | **gross self-employed income** |
| minus | $   20 | expenses |
| equals balance of | $ 980 | **net self-employed income** |

### *For Self-employed people:*
**Gross Self-employed Income** minus **Self-employed Expenses**
equals **Net Self-employed Income**

Keep in mind:
- For a self-employed, income tax is calculated on his net income.
- With his net income he buys food, pays the rent, goes to the theater – ***and*** pays taxes.
- When a bank loan officer asks a self-employed to state his income, the banker is asking about **net income.**

THE CONFIDENT INDIE
PART I: SELF-EMPLOYED - WHAT DOES THAT MEAN?

6

You'll learn more about income in **PART III** .

Now that you understand what distinguishes W-2 income from self-employed income you may think that you have it all figured out. Have someone pay you and withhold no taxes and KAZAM!! – you're an independent contractor. Oh, if only it were that easy! For as I'll show you in the next chapter: ***It is not the method by which one is paid but the nature of the business relationship that determines whether or not one is self-employed.***

## CHAPTER 2: IT'S ALL ABOUT RELATIONSHIPS
## What determines employee or self-employed status?

Many business relationships are straightforward and clear-cut. A fifth-grade teacher in the city school system is unquestionably an employee. If that same teacher tutors children on weekends and during the summer, in his home, with his materials, in the subjects he chooses – not out of the goodness of his heart but to earn enough to build an addition to his home – then tutoring is a self-employed endeavor.

However, in some work circumstances the lines get blurry. What if the school supplied the teacher with all the materials? What if the school scheduled the students' tutoring sessions? What if the students paid the school and then the school paid the teacher?

Or suppose Syd System, a software developer, leaves his job at the Callous Company, and then completes a project for the company for a flat fee? Is he truly self-employed or actually still an employee? And what if five years after leaving the company he is operating his own business but has always had and still has only one client – the Callous Company?

Employee? Self-employed? With both the teacher and the software developer the blurriness is real. However, in other cases the issue is deliberately obscured in order to save the business owner time, money and paperwork.

---

### REALITY √ CHECK

Ebenezer Ebay, although still working out of his home, can no longer handle all the business himself. But Eb is reluctant to take on the added hassle of payroll, withholding taxes, insurance and pension requirements, and the periodic reports required when a business has employees. So when he hires Peter Packer to come in five days a week, he has Peter sign a contract saying that he is an independent contractor. Believing that the contract is all that he needs to establish their relationship, he pays Peter as a ***consultant***. But anyone who examines the nature of their relationship would conclude that Ebenezer is an employer and Peter is an employee.

---

This contrivance of phony self-employment doesn't come up only in the nation's mom-and-pop-shops.

The largest case up to the present involved Microsoft. The IRS ruled that many of the people working at the company had been wrongly classified as independent contractors. They worked the same hours as other workers who were designated as employees, performed the same functions and reported to the same supervisors. As far as the IRS was concerned they were employees – despite words written in a contract – because Microsoft controlled the "manner and means" of their work. Microsoft and the workers had an employer-employee relationship – and it's the relationship that counts.

The IRS decision followed a lawsuit which ended in a $97 million settlement[6]. Workers at Microsoft, classified as non-employees, sued the company because they had been denied pension benefits and the right to purchase company stock at an employee discount. The 8,500 "permatemps," as they called themselves, received their share of a settlement agreement in 2005, and the individual payments (which ranged from $115 to $51,000) were classified as taxable income.

Time Warner, SmithKline Beecham, and the City of Fresno, California, among others, have also been involved in "permatemp" disputes.

As one of the attorneys for the plaintiffs in the Microsoft suit stated: "For those companies who haven't changed their policies, this settlement sends a message that it could be very expensive not to change."[7]

The same applies to indies who hire workers.

If Peter Packer, like so many misclassified workers, is an employee, then he and his employer, Ebenezer, need to face up to it and not stretch and squeeze the criteria to make his status look like that of a self-employed.

As the IRS goes looking for tax money that has been slipping between the cracks – whether through legitimate cracks or man-made fissures – it has been reclassifying many independents as employees.

The consequences of misclassification can be severe. If the IRS reclassifies independent contractors as employees, back payroll taxes and penalties can hit the employer hard.

The former independent, now classified as an employee, must file his tax return as an employee and may lose many of his business deductions or, if the deductions remain applicable to his new employee status, they must be moved from the self-employed section of his tax return to the employee section where their tax-reduction value dwindles. The reclassification could also eliminate his health insurance deduction and force him to give up his self-employed pension.

Beware of some old husbands' tales out there that say you're considered self-employed if:

- You have a contract.
- You're paid on commission.
- You have a business bank account.
- You work sporadically or part time.
- You work for more than one person.

None of these is sure-fire proof of self-employment. ***Take heed: If you claim to be self-employed you must be able to prove it.***

To cover both the contrived and the honestly complicated situations, the IRS has put together a guide to help determine whether someone is an independent contractor or an employee. To make its determination the IRS has focused the criteria upon a single issue: **Control versus independence.**

Does the worker perform independently? To what degree is his work controlled? It is a question of relationship, it is a matter of degree, and it is measured in three categories:

**Behavioral control**: Who directs and controls what will be done and how it will be done?

**Financial control**: Who directs or controls the business aspects of the work?

**Type of relationship**: What facts show the type of relationship?

Let's explore a few different business relationships.

## REALITY √ CHECK

The question of independence and control gives us more perspective on the case of Syd System, the software developer who left the Callous Company but for the following five years has had only the company as a client.

As the IRS sees it, having a single client suggests that Syd is really an employee. However, there are other factors that lend credence to his claim that he is an independent contractor with a home-based business:

He is paid an agreed-upon price for a job project and does not submit hourly bills; he works at home, using his own computer and other equipment; the Callous Company does not provide him with supplies; he is not required to or invited to attend staff meetings; when called to meet with company officials, the date is set at his convenience; he works no specific hours and determines his own work schedule except that he is required to deliver various phases of the work on dates set by the contract.

All these suggest that, although he works for a single client, he is a bona fide independent contractor.

## REALITY √ CHECK

Ted Tilesetter shows up for work, bringing his own tools, whenever the Confounded Construction Company calls him to a job. Sometimes he will work for five or six weeks at a time. He sets tiles in various houses in the order that the company specifies. The company supplies the materials, and pays him on a per diem basis.

Ted does not have a place of business and does not offer, advertise or promote himself to work for other construction companies. Although he cites the sporadic nature of his work as evidence of being an independent contractor he is actually a part-time employee.

---

**REALITY √ CHECK**

Lily Legal does corporate legal work for three companies, and bills them by the hour, sending invoices that itemize her work. The bills also include expenses for long-distance calls, faxes, photocopies, postage, and travel.

Does she have three jobs as a part-time employee? She claims to be an independent contractor, noting that she employs a part-time receptionist, and files a W-2 for that employee every year. She rents office space, owns her own office equipment, and pays for her membership in professional organizations as well as an online legal research service.

Although she has only three clients for which she works extensively, her relationship with them appears to be that of an independent contractor.

---

You can see that no single factor determines self-employed status. The IRS considers **all** evidence of control.

- Whether the worker is a self-employed or an employee depends primarily on the **extent** to which the individual or company receiving the service or product has the right to direct and control what the worker does and how he does it.

- The amount of instruction needed varies among different professions. Even if no instructions are given, sufficient behavioral control may exist if the person or company for which the work is done has the right to control how the work results are achieved.

- In highly specialized professions a business may lack the expertise to control the worker. That alone does not negate an employer-employee relationship.

- The greater the degree of control the more likely the worker is an employee.

- Independent contractors determine for themselves how the work is to be performed.

| WHAT'S YOUR BUSINESS RELATIONSHIP? | | |
|---|---|---|
| CATEGORY | SELF - EMPLOYED | EMPLOYEE |
| **BEHAVIORAL** **CONTROL** Who controls what is done and how it's done? | • Works how, when & where she chooses. <br><br> • Uses her own tools & equipment. <br><br> • Purchases her own tools & equipment. <br><br> • Uses her own methods. <br><br> • Chooses his own assistants. <br><br> • Decides who does which part of the work. <br><br> • Sets his own work schedule. | • Told how, when or where to work. <br><br> • Told which tools & equipment to use. <br><br> • Given or told where to purchase supplies. <br><br> • Given extensive training &/or instruction. <br><br> • Told what workers are to assist with the work. <br><br> • Told what work must be performed by a specific individual. <br><br> • Told what order or sequence to follow. |
| **FINANCIAL** **CONTROL** Who directs and controls the money? | • Pays his own business expenses except for specific costs set by contract, e.g. mileage. <br><br> • Has fixed ongoing costs regardless of whether the work is ongoing. <br><br> • Has a significant financial investment in the facilities. <br><br> • Advertises to his relevant market. <br><br> • Available to his relevant market. <br><br> • Maintains a visible business location. <br><br> • Paid by a flat fee for the project or service. <br><br> • May be paid an hourly rate, e.g. attorneys. <br><br> • Can make a profit or loss. | • Is reimbursed for expenses, although may have some nonreimbursed expenses. <br><br> • Has no fixed business costs if he has no work. <br><br> • Has no financial investment in his work facilities. <br><br> • Does not advertise his services. <br><br> • Works for one employer. <br><br> • Has no business location. <br><br> • Earns a regular wage. <br><br> • Wage or salary may be supplemented by commissions. |
| **TYPE OF RELATIONSHIP** How is the relationship between the parties perceived? | • Contract describes the relationship. <br><br> • Receives no benefits. <br><br> • Engaged for the length of contract or project. | • Job description is provided. <br><br> • Worker benefits are provided. <br><br> • Engaged permanently or indefinitely. |

The preceding table provides detailed comparison of the differences in business relationships between an independent contractor and an employee.

As far as the IRS is concerned, **if you claim to be self-employed you must be able to prove it.**

Yet even if you prove that you're self-employed, you're still only halfway through the IRS independent contractor maze. In order to treat your income as that of a self-employed on your tax return, you still must show the IRS that you're running a business not a hobby. The next chapter will show you how to do that.

THE CONFIDENT INDIE
PART I: SELF-EMPLOYED - WHAT DOES THAT MEAN?

14

## CHAPTER 3: FOR FUN OR PROFIT
### Is your endeavor a hobby or a business?

There are two conditions that must be met in order to be classified as an independent contractor by the IRS. As explained in the previous chapter, the first is establishing yourself as a self-employed rather than an employee.

The second is that you must be engaged in a business. It cannot be a hobby supported by Grandma's inheritance; it must be a real, honest-to-goodness business.

As pointed out in CHAPTER 1, there are different tax consequences for pay received by an employee and for that received by a self-employed. And, if the self-employed can show the IRS that he's running a business, not just puttering away at a hobby, the financial impact can be even more pronounced and he may end up with more money in his pocket.

---

### WHATTA CONCEPT!
#### Taxes As A Plus-Minus Formula

You receive various types of income – or "plusses." Examples: Wages; fees; commissions; pensions; savings account interest; stock sale gains; unemployment compensation; Social Security benefits; alimony received.

Various kinds of deductions – or "minuses" – reduce your income. Examples: IRA contributions; business expenses; union dues; charitable contributions; mortgage interest; alimony paid.

You subtract the minuses from the plusses. What you are left with is taxable income.

You pay tax on your income. That's why it's called income tax.
Therefore, the more minuses, the less tax you pay.

---

If your self-employed expenses are greater than your self-employed income you will have a net loss. That loss is subtracted from your other income (that is, from the part of your income that does not come from your self-employment). There are many reasons for self-employment, making money usually near the top of the list; but even losing money can be of some help – if it gets those **overall** plusses down so that you pay less tax!

If you receive $50,000 in income from Grandma's trust fund in the same year that you have a $10,000 loss in your self-employed business you get to subtract the $10,000 business loss from the $50,000 trust income. You are now looking at income of only $40,000 instead of $50,000.

However, if you lose money as a self-employed, you may deduct the loss from Grandma's trust income or from any other taxable income only if the IRS considers your self-employed activity a **business.**

Because of the two-part proof, even if you are very clearly not an employee, you must still be able to show that you are a self-employed **in business**. And the way to show that you're in business is that you must be in it to make money.

---

### THE IRS SAYS ABOUT BEING IN BUSINESS ...

In order for you to be engaged in a business rather than a hobby **the goal must be to make a profit!**

---

The IRS doesn't insist that you actually make a profit, but there must be a reasonable expectation of one. It could be either:

- A big chance of making a small profit

    or

- A small chance of making a big profit.

If the purpose of your endeavor is **not** profit, any loss you incur from it may not be a minus against other income. Said another way – your deductions are limited.

First, a look at a hobby.

THE CONFIDENT INDIE
PART I: SELF-EMPLOYED - WHAT DOES THAT MEAN?

16

---

### REALITY √ CHECK

Aunt Ada lives nicely off the income generated from her investments.

She enjoys quilting very much and every once in a while an acquaintance or relative buys something she's made. Ada keeps a hit and miss record of her expenses and does not advertise. She gives many of her quilts to her nieces.

Based on these facts, Aunt Ada has a hobby.

If Ada sells $1,000 worth of quilted pillows in a year she is allowed to deduct up to only $1,000 in quilting expenses, even if her costs were more than $1,000. Why? Because hers is a hobby, not a business.

|  | $1,000 | gross quilting income |
| minus | $1,000 | allowed expenses |
| equals | $    0 | net income |

---

Now let's look at a business.

---

### REALITY √ CHECK

Trixy Trinkets, unlike Aunt Ada, has no investments. To earn a living she must work as a W-2 person. She has a regular job as a buyer's assistant at a clothing store where she earns $60,000 a year. Evenings and weekends she designs and makes silver jewelry. She can't keep up with the requests of those who want to buy her unique pieces. So she cuts back on the hours at her job in the clothing store to devote more time to designing, creating and selling her jewelry. She's not sure how long it will take, but she's determined to leave the clothing store eventually and make a living as a jewelry designer. She was an excellent apprentice to a highly respected silversmith in her town and even helped him redesign his studio. She keeps careful records of how long it takes her to complete each piece and sets her prices by her records and the going market rate.

Based on these facts, Trixy is a self-employed jeweler. She is in business – even before she quits her regular W-2 job.

---

If Trixy sells $1,000 worth of jewelry, she may deduct as many business expenses as she incurs even if they amount to many thousands of dollars. If Trixy's net income is a loss, that loss can be deducted from her other income and could reduce her taxes.

$1,000   gross jewelry income
minus $3,000   expenses
equals - $2,000   net income

Said another way: Trixy has a $2,000 LOSS.

From her W-2 income of $60,000, she may subtract her $2,000 loss, to arrive at an earned income of $58,000.

## WHATTA CONCEPT!

What is negative income?

In accounting, subtraction and negative numbers are indicated by (parenthesis). For example, ($2,000) means negative $2,000 or subtract $2,000 or a $2,000 loss. Therefore the above example may be written as follows:

$1,000   gross jewelry income
( $3,000 )   expenses
equals  ( $2,000 )   net profit (loss)

As I said earlier: ***An activity is a business if its goal is to make a profit.***

If your activity ***always*** makes a profit, no problem – it's a business.

Or, if your activity makes a profit in ***three years out of five***, no problem – it's a business. That's because the IRS presumes it to be a business if there is a profit in three out of five ***consecutive years*** (2 out of 7 for horse breeding, training, showing or racing). The profitable years do not have to be consecutive but the five years during which they fall must be consecutive.

Let's look at two situations.

THE CONFIDENT INDIE
PART I: SELF-EMPLOYED - WHAT DOES THAT MEAN?

18

In the seven years since each started business Cheech had a profit in only three years; Chong had a profit in four years. However, in any five consecutive years Chong did not have a three year profit. By the three-out-of-five years IRS criteria, Cheech's endeavor would be considered a business, automatically. Chong would have to prove that his endeavor is a business.

| Cheech | | Chong | |
|---|---|---|---|
| **A Business**: | 2007. Loss | **Not A Business**: | 2007. **Profit** |
| | 2008. Loss | | 2008. **Profit** |
| | **2009. Profit** | | 2009. Loss |
| | **2010. Profit** | | 2010. Loss |
| | **2011. Profit** | | 2011. Loss |
| | 2012. Loss | | **2012. Profit** |
| | 2013. Loss | | **2013. Profit** |

> *Dear IRS,*
>
> *I'm self-employed and not making any money, but this is a business I'm running. Really!*
>
> *Yours truly,*
> *Irene Indie*

What if you've ***never*** made a profit? If you can't prove you're in it for the money, then the IRS says you're not a business! And, if yours is not a business then you don't get to deduct your business loss from other income. So how do you prove you're doing something to make a profit if you're not making a profit?

A number of books advise entrepreneurs that the best way is to just "show a profit." That's like telling Miles Mingus to trend on Twitter with his hit song three years out of five … or, if that doesn't happen, the mahogany-office accountant, Sammy Segar CPA, suggests that Miles forget about a lot of his expenses, pretend he made a profit and pay Uncle Sam more than is his due. ***Pretty bad advice!***

If you know that your self-employed business is going to make you rich someday (even though you've had a loss every year since you started your new venture) how do you prove to the IRS that your goal is to make a profit?

---

**THE IRS SAYS ABOUT PROVING A PROFIT MOTIVE ...**

A profit motive is indicated if you *treat your activity like a business.*

---

Just as the IRS provides guidelines for determining self-employed or employee status it also provides guidelines for determining if you're treating your activity like a business – and thereby in it for the money.

The following list will help you determine – in case you had doubts – if you're doing whatever you're doing to make a buck. No single item on the list settles or resolves the issue, nor is this a complete list used by the IRS in making a decision but these are the ones that are normally taken into account. The IRS considers **all** the facts surrounding an activity in determining if the activity is engaged in for profit.

## IF IT WALKS LIKE A BUSINESS AND TALKS LIKE A BUSINESS, IT MUST BE A BUSINESS.

1. Carry on the activity in a businesslike manner.
   - Are your books and records kept completely and accurately?
   - Is your activity carried on like similar businesses which operate at a profit?
   - If methods you used proved unprofitable did you change your methods or adopt new techniques in an attempt to improve profitability?
2. Expertise of the taxpayer or his advisors.
   - Have you prepared to enter this business by studying the accepted managerial and technological practices of those already in the field?
   - Are your business practices similar to others in your profession? If not, are you attempting to develop new or superior techniques which may result in future profits?
3. Time and effort expended.
   - Do you put more time into marketing your business than you put into fly fishing?

THE CONFIDENT INDIE
PART I: SELF-EMPLOYED - WHAT DOES THAT MEAN?

20

- Do you employ someone with the expertise you may not have or who puts in the time you are not able to?

- Did you leave another job to devote more time to this activity?

4. Expectation that assets used in the activity may appreciate in value.

   - The term "profit" encompasses appreciation of assets. Will the land, equipment or instruments used in your endeavor increase in value so that your future profit may be realized from the appreciation of your assets as well as from income?

5. Success in carrying on similar or dissimilar activities.

   - Have you taken a similar activity and converted it from an unprofitable to a profitable enterprise?

   - Have you had general success in running other kinds of businesses?

6. History of income or losses with respect to the activity.

   - Losses early in the history of a business are common. Are your losses due to heavy early expenses or have they extended beyond the normal time for this kind of activity to begin making a profit?

7. Amount of occasional profits.

   - There may be a disparity in the amount of profits that you make in relation to the losses you incur, or in the amount of money spent on assets used in your activity. The purchase of a $3,000 camera, but not one photo sale, may tell the IRS it's a hobby. Do you have an opportunity to make a substantial ultimate profit in a highly speculative activity?

   - A software developer may work on a project for years before it is viable. Is your business the type that will have an occasional large profit but small operating losses over many years?

### Be careful of the next two:

8. Financial status of the taxpayer.

   - If this is your only source of income, then you must be in it to make a profit.

   - If, on the other hand, you've got large income from other sources and this activity generates substantial tax benefits, this could indicate to the IRS that the activity is not carried on for profit but as a home-made tax shelter.

9. Elements of personal pleasure or recreation.

   - The IRS says "elements of personal pleasure or recreation" may indicate the lack of a profit motive.

## REALITY √ CHECKS: Actual Cases from The IRS Files

---

### The Artist's Road Is A Hard One

Stella Waltzkin, an artist, supported herself for some years by selling her art, teaching art, and designing fixtures for a lighting company.

After receiving an inheritance she no longer had to work, but she persevered at producing and selling her art. Over the next ten years Ms. Waltzkin continued to lose money on the sale of art. One year she claimed a $40,000 loss on $6,000 of gross income. The IRS ruled her activity a hobby.

But the Federal courts overruled the IRS decision. "It is well recognized," the court noted, "that profits may not be immediately forthcoming in the creative field and many artists have to struggle throughout their careers. This does not mean that serious artists do not intend to profit from their activities. It only means that their lot is a difficult one."

---

### The Fisherman Who Was at Sea

After six years out of the tuna fishing business, Fisherman Lamb decided to get back into it. He bought a boat and obtained a license. But by the third year of his business he still hadn't made a profit. That year he caught only one fish and his loss was a whopping $21,000! After taking losses on his tax return for five years, he quit the fishy business. Claiming that he did not have a profit motive, the IRS disallowed his losses in two of those years. The IRS noted that he didn't fish that much, but Lamb contended that there are only 15 to 20 good fishing days per year off the Maine coast. Lamb attributed his lack of success to diabetes, which had caused his eyesight to deteriorate.

The Tax Court ruled in Lamb's favor. It noted that he had substantial previous experience in the business and had shown evidence that he had gone back into it with a profit motive in mind. He kept records of weather and tide conditions and the locations of fish, obviously running the enterprise in a businesslike manner.

The court attributed the cause of Lamb's poor catches to his poor eyesight, not to a lack of profit motive.

---

## The Doctor Who Farms

The doctor spent his childhood on a farm. When he grew up he thought farming would be a profitable second business. For 17 out of 18 years he operated his farm at a loss. Not so surprising considering he worked there only on weekends. Guess the cows got pretty uncomfortable or the hay got pretty high. He intended to buy more land, increase the size of his herd, and devote more time to farming – in the hope that these changes would bring in more income. But he never bought the land and instead put more time into his medical practice. The IRS ruled that he was operating the farm for pleasure rather than for profit.

## The Lady Farmers

However, regarding another farm, the IRS was reversed when it disallowed nine years of deductions for a horse farm operated by a woman and her daughters. For nine years they bred, trained, raced and sold horses at a loss. The IRS disallowed the losses. Tax Court overruled the IRS, determining that the farm was operated with a profit motive because accurate records were kept, time and expertise were put into the work, and the women changed their procedures at the advice of experts.

## Yachting for Fun Or Losses

As with the farming doctor, once again concerned that the taxpayer might be having too much fun in his self-employment, the IRS has used personal pleasure as a factor to disallow business deductions. This case involved a yachtsman who leased his vessel to others, then deducted his losses in the yacht-chartering business. The IRS noted that the yachtsman enjoyed sailing and contended that he was just engaged in a hobby. The Tax Court found for the yachtsman. "A 'business' will not be turned into a 'hobby' merely because the owner finds it pleasurable," the court ruled. "Suffering has never been made a prerequisite to deductibility."

The IRS has won some and lost some. They look at the self-employment very closely if there's no financial need for the endeavor (Stella the artist or the farming doctor), or if it's a fun business (yachting).

Whichever one of the 41 million creatively self-employed you are you can make your life simpler by doing your best to meet IRS criteria. The real-life examples above should give you a sense of whether your manner of pursuing your activity is that of a self-employed in business or not.

Some people complain, and rightly, that the IRS intrudes into their businesses by forcing them to keep various kinds of records. But there is a more positive way to look at it. IRS regulations force you to take your business seriously, and that can only work to your business advantage.

## SELF-EMPLOYMENT AS TAX SHELTER

A number of books, articles, and websites advocate going into a self-employed business as a terrific way to get a lot of write-offs on your tax return. The epitome of this style is Jeff Schnepper, a well-known author and money guru, who glibly promises that "you can magically turn personal expenses into tax deductions." He asserts that his on-line bag-of-tricks will fool the gullible folks at the IRS[8] and that any taxpayer with his wits about him can't lose. Making up a self-employed business forms the centerpiece of his tax advice, in the book he reissues annually, **How to Pay Zero Taxes.**

Schnepper's signature phrase – "you can magically turn personal expenses into tax deductions"[9] – has been picked up by other writers, travel companies, and financial and insurance advisors with such frequency that you can find most of them by a simple Google search.

These writers are more interested in the tax consequences than in the business. At worst their advice may lead some people to set up a sham business to cut taxes – a move that could bring them up against the IRS with costly consequences. At best, it's putting the cart before the horse.

Here, according to these writers, is how it works: An employee, a W-2 person, creates a self-employed sideline that allows him to convert personal expenses into business write-offs. Or as an alternative scenario, one spouse works a W-2 job while the other spouse fabricates the self-employed job. All self-employed jobs are created exclusively to generate deductions to the point of zero taxes. "Which spouse should create the deductions?" is one of the questions these books pose.

In real life, decisions about self-employment are not made that way – one spouse may have a W-2 job for the sake of regular and steady income or health insurance coverage while the other tries a hand at the riskier and more irregular income of self-employment. Don't get me wrong – I'm for taking every deduction legally possible, but

THE CONFIDENT INDIE
PART I: SELF-EMPLOYED - WHAT DOES THAT MEAN?

24

going into business for that purpose is not what made America great or made any business succeed. Do you think Bill Gates or Oprah Winfrey got started in business in order to deduct their personal expenses? Or do you think it's because they saw great opportunities?

A reviewer in the New York Daily News called Schnepper's book "the IRS's worst nightmare." I doubt that, but it is a disservice to millions of indies. It's the glib and muddled counsel of the tax shelter promoters that gets the IRS breathing down our necks and gives us legitimate self-employed people a bad name. Remember, *for the IRS to consider your activity a business you must have a profit motive not a tax reduction motive!*

## TO SUM UP HOBBY VERSUS BUSINESS

- Even though paid as self-employed does not mean that you are self-employed.
- Specific factors determine whether you're an employee or self-employed. They have to do with the degree of control and independence in a business relationship.
- For the IRS to treat you as an independent contractor, being self-employed is only part of the picture; you must also be able to prove that you're in it for the money – that you're running a business.
- The more you treat your activity as a business the more likely the IRS will see it as one. The easiest place to start is right here with **THE CONFIDENT INDIE**.

THE CONFIDENT INDIE
PART I: SELF-EMPLOYED - WHAT DOES THAT MEAN?

25

## CHAPTER 4: THE BAD NEWS AND THE GOOD NEWS
## Employee or self-employed: Which is better?

Is self-employment for you? If you're still pondering that question, ignore the bad advice of the tax evasion gurus who urge you to do it for the tax breaks. Although taxes matter vitally once you're in business, taxes are not, and should not be, the defining factor in your decision to go solo.

Let's begin the analysis of the pros and cons by dropping the gushy prose about the joys of self-realization that abound in working for yourself and about how "the real you" will bubble up from the depths when you "control your own destiny." Instead I want to show you some of the considerations you need to face if you are thinking about going into business for yourself. And whether it is the right step for you.

Is it better to be self-employed or an employee? Let's look at several people who might be asking themselves this question.

---

**REALITY √ CHECK**

A reporter for the New York Times earning $160,000 per year with oodles of employee benefits including a pension and stock options who can no longer deal with incessant travel; she wants to adopt the life of a freelance writer with no editor dispatching her to Wichita on two hours' notice – but also no set income and no benefits.

---

**REALITY √ CHECK**

A guy who works in the local bakery getting paid a little above minimum wage who has kept his mom's Hungarian pastry recipes and is sure there'd be more satisfaction and more money in his own business; and he could name it Marika's Marzipan after his sweet mother.

---

---

### REALITY √ CHECK

A public relations executive making $300,000 per year, with mucho investments and even more client connections, tired of the rat race – yet thoughts about going out on her own give her a really awful stomach ache.

---

### REALITY √ CHECK

A woman with degrees in Russian, Spanish and Italian and lots of volunteer experience, whose youngest child is in school half a day; she wants to be home when her kids are home, and is thinking of starting a home business as a translator and language teacher.

---

For some the choice is not so hard; for others it is excruciating. There are a host of factors, personal and professional, in a decision about whether to go solo. Some of them are:

**Situational**: Do you have many family responsibilities? Do you have support from friends and family?

**Talent**: Do you have the skills to make it on your own?

**Psychological**: Do you have the temperament and the discipline necessary?

**Financial**: Do you have the money you need to get started? Or have enough saved to keep you afloat until your venture runs smoothly?

**Benefits**: Are employee benefits available through your spouse's employment? Can you afford the high bills of health coverage or can you take the risk of being without it?

**Legal**: Do you understand and can you handle your increased liability as an independent professional?

**Ownership**: Do you understand the differences as to who owns your work – the copyright or patent or recipe – if you create your creation as an employee? As a self-employed? As a work-for-hire?

**The Unknown**: How prepared are you for an emergency such as getting hurt while working? A long bout with the flu? A shortage of clients? Computer crashes? Car breakdowns? A no-show babysitter?

Whether to be self-employed or work for someone else: There is no right or wrong answer. It's a choice only you can make.

## DISADVANTAGES OF SELF-EMPLOYMENT

All the important disadvantages of self-employment can be summed as one big piece of bad news: *Nobody is taking care of you*. There's no big daddy to turn to. You alone are responsible for yourself – and often for a lot of others too.

You are not paid for sick days; you must come up with the money to pay for your own health insurance; if you have a question about pensions you can't run to the personnel office on the sixth floor to get an answer; there's no child care subsidy. I am not saying that every employee has this kind of coverage and benefits, but I am saying that *no self-employed has them*.

When you work for yourself you have no boss. You are both employer and employee and in your dual role you must pay both the employee's share and the employer's share of Social Security and Medicare tax, called **self-employment tax (SE tax)** (You'll learn more about taxes paid by a self-employed in PART V.)

As for your pension, every penny comes from you, whereas in many companies employers contribute to the pensions of their employees.

If you can't work or there is no work you don't get paid, and you can't apply for unemployment benefits. Nor can you get Worker's Compensation for a work-related injury.

*You are truly on your own.* It sounds daunting. But most independent professionals have faced all these considerations and have decided, as I also did, that (unless you believe in reincarnation) since you only live once, being your own boss is more fulfilling and more fun!

## ADVANTAGES OF SELF-EMPLOYMENT

And one big piece of good news about self-employment: There's no big daddy to tell you what to do, how to do it or when to do it. Nor can he fire you. *You alone are responsible for yourself.*

THE CONFIDENT INDIE
PART I: SELF-EMPLOYED - WHAT DOES THAT MEAN?

28

The same thing that makes self-employment difficult is what makes it attractive and adventurous. Nobody will take care of you, but instead of dwelling on that as bad news, embrace it as good news: It means you will be in charge. You will be responsible for yourself – and often for others too. You'll have more control of your time and your life. I'm talking practicality here, not psychobabble about women running with the coyotes or adolescent rebelliousness and your contempt for "the suits." (You may pick up a few "suits" as clients.)

Here's what I'm talking about. Do you want to work until three in the morning all week so that you can take four days off to go skiing? You can. Do you want to start the day late so you can have breakfast with your honey? You can. If you're not feeling great and want to work from your home in your pj's, you can. You can fit your schedule into the schedule of the rest of your family, maybe eliminating the need for expensive or inadequate childcare. If you have a great idea, you can try it. If it doesn't work, you are responsible for that too, but you can make changes and improve your idea without the need to play company politics with the sales department down the hall.

And with self-employment comes financial advantages. One of the less obvious advantages is the possibility of more money for the same work. Many companies have downsized (don't you love that word?) and former employees have been fired, then engaged as independent contractors. Why do you think that has happened? Money! It saves the company a big bundle – in payroll taxes and benefits – to hire someone as a freelancer rather than as an employee. So should you work for the same fee that you would be paid as an employee? No, you shouldn't. You should ask for more. You are costing them a lot less than would employee Dennis Dubya-Two, so how about splitting the difference? And if you're engaged by someone who has never run a business or never hired anyone to work for him, maybe you'll need to point out the financial savings to him and why he should use your services instead of those of the temp agency he's considering.

Self-employment comes with tax advantages as well. You are in control, so in many instances:

- You have more influence over business expense deductions.
- More business expenses are actually deductible.
- You get more flexibility in how much tax you'll pay and when you'll pay it.
- You get to decide when to spend money to help your business grow.
- You can influence when you receive income.
- You can distribute income to family members by hiring them as employees.

- You have a wide range of pension choices.

Some of these topics will be covered throughout **THE CONFIDENT INDIE**. Others are beyond the basic information included in this book. Nonetheless you're on your way to being able to take full advantage of them in the future. For now let's just look at two of the basic advantages: your own influence over business expense deductions and the greater deductibility of business expenses.

The IRS determines a business deduction as one that is "ordinary and necessary" to your profession. And who decides what is ordinary and necessary? The decision is based on a) industry standards and b) your employer. But as a self-employed *you are your own employer* and so you have a great deal of influence in determining which of your expenses are ordinary and necessary to your work. Therefore, as a self-employed your deduction vista is expanded. You may get to write off many more business expenses than if you were an employee.

The other tax advantage to the self-employed that we'll look at here is the greater *actual deductibility of business expenses*. In CHAPTER 1 you'll remember that Rick Reporter sold a feature story on sailing to both his newspaper and to a blog. If, in order to research the piece, he had purchased $100 worth of reference books and magazines on boating, then those PUBLICATIONS would be a business expense deduction. For this example let's say that the publications were his only business expense on his entire tax return. Without question it is a legitimate $100 business expense. He would have to split the expense – $50 against his W-2 wage and $50 against his freelance income.

However, the $50 expense allocated against his $1,000 W-2 income is deducted on a part of his tax return that must exceed a certain minimum. He would not have met that minimum. As an employee, therefore, the $50 PUBLICATIONS expense would not actually be deductible from his income. The deduction would be lost – and the entire $1,000 W-2 income would be subject to income tax.

On the other hand the $50 expense against his $1,000 self-employed income is deducted on a different part of his tax return where no minimum need be met. It would be fully deductible and so only $950 of the $1,000 self-employed income would be subject to income tax.

More control in determining *ordinary and necessary expenses* and the straightforward *deductibility of all business expenses* provide powerful advantages to being self-employed. When these factors apply to a large portion of your income they

THE CONFIDENT INDIE
PART I: SELF-EMPLOYED - WHAT DOES THAT MEAN?

30

are especially advantageous. Note that Rick Reporter's other expenses – such as the canoe trip with his buddy, the visit to the maritime museum, the 4 A.M. phone calls to his fishing partner about problems in renting the sailboat – are all totally or partially deductible against his $1,000 freelance income. Such legitimate increases in deductions lower the overall tax of a self-employed.

Please read on. **THE CONFIDENT INDIE** will help you clearly understand and intelligently weigh the advantages and disadvantages of the freelance life. I hope that you'll choose it over the W-2 life.

If you have already decided that you have what it takes to go out on your own, proceed to the next chapter.

However, if you're still undecided you may want next to read CHAPTER 6, an introduction to business expenses and CHAPTER 17 on self-employed income, as well as CHAPTER 26 on taxes paid by a self-employed. Each of these is the opening chapter of a PART in **THE CONFIDENT INDIE** and the information in them will help you make this life-changing choice. Then you can return here to read CHAPTER 5 which explains sole proprietorship.

THE CONFIDENT INDIE
PART I: SELF-EMPLOYED - WHAT DOES THAT MEAN?

31

## CHAPTER 5: THE MOST SIMPLE BUSINESS STRUCTURE
### Sole Proprietorship

If you've decided an indie business is for you, congratulations! But, now what do you do? Well, according to the majority of books on entrepreneurship, the first step is to talk with a lawyer about incorporating. The lawyers – no surprise – say the same.

Incorporating is not the thing to do!

Every business conducts its affairs as a particular kind of **business entity** (or **business structure**). The organizational form that you choose determines which tax and legal regulations will apply. For tax purposes the IRS gives a choice of the following kinds of business structures:

- Sole proprietorship
- Partnership (several types)
- Corporation (two types)


If you're a self-employed in business and you have done nothing about a business entity, your business is already structured. It is a **sole proprietorship.**

**THE CONFIDENT INDIE** is a book of basics. There is no need to complicate when simplicity will suffice. For all but a few newly-hatched solo ventures a sole proprietorship is the way to go. And although most of the information and guidance in **THE CONFIDENT INDIE** applies to all business structures, I'll focus on sole proprietorships.


## WHAT IS SOLE PROPRIETORSHIP?

A sole proprietorship is the most simple business entity. Did you have a lemonade stand when you were a kid? Or as a teen, did you babysit or do yardwork? If you were doing it to make money then you were a self-employed in business and your business structure was a sole proprietorship – and you probably weren't even aware of it.

## How to Become A Sole Proprietorship

It's simple. Just say, "I am a business."

As soon as you sell or attempt to sell your service or product in hope of making a profit you have "formed" a sole proprietorship. There are no papers to complete, no agency to contact. You simply engage in your business activity.

Rick Reporter from CHAPTER 1 did that. When he decided to try to freelance his sailing story he became a self-employed in business and his business structure was a sole proprietorship. Even were Rick unable to sell the piece, and ended up with enough rejection letters to paper his walls, as long as he intended to make a profit as a freelancer he'd be a sole proprietor. He doesn't need a business name. He is as legit with a business card that simply states his name and contact information as he'd be were he to call his business Rick's Real Good Writin' and rent office space and open a business checking account, and do other such foolish things.

Don't pay much heed to the pros and the how-to-be-a-business websites and books that insist you have need of an accountant, a lawyer, a banker, an insurance agent, and a marketing consultant to become a business. Depending upon the kind of project you are embarking on – if you're a solo trucker shipping hazardous materials across state lines, for instance; or an event planner concerned about liability; or as your business grows or tax laws change – some or all of these professionals may be useful to your business, but they are not necessary for the instant formation of your business as a sole proprietorship.

## Wait. Wait. Wait.

You may never need to incorporate. The feds say that nearly four out of five businesses in the United States are sole proprietorships. Yet just about every lawyer advises a budding indie to incorporate. In my many years of experience I have found only one attorney who didn't answer, "yes," when asked: "should I incorporate?" And every new client that has come to me already set up as a corporation said he or she did it because "my attorney (or my accountant) told me to do it." None of them had a clear idea of why incorporation was supposed to be an advantage.

Once in a while there may be a good reason why a self-employed should incorporate, but, if advised that you must do it, find out why. Be sure the professional explains to your satisfaction – and also to the satisfaction of a savvy friend, colleague or relative – what makes incorporation necessary.

Look at some facts to stifle old husbands' tales. All business structures:

- Allow you to deduct business expenses.

- Allow some or all deduction of medical insurance.

- Allow for contributions to pension plans.

- Allow you to hire employees or subcontractors.

- Allow the other guy to sue you.

- Do not allow you to hide income.

- Do not allow you to write off personal non-business expenses.


## The Characteristics And Advantages of A Sole Proprietorship

- You and your business are one and the same.

- A sole proprietor and his business use the same tax year.

- Its income or loss is your income or loss. (This is referred to as pass-through, which we'll look at in a moment.)

- Its debts and assets are your debts and assets.

- Assets, originally for personal use, can immediately be used in your business without paperwork and without negative tax consequences. And, there can be positive tax consequences without any cash outlay.

- It's the easiest, quickest and cheapest business structure to set up and maintain with regard to recordkeeping, accounting, legal procedures and fees.

- The most flexible business structure is a sole proprietorship.

- It is the only business tax entity that does not require a separate tax return. A federal **Schedule C: Profit or Loss From Business** and a few other pages are added to your personal tax return. These pages show the income and expenses of your independent endeavor.

- Only a sole proprietorship allows for a simple, direct deduction of home office expense.

- A business loss can immediately reduce your other taxable income.

- Taxes are not paid twice on the same income – as can happen with a corporation.

- Recent tax law changes have made sole-proprietorship the most tax-advantageous pass-through tax structure for a one person business.

- A sole proprietorship allows for the most advantageous tax remedy when husband and wife work in the same business.

- It is easy to change from a sole proprietorship to another business structure – such as a partnership or corporation – when your situation warrants it.

**Three Disadvantages of Being A Sole Proprietor – And Three Antidotes**

1. You are personally liable. Yes, they can take your house if your massage oil gave someone a skin rash that ruined her performance at the piano competition and so destroyed her future earning potential. ***Antidote:*** Get adequate liability insurance appropriate to your business activities and assets. Insurance can be much less expensive than incorporating.

2. And the reverse: Business assets can be confiscated to pay personal debts. Yes, they could take your computer if you owe money on your credit card or to your dentist. ***Antidote:*** Watch your spending.

3. Audit rates are higher than for other business entities. ***Antidote:*** Don't flinch. Good records will get you through an audit. **THE CONFIDENT INDIE** will lead the way.

# A GENERAL VIEW OF TAXES AND INCOME IN A SOLE PROPRIETORSHIP

Any profit made by a sole proprietorship is income made by the indie. It is directly added to the other income on the tax return of the self-employed.

Any loss is subtracted from other income on the tax return. If the loss exceeds all the other income on the tax return it can be used against previous or future earnings. This is a net operating loss (NOL) and must be handled by a tax professional.

Because of this kind of treatment of income a sole proprietorship is called a pass-through entity. The income passes through the business directly, dollar for dollar, to the individual taxpayer.

The sole proprietor – that's you, the indie – gets no wages or salary. Whatever profit or loss the business makes is the sole proprietor's, or owner's, **net income**. You can think of **profit** and **net income** as the same thing. Net income gets taxed.

The owner may end up with more or less money at her disposal than the amount shown as a profit or loss. For instance, let's say that Caitlin Caterer charged a $3,000 oven to her credit card and made a single payment of $500. She would have a $3,000 business expense deducted on her tax return even though she shelled out only $500.

**Think of Caitlin's money this way ...**

Gross Sales $10,000

Cost of Oven ( 3,000 )

Net Income on Tax Return $ 7,000

**... or this way:**

Money In $10,000

Payment on Oven ( 500 )

Money in the Bank $ 9,500

A sole proprietor is responsible for paying all his own taxes on his net income. However, unlike a corporation where the tax liability is calculated solely on the activities of the business, the tax liability of a sole proprietorship, because it is calculated as part of your entire tax return, is determined by all circumstances on your tax return, such as other income, personal expenses, whether there's a working spouse, and the number of dependents.

**PART V** will present a complete explanation of taxes.

*Regulatory Chores That May Be on A Sole Proprietor's Do-List:* A sole proprietor may need to look into permits, licenses, or other regulations.

---

### REALITY √ CHECK

P.R. Bernays saw the storm approaching. The public relations firm where he worked had new management and was slowly sinking. P.R. had worked there for five years, long enough to learn the hype and hoopla of the business. He quietly took on a few clients of his own, working for them on weekends, evenings, and using a few of his "personal and sick days" too. Although he was still an employee of the troubled company, P.R. was also a self-employed in business. By the time the firm went under his own business was growing. P.R., already a sole proprietor, had to do nothing about his business structure; but his decision to call his business "The Perfect Spin" rather than to simply use his name meant he had to register the business name with the county clerk. The purpose of registration is to make sure that no two people in the same county use the same business name. P.R. also decided to convert his three-bay garage into an office and so he had to deal with the friendly and courteous bureaucrats of several local agencies about zoning and construction permits.

---

All independent professionals, depending upon:

- The product they sell.
- The service they provide.
- The location of their businesses.
- Whether they use a name other than their own as their business name.
- Whether they have employees or hire subcontractors.

*May* have to:

- Obtain various permits from state and local governments to comply with zoning or health code regulations.
- Obtain various licenses, perhaps registering the business with the state.
- Show proof of insurance.
- Register to collect and/or pay state sales or gross receipts tax.
- File for the use of a trade name. Often referred to as a DBA, "doing business as."
- Contact a federal agency about federal regulations for various kinds of businesses; for instance, a weaver who raises his own sheep must comply with textile regulations, and the maker of Bobbie's Beef Pot Pies must observe regulations on the preparation of meat products.
- Obtain a Federal (Employer) Identification Number, EIN[10].

We'll look at why you may need to obtain a Federal Identification Number below. Most of the other governmental rules that apply to various aspects of your solo business are required and administered by local and state agencies, not by the feds. You will have to make calls, check on the Web, visit your library and consult your county tax office to find out the full scope of your responsibilities. Bear in mind that these rules apply to partnerships and corporations as well as to the sole proprietor.

---

**ALERT!**

Every jurisdiction overflows with rules and regulations. Some you must follow closely while others you can let slide because nobody pays any attention to them. Don't slap down $500 for a certain permit and later discover that you are the first to apply for it in 50 years. On the other hand don't skip a $200 license the lack of which could shut you down. Get in touch with business associations for such information – many of them allow you to attend one meeting as a visitor without being required to join and pay dues.

---

# FEDERAL EMPLOYER IDENTIFICATION NUMBERS (EIN)

Use your Social Security number as your sole proprietorship's identifying number, unless:

- You must withhold taxes from a subcontractor you've hired.
- You hire one or more employees.
- You set up a self-employed retirement plan.
- You deal in products that require you to file a federal excise, or alcohol, tobacco and firearms return.
- You choose not to use your Social Security number in your business transactions.

If one or more of the above applies to your business, you will require a nine-digit employer identification number (EIN). Since all these situations are beyond the basics covered in this book be sure to consult my website, http://junewalkeronline.com/, or your tax pro should any of them arise.

If you obtain an EIN use it for all your business correspondence with the federal government. Don't use your Social Security number for this purpose unless specifically asked for both numbers. Never use someone else's EIN. If you buy a business you cannot use a previous owner's EIN.

# OTHER BUSINESS STRUCTURES

If four out of five businesses in the USA are sole proprietorships that leaves one out of five that's structured differently. The other choices are: **partnerships** (a sole proprietorship is a one-owner business, a partnership is for more than one owner and is a pass-through entity) and two kinds of corporations (a regular, called a **C-corporation**, is not a pass-through entity; an **S-corporation** is a hybrid – part partnership and part corporation). I do not want to confuse you by going into detail about these other business entities since they will not apply to you at this time. If you are considering a business structure other than a sole proprietorship be sure to get sufficient and clear advice before traveling down that road.

### LLC: Best Thing Since Sliced Bread

It's not. The important thing to understand about a **Limited Liability Company** (LLC) is that it is not a federal tax entity. ***An LLC is a legal business structure*** set up under the laws of each state. Because LLCs are formed under 50 different sets of state law the tax and legal treatment of an LLC may vary from state to state. It also may vary from federal to state.

Many indies go online and set up an LLC lickety-split and then erroneously assume that they have built a thick wall of liability protection around themselves. Not so. There is a lot more to it than that. If you ever consider setting up your business as an LLC or already are an LLC be sure that you understand the requirements of maintaining LLC status as required by your state. Only if you follow them will you have liability protection similar to that enjoyed by a corporation. If, as a sole proprietor, you foresee potential liability problems because of the kind of business you are in, then speak to an attorney about forming an LLC.

For tax purposes, a one-person LLC may be structured as a sole proprietorship (known as a **disregarded entity** in tax jargon). If more than one person formed an LLC they could choose a partnership or an S-corp or, in some states, a C-corp structure for federal tax purposes.

Some states recognize another legal entity called a Limited Liability Partnership (LLP). This is available in certain states to certain professions such as doctors or attorneys or accountants. An LLP bears many similarities to an LLC.

Remember: LLCs and LLPs are legal designations, not tax structures. Setting up an LLC requires professional help, a setup expense, and in many states a hefty annual fee.

As your indie business grows and changes you may want to review your business structure, but for almost all independents, sole proprietorship is the right first choice.

**PART I** has laid out the basic principles and the initial steps of self-employment. As you continue **THE CONFIDENT INDIE** you'll learn about the day-to-day operation of an indie enterprise. The rest of the book, therefore, is material you will certainly consult over and over as your business develops.

# PART II: BUSINESS EXPENSES

How-to books and IRS manuals for the self-employed generally start with an explanation of income. Yet anyone who has ever been in business knows that expenses come first. A landscaper doesn't get paid before he buys the equipment; he's paid after he cuts the grass. **THE CONFIDENT INDIE** starts where it makes the most sense, with expenses coming before income. Let's start with the pleasures of taking deductions. Income will be covered in **PART III**.

## CHAPTER 6: INDIE POWER MINDSET
## An Introduction to Business Expenses

What makes an item or event a business expense? Common sense (you know, that's the commodity your mother wished you had) would tell you that business expenses are the costs you incur to run your business – the money you must spend in order to make money.

---

**THE IRS SAYS ABOUT BUSINESS EXPENSES ...**

To be deductible, a business expense must be ***both ordinary and necessary***. An **ordinary expense** is one that is common and accepted in your field of business. A **necessary expense** is one that is appropriate and helpful for your business. An expense does not have to be indispensable to be considered necessary.

---

Okay, but what is ordinary to an astrologer? What is necessary to a computer games inventor?

The answer: Anything you do that relates to your work, that stimulates or enhances your business, nurtures your professional creativity, improves your skills, wins you recognition, or increases your chances of making a sale may be a business expense and therefore deductible.

---

### REALITY √ CHECK

When Astrid Astrologer goes to another astrologer for a reading, that isn't a personal expense; that's a business expense, and deductible. It's just as legitimate a deduction as the one a management executive takes for attending a seminar on product presentation.

---

### REALITY √ CHECK

Ivan Inventor – of computer games that is – shouldn't assume that buying someone else's computer game can't be a business expense. Even if he stayed up half the night fighting invaders from another galaxy, he was researching the competition. The purchase of the game is a business deduction.

---

Astrid and Ivan are independent professionals. When Ivan fills out a form that calls for his signature and "title" he writes "owner" next to his name. Both Ivan and Astrid are in business. Ivan's business is inventing computer games. Astrid's business is reading horoscopes for clients. Very simply, Ivan's business is Ivan. Astrid's business is Astrid. There must be in the life of every self-employed a moment of illumination, a shift in understanding, a reconfiguration of brain circuits, a vision of herself or himself as a business – a solo act, but a business nonetheless. It's a new way of thinking that is essential for an independent professional. It is an indie power mindset.

With this chapter begins the presentation of a lot of information about business deductions, but what underlies this material is more fundamental than information. It is an invitation to adopt the thinking habits of a solo entrepreneur. With that mindset you will know that you are a business – that whenever you reach into your pocket for money, write a check, purchase on your iPad, or slip out your credit card you may be engaging in a business transaction. In the instant that you come to understand what it means to profess that you are a business, and that the work you do is blended into every aspect of your life – well, that may well be ***the most important moment of your indie business life!***

# THE INDIE POWER MINDSET

It guides you to embrace a new and powerful way to relate to your business, your work, your creativity.

### First: Define your business as broadly as you honestly can.

The more multi-faceted and inclusive your field of endeavor, the more wide-ranging your expenses can be and therefore the less taxes you'll end up paying!

- A photojournalist can deduct a more extensive variety of expenses than can a wedding photographer.
- A website designer and social marketing developer will have more diverse expenses than does a website builder.
- A generalist writer – someone who might write about anything – has more assorted expenses than a sports writer.

### Second: Look at all your activities from the vantage point of your new entrepreneurial indie power mindset.

Don't be so sure that there is a well-marked difference between work and family, and play and chores, or that you know what the difference is. The business life of an employee has clearly established boundaries, but the business life of a self-employed like yourself is intertwined with your personal life. If your business is broadly defined and your life is richly complicated, it can make for an intertwining that gets pretty tangled. If you're caring for your parents while running a day care business, or dropping off your children at different locations while delivering products to clients, or struggling to find time for your new independent venture while holding down a full-time job, the interplay of your business and other interests can be intricate. On the other hand, if you live the life of a loner, without commitments or obligations, the boundary between business life and personal life might be remarkably simple.

Whether an expense is personal or business is often decided by the circumstances.

- A musician who is single and without children may do very little that is not considered ordinary and necessary to his business – travel, purchase entertainment system equipment, attend concerts.
- An alarm-system installer with four children who spends all his free time fishing, by himself, will have limited business expenses.

- A visual artist attends a Broadway performance. She scrutinizes the sets and costumes, makes notes about on the set designer's bio. She deducts the cost of the theatre ticket as a business RESEARCH-STUDY expense.

- A structural engineer drives through Millionaire's Mile looking at the period architecture of the houses. Stops to sketch and take notes. Since this is research for him the drive is a business event and the mileage there and back is a business AUTO expense.

- The proprietor of a shop that sells hand-made clothes for children deducts as a PUBLICATION expense every magazine she purchases that has any clothing, children, or textile industry trends in it.

### Third: Review your relationships.

Your new indie power mindset may present a different aspect to the link between what you do and the people with whom you do it. Anyone who has a connection with your business may be ***primarily a business associate*** even though in some cases he or she may also happen to be a college classmate, friend, parent, child, or spouse. Friendship with a business associate does not necessarily rule out a business deduction. You'll just have to show that the predominant motive for the activity that warranted the expense was business-related.

- A dance instructor ***calls his friend*** to invite her to a movie and, also, to ask her to bring her notes from the marketing webinar she attended so that they can discuss whether he should attend the next webinar session to get ideas for promoting his business. The movie tickets and phone call are business expenses. And so too are the drinks they had afterward where the business discussion continued.

- A carpenter deducts not only the tools that she buys, but also the expense of dining out. Why? Because during the meal ***with her husband***, an ad agency exec, she explains the timetable for her new business, gets his input on questions of scheduling, picks his brain about various proposals, and tests his reaction to her brochure. She could not have had this business discussion at the family dinner table with her three children in attendance and so the gift given ***to her brother*** as thanks for baby-sitting while she was at this business dinner is also a business expense.

## TO SUM UP THE INDIE POWER MINDSET

To achieve the best possible advantage regarding business expenses:
- Define your business as broadly as possible.

- Re-examine all your activities. It may be that many of them have a business element.
- Whatever you do, and whomever you do it with, consider the possibility of a business connection.

The next nine chapters discuss individual expenses. Each expense will be sufficiently presented to help you through just about every situation that may arise. This is a book of basics and so there may be a complex event that takes place in your solo venture that is not covered here for which you will need special guidance. **THE CONFIDENT INDIE** gives you such a strong foundation that you will know when you need special help. On the other hand, you may find that a particular expense has no bearing on anything you have encountered in your solo activity. If so skip that section and move on. It will always be here should a new circumstance come to pass. Don't burden yourself with information about situations that may never apply to you.

In **PART IV** you will get a foundation in recordkeeping. You will learn why recordkeeping is important, which records to keep and for how long. You will then be able to walk with confidence to the next step – actual recordkeeping, whether you prefer manual, digital, or a combination of methods. The most important step you must take in any recordkeeping system you setup is the following one: From this moment on get backup for everything you spend. Pay for everything by check or credit card, or, if you must pay with cash, get a receipt. If you purchase online, printout the order record. If it suits you scan the receipt. Everything? Yes, everything – from computers to toothpaste! That is one step of **Five Easy Steps** and my **Most Simple System** of recordkeeping. You can later decide if you want and need the other four steps.

Let's now take a look at business expenses in a way you've never looked before. You are on your way to learning how to simply and easily miss not one business deduction and thereby pay the least tax legitimately possible. As we move ahead I urge you to keep in mind a quote directly from the IRS: ***"There is no reason to pay more tax than the law requires."***

## CHAPTER 7: UP AND RUNNING
### Business Start-up Costs

Business START-UP COSTS are one category of expense that falls on the far side of complex. There is another, TRAVEL expense, but we'll look at that later.

Be assured that everything you spend to get a business up and running, is deductible– although via some knotty rules – if you do get that business up and running. Here's an example.

Billy Bridesnapper was getting itchy about his job at Phil's Photos. He traipsed all around the county, in his own van, hauling his own equipment, getting shots that wowed everyone, yet he was earning only a small hourly wage and a small percent of each photo shoot he did while Phil made the big bucks. Over the course of several years Billy had learned a lot, mostly through observation, about the management end of the business; and via word-of-mouth he'd become known for his untypical black and white photos of typical family occasions. Friends and colleagues encouraged him to strike out on his own but being a savvy businessperson (for a photographer, that is) he decided to first weigh the pros and cons by evaluating the market for his kind of photos and getting estimates of the cost to set up his business. Also, Billy didn't feel right going into direct competition with Phil, yet all his contacts were in the same geographic location. He'd have to do a lot of planning *before he started his own business.*

Many of the expenses that Billy would incur in the organizing and planning stage of his new venture may be classified as START-UP COSTS. They might include items as diverse as a survey of potential markets, advertisements for his grand opening, or a legal fee paid for a review of his rental lease contract.

> ### THE IRS SAYS ABOUT START-UP COSTS ...
> Business START-UP COSTS are the costs you incur when investigating the possibility of creating or acquiring a trade or business, or they are the costs of setting up a trade or business.

To qualify as START-UP COSTS, expenses must meet **all** the following guidelines:

- The expense has to be one you could deduct if you were already in business.
- They must be paid or incurred for a trade or business that actually gets started.
- You must pay or incur the costs before you begin business operation.

START-UP expenses are many and varied, and fall into two types:

1. **Exploratory Or General**: A person looking to go into business for himself might explore various fields of endeavor, as well as general questions of self-employment such as tax advantages, pension consequences, workspace problems.

2. **Investigative of A Specific Business**: After determining that self-employment is a viable and reasonable course for him to pursue, he might then investigate a specific business by traveling to a potential location or paying for a market survey.

The list of possible START-UP expenses is as long and varied as a list of expenses for an existing business. The following is a small sampling:

- Survey of potential markets
- Analysis of available facilities, labor, and supplies
- Travel to look over business sites
- Fees for the professional services of accountants and lawyers
- Salaries and fees for consultants
- Training employees
- Office supplies
- Repairs
- Utilities
- Travel to find customers, suppliers, or financing
- Advertising for the grand opening

What's the big deal? Keep in mind that any expense that would qualify as a business deduction once you are in business qualifies as a start-up cost if you incur it before you launch your new venture. That's pretty simple, isn't it?

You may be thinking: If it's that simple, and if the criteria for regular business expenses and start-up expenses are the same, whatever is the reason for classifying them as start-up costs anyway? Why not just deduct them along with all the other business expenses?

Because the IRS won't let you, that's why. You can deduct all of your regular business expenses in the year they are paid or incurred, but to the IRS start-up costs are not regular business expenses; they are considered *capital expenses*. Capital expenses cannot be deducted in the year you pay them; instead they become part of the basis of your business. And because of that they have to be deducted in a different way: Sometimes over a period of years, sometimes not until you sell or dispose of your business.

Before going any further into start-up costs it will be helpful to introduce you to two more accounting terms.

---

### WHATTA CONCEPT!
### Capital Expense And Basis

Your **basis** in something is simply what it cost you. If you paid $200 for a bicycle, your basis in that bike is $200. If you paid $200,000 for a warehouse to store your widgets your basis in that building is $200,000. The bike would be a **capital asset** of your messenger service business; the warehouse would also be a capital asset of your widget-making business. Your business is a capital asset. Its basis is another way of saying how much your business cost you, and whether we're talking about a million dollar widget-manufacturing venture or a $5,000 cookie-making venture, each entrepreneur who lays out money for capital assets has a basis in his business.

A **capital expense** is a cost related to the buying of a capital asset. The purchase of the bicycle is a capital expense, as are the snakeskin straps that you bought to attach to the pedals, thus becoming part of the basis (cost) of the bike. The warehouse is a capital expenditure, as are the legal fees associated with its purchase, all adding to the basis of the building.

---

START-UP COSTS **are capital expenses**. Some expenditures, even if incurred before you embark on your new enterprise, are not classified as START-UP COSTS. They are business expenses and are deductible in a different fashion than are START-UP COSTS.

Pre-business opening expenses not considered START-UP COSTS:
- Loan interest
- Taxes
- Research and experimental costs
- Computers, machinery or office equipment

You will learn more about these specific expenses in forthcoming chapters.

Now let's get back to Billy Bridesnapper. Although only 27 years old he managed to save up enough money to get started in his own business. (I told you he was unusual for a photographer.) When Phil announced he was going to sell the business to his brother Phineas, Billy really got busy, because he knew he did not want to work for Phineas.

In a few months Billy spent $8,600 on locating and doing some repair work on a studio (with the help of his cousin, a carpenter), updating his blog that was a visual diary using his own black and white photos, and printing high quality promotional literature which accentuated the merits of his exclusive use of black and white photographs for all his assignments, including weddings, bar mitzvahs, retirement parties, and more, and that also included 10 Tips on the Best Make-up and Attire for Great Looking B&W Photos.

His decision to concentrate exclusively on black and white photography sets him apart from and avoids competition with Phineas; customers who want the color photograph treatment he can send to Phineas, who can reciprocate by sending to Billy those interested in black-and-white photos. They shake hands, part company, and Billy heads out on his own.

### Will Billy get to deduct all his START-UP COSTS?

Because Billy's investigation and planning were successful and resulted in an up-and-running business he can deduct all those pre-opening expenses, but because they are START-UP COSTS, the method of deduction differs from that used for most business expenses.

Billy may deduct up to $5,000 of his total START-UP COSTS in the year he starts his photo business even if his grand opening were as late as December 31.

The remaining $3,600 may be deducted over the next 15 years (180 months). If Billy started his business on January 1, he would get to deduct one-fifteenth of his expenses every year for 15 years. That is called **amortization**.

Here are the numbers. Billy's expenses total $8,600. If he deducts $5,000, he still has $3,600 left to deduct over 180 months. If we divide $3,600 by 180 months, we get $20 per month. One year's worth is 12 times $20 = $240. That is Billy's yearly deduction.

January 1 is a good day to open a photography business, because there are a lot of weddings in February. However, Billy had everything in place by November and was hoping to get some of the holiday trade, and so his grand opening was November 1. Billy may deduct the entire $5,000; however, since his amortization period begins the month in which his business opened, he gets to deduct only an additional $40 in his first year. That two months, November and December, times $20. He gets a full 12 months' deduction the following year.

**What if Billy sells his business?**

If Billy disposes of his business before the end of the amortization period his leftover START-UP COSTS remain as part of the **basis of his business**.

Let's hope that Billy sells his business at a profit, in which case the remaining START-UP COSTS would help to reduce his gain. If, however, he gives up and walks away from the business, or sells it at a loss, the remaining START-UP COSTS would increase his loss.

**What if Billy never starts his business?**

If Billy's business makes it past the starting gate he gets to deduct all the START-UP COSTS involved in the launching of his new venture, albeit he has to follow the rules of how much to deduct and when. Now I'll show you what Billy is allowed to deduct if his undertaking never gets beyond the planning stage.

Looking at the IRS guidelines on START-UP COSTS for a business that never gets off the ground, it's quite clear that the agency wants to rein in people who have a notion to explore the possibility of going into business for themselves, but only as long as they can write off the search at the expense of their fellow taxpayers.

If a business never gets started then exploratory or general expenses never can be deducted; but investigative and specific expenses always can be deducted – one way or another. Be aware that when the IRS says "specific business" it means just that – that the costs are incurred trying to start a new business or buy an existing one. It does not mean exploring a specific type of business. Therefore, an aspiring indie can be assured of deducting some of his START-UP COSTS if he settles on a business and makes concrete moves toward starting it up, whether the business actually gets started or not.

---

## THE IRS SAYS ABOUT START-UP COSTS IF THE BUSINESS NEVER GETS STARTED ...

If your attempt to go into business is not successful, the expenses you had in trying to establish yourself in business fall into two categories:

**Exploratory Or General:** The costs you had before making a decision to begin or acquire a specific business. They include any costs incurred during a general search for or preliminary exploration of a new venture. These costs are personal and nondeductible.

**Investigative of A Specific Business:** The costs incurred in your attempt to acquire or begin a specific trade or business. These costs are capital expenses and you can deduct them as a capital loss.

---

## REALITY √ CHECK

Grace Granddaughter tried to start up one business, but ended up in a different business. Let's see how her expenses get deducted. Grace decided to start baking and selling Grandma's secret recipe mouth-watering chocolate oat cookies. She put a nonrefundable deposit on professional bakeware, gave a month's security on renting a restaurant kitchen during its off hours. But her plans were disrupted when Grandma became ill and Grace had to care for Grandma. Grandma died, leaving Grace no inheritance, but with some experience in caring for the elderly. At that point Grace decided that the cookie-making business had crumbled. With her new skills she established herself as a home health aide for old folks. START-UP COSTS for Grace's cookie-baking business were *for a specific business* and so can be deducted on her tax return – as a capital loss.

---

## ALERT!

If your clever friend – the one that always has a scheme up his sleeve – suggests flying to Hawaii, to do some scuba diving and then flying back to Colorado to do some skiing, and he tells you that you can deduct everything by claiming that you were investigating the possibility of starting a scuba diving and/or a ski instruction business, tell him to forget it. The IRS is very unyielding about allowing such deductions – unless, that is, you in fact do start one of those businesses.

Let's look at what would happen if Billy Bridesnapper had spent all his time, effort and money and then decided not to go into the photography business. How and which START-UP COSTS can he deduct?

---

### REALITY √ CHECK

At the last minute, Billy Bridesnapper got cold feet – deciding that the pressures of running his own business would be too much for him. Nevertheless, Billy's expenses for making ready the studio and his blog and promotional material, which totaled $8,600, are deductible. However, the amount is not deducted as START-UP COSTS, but as a capital loss, in much the same way as money lost in a bad stock market purchase is deductible. If, instead of repairs and promotional material, Billy had purchased a camera, an 85 mm lens, a printer, and a flatbed color scanner for a business that he never started he could not deduct the cost of this EQUIPMENT until he disposed of the items. For instance, if he sold the scanner for $1,000 less than he paid for it he would have a $1,000 capital loss, which has the same tax effect as having lost $1,000 on a stock market sale. If he sold the camera for $200 more than he paid he'd have a $200 capital gain, and would report it as such on his tax return. If he gave the lens to his cousin he'd have neither a gain nor loss on the lens. If he gave the printer to the Community Teen Center's photo lab he'd get a charitable contribution deduction on his tax return.

---

You're not alone if you find START-UP COSTS complicated; they confuse many writers on self-employment, who then run out and publish misinformation. One addled writer of a well-known book on self-employment, for example, tells his readers that the expenses for an abandoned start-up business are investment expenses and should be itemized on Schedule A of your tax return. That's incorrect. Be careful.

## THE SMART WAY TO DEAL WITH START-UP COSTS

If you are planning to go out on your own, or maybe just thinking about going solo, here's a way to look at your position to help you decide whether you're ready to spend some money on searching out your new indie business.

Depending on your choice of business, going out on your own could be an expensive proposition. I want to show you some ways to interpret the rules on START-UP COSTS that you can apply to your situation and perhaps lighten the tax burden of your journey into independent professionalism.

## Run These by Your Tax Preparer

In this book I do not give advice on how to prepare your own tax return but here I'd like to give you a couple of items to run by your tax preparer, to make sure nothing slips through the cracks:

- If, when your tax return is prepared, you neglect to make the decision to amortize your START-UP COSTS (At IRS cocktail parties this is known as "making the election to amortize"), you may amend your tax return to choose amortization, but only through the October 15 extension deadline for that year.

- If you do not make the election on time you cannot deduct the costs until you sell or otherwise go out of business. That is, these costs remain part of the basis of your business.

Just about every tax treatment offers a variety of approaches – as my brother used to say, there's more than one way to skin a rabbit. That's where the tax professional comes in – to advise you on which approach makes the most sense at your particular financial position.

START-UP COSTS are a perfect example of the choices involved in deducting business expenses. Are you going to take the largest deduction in the quickest possible time – $5,000 plus amortization – right now? Or should you stretch it out the deduction and forgo the immediate $5,000 deduction? Are you living high off Aunt Ada's trust fund and need some tax deductions this year? Or do you have so little income and so many deductions that you'd like to save the deduction until you sell the business?

## Think Ahead

What if it's November when you leave your high-paying W-2 job to start your new independent venture? You have a high tax liability because of your wages for most of the year and you are looking for a way to deduct all the expenses of setting up your new business. You want to take the deductions right away, instead of amortizing them over five years? If only, you think, there were some way of turning your START-UP COSTS into regular deductible business expenses.

Maybe there is. Depending on the business, it may even be easy.

Let's write a script for Billy Bridesnapper that illustrates my point. He's changed his mind again. Billy knows that he can't get along with Phil's brother Phineas, and so he is going full force into his own photography business after all. But he's really worried about being short of cash because the $8,600 he spent for his studio and on advertising has emptied his piggy bank.

Well, here's a way out for him. As you know Billy has developed a reputation for his untypical black and white photos of typical family occasions, but did you know that his reputation developed over the years because he's been taking photos of family and friends and getting paid for it? The profit enabled him to buy his new digital camera body and lens. This year alone he took photos of his sister's wedding and was paid for his work. A friend paid him for the photos he took of his bachelor party, and he was given an honorarium for the pictures he took of the school PTA pet show. Well, if Billy's been taking photos with the purpose of making a profit so that he could buy more photo equipment, sounds to me like he's been a paid photographer, in business. His self-employed earned income is evidence that the IRS tends to accept as proof of being in business. If he dates the launching of his business from the day he first got paid for his photos, and the $8,600 for the studio and other projects were for an expansion of his business then those costs are not START-UP COSTS but expenses of an *existing* business. That makes them deductible in the year Billy incurred the expenses.

If you can credibly show that your business started some time ago, no matter how small that beginning may be, you can argue that later expenses are an expansion of your already-existing business, and those costs can be taken as deductions in the year that you incur them.

## TO SUM UP START-UP COSTS BY MEANS OF THREE SCENARIOS

**First scenario**: Ken's company has informed him that he's being downsized. He begins to explore the possibility of self-employment in a general way. The company changes its mind and Ken abandons all plans at self-employment. Any general expenses incurred are not deductible; the IRS considers them personal expenses.

**Second scenario**: It begins the same way. But Ken, after generally exploring self-employment, makes plans to become a website designer. He incurs some expenses, including legal fees. The company changes its mind and Ken still has a job. He drops his plans for the website business. He cannot deduct the costs of general exploration of self-employment; those are personal expenses. But he can deduct the expenses connected with his pursuit of the website operation. They are deducted as a capital loss.

**Third scenario**: Ken's job is terminated and he sets up the website business. He can deduct all of his expenses, both the exploratory look at self-employment and the specific focus on the website design business, including the legal fees. But all of those expenses are START-UP COSTS and thus capital expenses. He must follow the special rules for deduction.

## CHAPTER 8: AN INDIE BUSINESS MEETS AND GREETS THE WORLD
### Advertising, Goodwill, Lobbying, Gifts, Meals & Entertainment

In order to be successful, solos have to get themselves known, attract customers, entertain clients, develop networks, thank their colleagues, influence government agencies, and engage in a variety of activities that promote their businesses. Such activities are common to all business, however big or small, and most of the expenses incurred can be deducted if you follow the rules, however peculiar they may be. Let's take a look at how a solo makes his mark in the community.

## ADVERTISING, PROMOTION AND MARKETING EXPENSES

What is advertising? It's attracting clients or customers, or showing that your service beats the competition, or getting out word that a sale is going on, or even nothing more than reminding the public that your business exists. Advertising executives may make distinctions between advertising, marketing, and promotion, but for tax purposes they are all the same thing. ADVERTISING expenses include:

- A website designer hired to present you or your product virtually to the universe
- Google Ads on your website or FaceBook Ads
- An ad for your service in the local paper, trade journals, on radio or television
- The cost of a marketing mentor who gets your byline on a lot of blogs
- A graphic designer's fee for sell sheet design
- Advertising space in your child's yearbook or a friend's social club directory
- Contest costs and their prizes (not if open to your employees)
- T-shirts printed with your business logo
- Signs (If a sign will last longer than one year, then it is an EQUIPMENT expense.)

Even if people may not respond until next month, next year, or maybe five years from now, whenever you promote or advertise yourself – your business, your product, or service – your costs are deductible.

At one time the IRS insisted that deductions for advertising costs would have to be spread over several years because of the long-term effects of most advertising. But the

IRS was taken to court on that, and lost. Now the IRS allows advertising to be deducted in the same year that the advertising funds are spent.

---

### THE IRS SAYS ABOUT ADVERTISING ...
You generally can deduct reasonable ADVERTISING expenses if they relate to your business activities.

---

## Expense: Reasonable As Can Be
The IRS likes to insert a "generally" into just about every rule it makes as a hedge against exceptions. But you need have no fear of a disallowed deduction if your advertising expenses are reasonable and business-related.

Business cards? Having them printed is a reasonable form of promotion. An advertisement in a community newsletter? That certainly is tied to business activities. Your name or product up on a billboard? A straightforward business expense.

## Expenses: Use A Little More Care
But some marketing expenses aim at a result more indirect than business cards and billboards. Instead of being geared for some immediate result they foster a warm fuzzy feeling about your business, a positive image that promotes your business on a long-term basis.

Sponsoring your daughter's soccer team – which might include paying for uniforms or the cost of the away bus – is a valid promotional expense. But to ensure that the IRS sees it as deductible, establish a clear connection to your craft, trade or business. See to it that the name of your business is on the uniforms and be able to show that your sponsorship will benefit your business in some material way.

## Out of Bounds Expenses: Not Deductible
And then there are the expenses that will never make it past Uncle Sam, however hard you try. Every single person that Lorenzo Landscaper invited to his daughter's wedding was a business associate, client, or potential client. Can he deduct the cost of the wedding? No, that is a personal expense, not a promotional cost.

What if "Astrid Astrologer Tells the Future" is painted in day-glow yellow on both sides of her car? Sure, that's a legitimate advertising expense and she can deduct it – the cost of having the lettering done, that is. But day-glow paint doesn't change her personal car into a business vehicle. (See CHAPTER 10 for more information on auto expenses.)

## Foreign Expenses: There Are Some Special Rules

If you plan to advertise on foreign radio, television, cable stations, websites or blogs, check with your tax advisor before assuming they are deductible business costs – they might not be.

## Dining Expenses: Not What You Think

As I suggested, while people in marketing may make distinctions between advertising, promotion and public relations, to the IRS they are all the same. On the other hand, what you may think of as promotion and therefore as a deductible ADVERTISING cost, the IRS may categorize as a different kind of deduction. MEALS & ENTERTAINMENT is one of those costs. Regardless of your business reason for paying for the meal or the recreational event the cost may not be treated as an ADVERTISING expense. You will see later in this chapter why the expense category distinction is important.

## Advertising Expenses: In Hiding

As an indie business you're changing the way you think about what you do and the people with whom you do it. For instance, all those Christmas cards you bought and mailed, did you send them to friends? Or did you send many of them to clients and prospective clients?

Also keep in mind that, if you are engaged in an activity that is not in the normal course of your business but related to it, the ADVERTISING expenses are deductible. For example, if Marketing Martha, in response to many requests, teaches a Saturday morning seminar "Social Networking for Business," the cost of any advertisement, in any medium, associated with attracting people to attend the seminar is deductible. That holds whether or not there is a charge for admission to the seminar or whether Martha is paid for the seminar presentation.

There's more to advertising than meets the eye … and then there's even more!

Besides giving exposure to your business, there's another benefit to advertising: the very fact that you advertise your product or service helps to establish profit as a motive for doing what you're doing. It's evidence – even if you're not making any money – that you're not just indulging a hobby. And, remember, if it's not a hobby you get to deduct your expenses even if they far exceed your income.

Topics related to and sometimes confused with advertising that will be covered in this chapter are:

- Goodwill
- Lobbying Expenses & Political Contribution
- Business Gifts
- Meals & Entertainment

Each will be covered in this chapter.

## SPREADING GOODWILL. THEY GOTTA LOVE YA!

As far as the IRS is concerned, there is no such thing as a GOODWILL expense.

---

**THE IRS SAYS ABOUT GOODWILL ...**
Goodwill is the value of a trade or business based on expected continued customer patronage due to its name, reputation, or any other factor.

---

What does the IRS mean by this? Well, they're not talking about peace on earth and goodwill toward men. What they are talking about is the worth of an intangible – putting a dollar amount on something that can't be touched or held or seen. Let me explain it this way.

If you were asked to put a dollar value on a friend's house – a house is a tangible – you might make a good guess. If you were pressed to be more precise, you could check on recent sales of comparable properties, make some calls, and come up with a more accurate appraisal. But if you were asked to put a dollar value on your friend's standing in the community – an intangible, his reputation – could you come up with an amount?

It's the same with a business. If Martha Marketer were to sell her business to a longtime highly-skilled employee it would be possible to put a value on the assets of his business – computers, scanners, office furniture, etc. But what value could be put on her business's reputation? How much is her name recognition worth? Her dependability? Her long-standing relationships with clients? In business circles these intangibles are known as goodwill.

As I noted about ADVERTISING expense, the IRS makes no distinctions between advertising, marketing and promotion. Many people think that goodwill is also in the same expense group – as a fourth item. That's not exactly so.

Goodwill is a value that is applied only when a business is sold – but you create it as you go along.

Whenever a self-employed spends money working on his own image and the image of the business, fostering a favorable public impression of the business, he is creating goodwill. Although there is no such thing as a goodwill expense per se, the money spent to foster the image may be deductible as an ADVERTISING expense or as some other business cost, depending on circumstances.

Some examples of creating goodwill:

- If Lorenzo Landscaper services his customers promptly, efficiently and with a smile he is engendering a feeling of goodwill about his business – at no expense.

- If he gives workshops at a nursery on Saturday mornings about xeriscaping in the desert, he can deduct any of his costs as ADVERTISING expenses.

- If he takes a member of the Chamber of Commerce program committee out to lunch with the aim of being scheduled as next month's speaker, Lorenzo can deduct the cost of the lunch as a MEALS & ENTERTAINMENT expense.

- If Lorenzo gives landscaping advice on his website, that's a soft sell approach that may cost money now in exchange for name recognition that may attract customers in the long run. Those costs are ADVERTISING expenses.

- Graphic design costs for his new seed packets are an ADVERTISING expense. His costs for the seed packets that he mails out free with his spring newsletter – to promote goodwill – may be a SUPPLIES expense, or cost of goods sold as part of his INVENTORY, or an ADVERTISING expense. The costs of mailing would be a POSTAGE expense.

- If Lorenzo gives a $25 local restaurant gift certificate to Clyde Client in thanks for Clyde sending him a customer, that is a BUSINESS GIFT expense.

So you see, when fostering goodwill you may encounter any number of different kinds of expenses. And although Lorenzo does not expect to see results from his goodwill efforts for many months or years down the line he can deduct the costs as certain specific expenses in the year that he incurs them. But he can't deduct them as a goodwill expense because there is no such thing.

If Lorenzo's longtime employee did buy the business from him, and if part of the selling price were based upon Lorenzo's reputation and good customer relations, that part of the selling price is called goodwill – and that's what the IRS means by the term goodwill. In some parts of the country it's called "Blue Sky," possibly because the value set on these kinds of things is determined by looking up and pulling a number out of the blue.

If goodwill is a component of the sale price of a business the purchaser must amortize – spread out – the goodwill amount and deduct it over 15 years.

## Giving It Away for Free

I want to mention one final point about goodwill: If a self-employed provides free services in order to promote goodwill, he cannot deduct the value of his time as a business expense.

If Lorenzo cut the grass of the local community center for free, his deductible costs would be his actual expenses only, for example, gas for the mower. If his usual fee for this service is $100 he cannot take $100 as a tax deduction; in other words, he cannot deduct anything for his time.

Although Astrid Astrologer promoted her business by giving away free astrological charts she cannot take as any kind of deduction the value of her time in preparing the charts (although she could deduct the cost of the paper on which they were written).

On the same principle, in a recent case the Tax Court disallowed the deduction of a physician who took the value of his services as an ADVERTISING expense after providing free medical services to the public. The court ruled that the doctor's uncompensated services were not an expense.

*Unfair, you say!* I know you say that, because this is one of the topics about which I get the most emails. Indies just can't believe it. They think I'm wrong. I haven't really researched it. They should be able to deduct for the value of their time. No. No. No. Can't do it.

Here's a way to look at it that, although may not make you feel better, may help you understand why it is the way it is. You cannot take a deduction for something that did not cost you or someone else any money.

Lorenzo cuts grass for Mr. Green; he gets paid $100; he pays tax on the $100. Then Lorenzo donates the $100 to the Children's Society; he gets a *personal charitable deduction* of $100 on his tax return. His tax paid on the $100 income is more than the tax saved by the $100 contribution.

Rather than donate $100 Lorenzo decides to cut the grass around the Children's Society office building. He does not get paid for his time; he cannot deduct the value of his time on his tax return as a charitable deduction; he may deduct the cost of any out-of-pocket grass-cutting expenses he had as a ***personal charitable deduction***.

In the long run, however, it may still be of value. Even though you cannot write off the value of your time as a tax deduction, remember that what goes around comes around, and by building up goodwill you may profit by getting new clients, or end up with more money in your pocket when you sell your entrepreneurial business because of the "blue sky" component, or, it just may make you feel good!

## LOBBYING AND POLITICAL CONTRIBUTIONS

Lobbying is often thought of as a derogatory term. Stripped of its negative connotations, though, lobbying just means attempting to influence government legislation or policy. And there's nothing wrong with that – having access to government and being able to influence its officials is an important factor in a democracy.

Most of the tax guides are wrong about business deductions for lobbying. The source of the trouble is the official Internal Revenue Service tax code. And that brings me for a moment to a broader subject: One reason that much of what you read on the subject of taxes all sounds alike and offers the same advice is because by and large the authors just rewrite IRS material. That's why so much of it is wrong. Remember, one of the first things I told you was that the tax laws are not written with self-employeds in mind. So when I say that much of what you read is wrong, I don't mean factually incorrect. I mean wrong in the sense of being misleading and off target because the point of view is not that of a self-employed.

LOBBYING expense is a case in point. Just about everything you read on the kinds of business deductions allowed for lobbying starts with the following opening sentence: "Generally lobbying is not deductible as a business expense." (There's that "generally" again.)

That's a sentence taken right out of an IRS publication. Then follows a statement with a list of the various LOBBYING expenses that cannot be deducted. They include such admonitions as – you can't deduct your cost for contacting the President or your costs for trying to directly influence the views of the Vice President. And so on. In doing so the authors show more familiarity with the IRS manual than they do with the real life of a sole proprietor.

But if you look at the genuine concerns of a self-employed, you'll find that there is a considerable amount of LOBBYING expenses that can be deducted.

Most entrepreneurs and indie businesses – at least the ones who make up the bulk of my readers – have little to do with attempts to influence the President, the Vice President, a Cabinet member (the IRS tax code calls them "covered executive branch officials") or the Speaker of the House. There are numerous occasions, however, when free agents and entrepreneurs are trying to be heard on a local level – at City Hall.

And as far as the issues that come up at the Mayor's office or at the City Council meeting are concerned, you can deduct your LOBBYING expenses.

If the local government is planning a zoning change that would be detrimental to your business, or if you want the city council to allow home businesses in the area in which you live, or if you're a restaurateur who's opposed to their proposed ban on smoking or live music – all your efforts in those areas are deductible. You can argue with the building inspector, attempt to be arrestingly persuasive with the police chief, and exchange heated views with the fire marshal, and you can deduct all the expenses incurred. So the stuff that the other guys write, while they may not be formally wrong, are highly misleading – because they're not in touch with the nitty-gritty of self-employed people.

---

### WHATTA CONCEPT!
#### Branches of Government

For the sake of those who are not familiar with government, let me point out that at both the federal and state levels there are two separate branches of government that are lobbied – the executive branch, which runs the agencies and departments of the government; and the legislative branch, consisting of lawmakers called Senators, Congress members, Legislators, Assembly members, or other names depending on the state.

The legislative branch makes the laws, the executive branch enforces them. The third branch of government, the judiciary, is not subject to lobbying.

---

## Lobbying Expenses You Can Deduct

*Local Or County Government:* You may deduct up to any amount for expenses of appearing before, or communicating with, any local or county council or governing body concerning its legislation, ordinances, or other official actions of direct interest to you. These governing bodies include boards of education, municipal or county planning or zoning boards and local commissions. Your expenses, including travel, in meeting with any municipal or county official – from the mayor to the county clerk's secretary – are deductible if they involve your business.

Of interest to my fellow New Mexicans: An Indian tribal government is treated as a local council or similar governing body for the purposes of lobbying expenses.

My interview of an IRS attorney confirmed my reading of a peculiar loophole in the IRS regulations regarding LOBBYING expenses. You may deduct any expenses (you are not limited to the $2,000 maximum, see below) of communicating with state officials of the executive branch as long as your lobbying does not involve legislation. That means, as long as you are not trying to influence the law.

So although you are limited in deducting the costs of lobbying your state legislators about a piece of pending legislation, once a law is on the books you are not limited in deducting the costs of trying to influence a state agency regarding enforcement of the law. For example, you may deduct all cost of trying to influence your State Environmental Protection Agency regarding an existing regulation that affects your business. The loophole demonstrates once again that you shouldn't look for logic in IRS Tax Code.

*In-house Expenses of $2,000 Or Less:* You may deduct up to $2,000 in expenses at the state and federal level, including communicating directly with the President and the Vice President, if the expenses are in-house – which means if it's done in your office by you or someone who works for you.

For example, if you wished to make your views known about a proposed state bill involving air pollution, you could deduct your expenses, including travel to the State Capitol to attend legislative committee hearings. Since the deductions only apply to in-house expenses, you could not deduct the expense if you were to hire a lobbyist to do it for you, or if an organization to which you belong did it.

## Lobbying Expenses You Cannot Deduct

These allowable deductions aside, it is true – just as the tax columnists and IRS publications say – that when you get to the upper reaches of expenses and the upper layers of government, much lobbying is not deductible.

The following in-house expenses cannot be deducted if they exceed $2,000:
- Influencing proposed state or federal legislation.
- Attempting to influence the public about elections, legislative matters, or referendums.
- Communicating directly with various federal high-ranking members of the administration, including Cabinet-level officials and their immediate deputy directors, in any attempt to influence their official actions or positions.
- Participating in any political campaign for or against any candidate for public office.

*Political Contributions by Sending A Check:* Just to be clear about political participation, you cannot deduct direct financial contributions to political parties or candidates as business expenses, even if it is under $2,000. A check flying out the door is not an in-house expense. (FYI: You cannot deduct political contributions as a personal itemized deduction either.)

*Is it lobbying or promotion?* And, because some self-employeds confuse lobbying with business promotion, I must add that you may not deduct indirect political contributions either. By which I mean things such as the following:

- Advertising in a convention program of a political party, or in any other publication if any of the proceeds from the publication are for, or intended for, the use of a political party or candidate.
- Admission to a dinner or program (including galas, dances, film presentations, parties, and sporting events) if any of the proceeds from the function are for, or intended for, the use of a political party or candidate.
- Admission to an inaugural ball, gala, parade, concert, or similar event if identified with a political party or candidate.

Let's explore deductible and non-deductible LOBBYING expenses.

---

### REALITY √ CHECK

Fred Fixit **cannot** deduct that portion of his dues to the Santa Fe Handyman's Association that is used toward trying to convince state legislators to give handymen a special tax break. Reason: Fred is attempting to influence state legislation and his dues are not in-house costs.

---

### REALITY √ CHECK

However, Lorenzo Landscaper can deduct that portion of his dues to the Landscapers' Association that is used to lobby the county government to try to dissuade the county from raising fees at the county dump. Reason: Lorenzo is lobbying at the local level and therefore there is no limit on his deductible expenses.

---

### REALITY √ CHECK

Endie Naturopath, a naturopathic physician, is fighting to get licensing for naturopaths in New Jersey. She may deduct up to $2,000 per year of in-house costs for phone, travel, printing, and other items involved with her campaign to get favorable legislation enacted. Reason: Lobbying to influence legislation at a non-local level is limited to $2,000 of in-house expense.

---

Pretty complicated, wouldn't you say? Before putting any big bucks into lobbying, check with your tax professional. And ask her enough questions to be sure she really understands the fine points. I always have to check my notes!

## TO SUM UP LOBBYING EXPENSES

- You can deduct any amount for LOBBYING local or county government.
- You can deduct up to $2,000 for in-house LOBBYING of the state or federal government if attempting to influence pending legislation.
- You can deduct any amount spent on LOBBYING at the state level if attempting to influence enforcement of the law.

Of course, if you are a professional lobbyist all business expenses that you incur in your business on behalf of a client are deductible for you (although not necessarily for your client).

## BUSINESS GIFTS

Rob Rolf has just about finished converting his garage into a two-room office where he intends to see patients in his massage therapy practice. Friday promises to be a crowded day – after meeting with a plumber first thing in the morning he has to rush across town for an eight-hour hands-on workshop. Nevertheless Friday is the only day that the truck will be in his area to deliver his new massage table. His next door neighbor, Ned, also works at home, and they've been quite friendly since they helped each other dig out of a snowstorm. So Rob asks Ned if he would watch for the truck and let in the deliveryman with the table.

No problem, Ned says. Everything goes well, the table is delivered, and Rob buys Ned a bottle of wine as a thank you present. Rob can deduct the cost of the wine as a BUSINESS GIFT.

---

**THE IRS SAYS ABOUT BUSINESS GIFTS ...**
If you give BUSINESS GIFTS in the course of your trade or business, you can deduct all or part of the cost of the gifts.

---

Don't be too quick to rush out and buy that potential client a set of golf clubs. Sorry. Two packs of golf balls are more like it. That's because ***there is a $25 per-year-per-person limit on*** BUSINESS GIFT ***deductions.***

No matter how much you spend on gifts for a particular business associate over the course of a year you may deduct only $25. If Rob Rolf had bought Ned a bottle of Grand Marnier for $30, he could deduct only the $25 limit. If instead he bought Ned a $10 bottle of Merlot, Rob could deduct the $10, and could give Neighbor Ned another gift before the year was out, and could deduct $15 of the cost of the second gift.

***Twenty-five dollars, you've got to be kidding!*** The Soviet empire has collapsed, a new millennium has arrived, apps have taken over everything, and yet the IRS gift limit was, is, and probably will be $25 until well into the future. Get used to it.

However, the IRS does allow you to deduct related incidental costs beyond the $25 limit – costs such as engraving on jewelry, or packaging, insuring, and mailing. A cost is incidental only if it does not add substantial value to the gift. For example, the cost of gift-wrapping is considered incidental. The purchase of an ornamental basket for packaging fruit is not an incidental cost if the value of the basket is substantial compared to the value of the fruit.

Are you allowed to deduct a gift basket of fruit to Grandma?

Of course you can – if Gram has some connection to your business. Did she show you how to hook up your printer? Make curtains for your office? Explain how to use Track Changes in Word?

Your business relationship with Grandma brings up the recurring subject of how a self-employed needs to continue thinking as an indie business. Which is particularly pertinent in gift-giving. Of course, if you bought your client a basket of fruit as a birthday present you would treat it as a BUSINESS GIFT deduction. But what about your friends with whom you have a business connection? You need to maintain an awareness of all the business connections between yourself and others. If your marketing consultant, who is also a friend, invites you to her place for dinner and you bring a gift for the hostess, in this instance, is she primarily a business associate or primarily a friend? Be sure you're wearing your indie think cap. A gift to a business associate is deductible. One to a friend is not.

As with other client expenses, a gift may be deducted as a business expense when it is given *in the ordinary and necessary course of your business* to a business associate. Those associates include clients, customers, dealers, distributors, employees, Neighbor Ned, your website designer friend, Grandma – anyone who has helped to nurture your enterprise.

The gift counts toward the $25 per year, per person limit whether given directly, or indirectly, to a business associate. Therefore, if you send something over to the Callous Company – like a $25 cheese and nut sampler because Reggie Receptionist has been so pleasant and helpful to you – it's obviously intended as a gift for Reggie. If later in the year you give him a box of chocolates on Secretaries Day – it's nice of you, but you've already used up your gift deduction to Reggie for the year. You get no business expense deduction for the chocolates.

The same holds for a gift to a spouse or child of a business associate. Finger paints for the child of a business associate are considered a gift to the business associate. If you've already given a client a gift that cost at least $25 and you are then invited to your client's daughter's wedding, you get no BUSINESS GIFT expense deduction, regardless of the value of the present. This rule does not apply if you have a bona fide, independent business connection with that family member – in this case, the bride (or maybe the groom).

If you and your spouse both give gifts to the same business associate, both of you are treated as one taxpayer and so together you can deduct gifts of only $25 per recipient. It does not matter whether the two of you have separate businesses, or whether each of you has an independent business relationship with the recipient. (There's IRS logic again.)

## Gift Chronicles

When I was a child one of my sisters-in-law kept a record of every gift she ever gave to anyone. (I think she is still compiling it.) You would do well to copy her careful watchfulness, but as I'll show you, there is a particular method you must use in keeping records of BUSINESS GIFTS.

If, during an IRS audit, you are unable to produce records of certain business expenses, in many cases the IRS will estimate the amount of your expenses and allow you to deduct them. The estimate is allowed if it is clear that the expenses have been incurred – as for example in the purchase of business equipment or telephone use.

No estimating allowed, however, with BUSINESS GIFTS or with business MEALS & ENTERTAINMENT expenses. Because the IRS suspects that such expenses are often invented or inflated, you are required to have records. If you have none, the deduction will be disallowed in an audit.

When you give a business associate a gift, to ensure that you will get the deduction, on the receipt write the following information:

- Date the gift was given.
- Cost of the gift.
- Description of the gift.
- Name & business relationship of the person to whom you gave the gift.
- Business reason for the gift, or the business benefit you expect to gain.


Gifts should always be documented and annotated. If a collection is taken for a baby shower for a business associate, for example, it's best to write a check. If that's impossible or inappropriate, and you contribute in cash, be sure to note the required information on your monthly minder, or iCal, or on a piece of paper that you will later use as your "receipt."

Rob Rolf would have written on the receipt from the liquor store:

5/5/13
Thanks
Neighbor Ned
table delivery

### That's Entertainment? Or Is It A Gift? Does It Matter?

What if Rob had thanked Neighbor Ned by taking him to a Knicks game, or to hear the Tony Trischka Band? Would that be a MEALS & ENTERTAINMENT expense or a BUSINESS GIFT expense for Rob? And why does it matter? It matters because it may affect the amount of taxes that Rob pays.

Let's look at the numbers in various scenarios.

*First Scenario:* It doesn't matter how you categorize a $50 concert ticket for a business associate – as gift or entertainment – you end with the same deduction. Here's how:

- No matter what the cost of the gift you can deduct only $25.
- As you'll see in the next section you may deduct only 50% of a MEALS & ENTERTAINMENT expense. A little arithmetic here: 50% of $50 = $25.

So in this case, the deduction is the same however you classify the concert ticket.

*Second Scenario:* What if you treat your client to a ringside seat at the heavyweight championship fight for $400? Let's look at your choice then:

- No matter what the cost, if it's a gift you get only a $25 deduction.
- But as an entertainment expense, it's 50% of $400 = $200 deduction.

Big difference in what you can deduct as the price moves up. At which point, how you classify the expenses – BUSINESS GIFT or MEALS & ENTERTAINMENT – does matter.

As you probably guessed, you don't have total leeway in choosing which kind of deduction you take. The IRS has set up specific rules to govern the BUSINESS GIFT vs. MEALS & ENTERTAINMENT expense, as follows:

- If your client eats or drinks your gift of foodstuffs and liquor at a later time and *without sharing them with you*, that's a BUSINESS GIFT expense.

- Whenever you accompany your guests to the concert or game, you must deduct the cost of the tickets as a MEALS & ENTERTAINMENT expense.

- If your client attends the concert or game without you, the tickets you gave may be treated as either a BUSINESS GIFT expense or a MEALS & ENTERTAINMENT expense, whichever is to your advantage.

## It's The Little Things That Don't Count

There is no $25 per person limit for deductions on some things that you give away – as long as they're cheap, that is.

Promotionally savvy Rob Rolf gives to potential clients small bottles of massage oil. In addition to information about the herbs used in the oil the labels also have his new address on them. These nominal gifts are not included in the $25 per person limit.

There is no per person limit as long as a gift item:

- Costs $4 or less.
  and

- Has the name of the self-employed or his business clearly printed on it.
  and

- Is identical to a number of others distributed to many clients or business associates.

You've all received pens, calendars, desk sets, magnets, baseball caps and the like; now you know that they probably cost the smart entrepreneur no more than $4 each.

## When Is A Gift Not A Gift?
*Free samples are not business gifts.*

If you give samples of your merchandise to prospective buyers or to people who might review or publicize your products – whether it's a widget or a book – they are not subject to the BUSINESS GIFT cut-off amount of $25, because they are not considered gifts.

Your cost for the free samples gets deducted in another expense category, usually as SUPPLIES or are deducted from INVENTORY as part of COST-OF-GOODS-SOLD. These giveaway items will be deducted at your cost, not at the amount you would receive were you to sell them.

*A gift to a charitable organization is not a* BUSINESS GIFT.

A sole proprietor cannot deduct, as a BUSINESS GIFT, money he has given to a charity. Such a contribution is a personal deduction.

# MEALS & ENTERTAINMENT

Now let's see, does the dessert fork go to the left of the salad fork? Is it OK to eat a chicken wing with your hands? May you start eating before everyone is served? Do you pass to the left or to the right?

If you think the rulebook of dining etiquette is thick and complicated, wait until you get a load of the rules on the deductibility of dining and entertaining expenses for an entrepreneur. Believe me, it's not "Eat, drink, and be merry, we can deduct it."

However, life's ordinary guideposts can often lead us through the maze of IRS regulations. Think back to when you went to your first party all by yourself and your mama told you, "Now, just behave yourself and everything'll be fine." Mama's early advice applies to your attendance at the mayor's dinner party as well as it applied to your friend's fifth birthday party: Follow the generally accepted rules of conduct that apply to all interpersonal relationships – like courtesy, attentiveness and tact, and even if you haven't mastered the finer points and myriad rules of elegant dining, you'll most likely not embarrass yourself or your host.

The same logic applies to MEALS & ENTERTAINMENT: Follow the generally accepted rules regarding business expenses and you'll most likely do OK.

The IRS says an allowable deduction is one that is (a) common and accepted in your field of business, trade or profession, and (b) not extravagant, and (c) helpful and appropriate, although not necessarily indispensable, for your business. As I said in CHAPTER 6. UNDERSTANDING BUSINESS EXPENSES: Business expenses are the costs you incur to run your business – the money you must spend in order to make money. If you apply these principles to MEALS & ENTERTAINMENT expenses, you won't stray very far from what is an allowable deduction – unless, that is, your deductions get too creative.

### What's Entertainment And Whom Can You Entertain?
*Business meals or entertainment are deductible as a business expense if you talk business before, during, or after the meal or entertainment.*

If Hilda Headhunter takes a client to lunch to discuss the personnel needs of the client, Hilda gets to deduct the cost of lunch. But what if Hilda treats her sister-in-law Selma to Aida? And what if she then claims an entertainment deduction because during intermission Selma tells her about a company in her building looking for human resources help? Nothing doing! That's a bit too creative for the IRS.

But don't assume that opera tickets are not deductible. For many business occasions the ticket price can be deducted, and it is important for you to know how and when those occasions and situations arise.

## What kind of activity is deductible?
Any activity considered refreshment, entertainment, amusement, or recreation.

## Where can the activity take place?
- At your place of business
- At a business convention or reception
- At a restaurant
- At bars, theaters, country clubs, social or athletic clubs, sporting events
- At home
- On hunting, fishing, vacation, or similar trips

## What kinds of expenses are allowable?
- Meals you provide to customers or clients, whether the meal is the whole deal or it's a part of an entertainment package (for example, refreshments at a football game)
- Tickets to sporting events, concerts, theatrical presentations, movies, etc.
- A meal expense includes the cost of food, beverages, taxes, and tips
- Meeting personal, living, or family needs of individuals, such as providing meals, a hotel suite, or a car to customers or their families
- The costs you incur if a business associate visits and stays with you (cost of meals you serve, etc.)

## With whom can you dine and party?
Any business associate, established or prospective. Broadly defined this includes:
- Customer or client
- Supplier
- Employee
- Agent
- Collaborator

- Professional adviser
- Colleague

## What kind of record must you have?

You must have a record that clearly shows:

- Amount
- Date
- Name of the place
- Type of entertainment, if not obvious
- Business purpose
- Business relationship

The easiest way of substantiating business meal expenses is to staple the business card of your associate to the restaurant receipt. See below for a typical handwritten receipt.

---

**REALITY √ CHECK**

Tessie Tripp is trying to win a contract to handle travel arrangements for a major cable TV station. She invites the suits who will make the final decision to her mountain lodge for a weekend of negotiations. She pays all the bills for the weekend (maid, catered meals, etc.).

Tessie gets to deduct the expenses.

---

**REALITY √ CHECK**

Nadine Novella has dinner with someone she is interviewing for a short story she is writing. She interviews during dessert. Nadine pays for the dinner. She gets to deduct the cost. She writes on the receipt:

> *6/14/13 with Sally Source*
>
> *info re 1920s fashion*
>
> *dinner @ Diners Delight $93.00 w/tip*

---

> ### REALITY √ CHECK
> Charlotte Salesrep treats the local dentist to dinner, during which time she explains the instant access and lower radiation benefits of digital x-rays – hoping to get make a sale. Charlotte's expenses are legitimate deductions.

The best way to ensure that the entertainment is directly related to business is to put it in a *clear business setting*. Like these:

- Billy Bridesnapper provides a hospitality room at a photography convention where he displays his unconventional black and white photos of conventional family events.
- Prudence Pas de Deux invites local civic leaders – none of whom has she ever met – to the opening performance of her dance troupe, "The Young Ones." She also provides them with coffee, other beverages and dessert during intermission.

*Hold on A Moment:* Before continuing in this section take a moment to think about your business. Sarah Sculptor spends all her time in her studio, rarely dines out and her agent does all the socializing necessary to sell her work. Sarah need read no further in this section. On the other hand, architect Frank Boyd White feels that more of his time is spent wheeling, dealing and cajoling than designing. Frank needs to keep on reading about deducting the costs of the social distraction side of his business. Where does your business fit? Is there much business socializing? Is your home office not the best place to bring clients and so much of your work is done in town? There is a BUSINESS MEALS AND ENTERTAINMENT EXPENSES chart on page 84. You be the judge of how much you need to know at this time about MEALS & ENTERTAINMENT deductions.

### Now Some Finer Points of Dining for Deductions

Many self-employed are convinced that the IRS tax code is arbitrary, but in the case of MEALS & ENTERTAINMENT deductions, the reason for the agency's beady eye is clear – the IRS is trying to weed out the invalid business deductions in an area that seems to invite abuse. And while taxpayers have the right to explain their honest differences of opinion with the IRS, guess whose opinion usually prevails?

Before taking a look at what the IRS says about MEALS & ENTERTAINMENT expenses let me tell you a secret about that monstrous document, the IRS Tax Code. You've probably heard our politicians orating about the thousands upon thousands of pages of the Code that is reputed to be so formidable and intimidating. Well, it is. But the tax code that they are complaining about is a different animal from the numbered publications that are available online or some of them at the local IRS office. These taxpayer-friendly IRS pamphlets – which explain how to do our tax returns and whether we can take Grandma as a dependent – are actually IRS employees' interpretations of the tax code, reorganized and put into plainer language to guide the taxpayer through the maze of tax regulations. Does the official IRS Tax Code really exist? Yes, it does. It's about 10,000 pages long and it's published in very small print. Few have ever actually read a paragraph of it. Now for the secret: Many of the people who write about taxes haven't read the code either. Like the general public they rely on those little IRS publications – interpretations of the tax code. They then interpret the interpretations. Sometimes they even crib and hastily rewrite the interpretations of what others have written. The result can be something like the child's game that's played by whispering a story from one ear to another and another and another – what we end up with is often far from the original article.

Although it's a tiresome process, and a strain on the eyes, I do read the IRS Code, because I believe in basic research – going back to the source. That said, here's what the IRS presents in one of its interpretative publications.

---

### THE IRS SAYS ABOUT ENTERTAINMENT EXPENSE …

You may deduct business-related entertainment expenses that you have for entertaining a client, customer, or employee if the expenses are both ordinary and necessary and meet one of the following two tests:

    1. Directly-related test

      or

    2. Associated test

The amount you can deduct is usually limited to 50% of your meal or entertainment expense.

---

Most of the writers about taxes go on and on about how you can get a passing grade on one of those tests or the other. If you can't show that the entertainment expense meets the directly-related test, there's always the associated test. But my guess is you don't care a hill of beans whether you meet one test or the other test. Your only interest is to write off as much of your dining and entertainment costs as you legitimately can, and I'm going to show you how to do that.

Well aware that MEALS & ENTERTAINMENT expenses are a vital part of the conduct of business, the Tax Code gives the taxpayer considerable leeway in claiming legitimate expenses. The IRS gives you a reasonable series of alternatives. Let's take a look:

Either

A. *Business was the main purpose* of the meal or entertainment,

or

B. The meal or entertainment *was associated with your trade or business*.

Either

C. You *engaged in business while entertaining*,

or

D. The business discussion or event *directly preceded or followed the entertainment*.

Either

E. You had more than a general *expectation of business benefit or income* resulting from the entertainment.

or

F. A *substantial business discussion* took place.

Let's take a look at each of these and see how they relate to the business life of a self-employed and also how they differ from one another:

*A. Business is the main purpose for the entertainment:* Be careful when making this claim. Business as the main purpose seems unlikely when you're watching showgirls dance or Chippendales prance, or sailing on a yacht. A dinner with business as the main purpose is more credible.

Would you talk business at the opera? Between the acts of a play? For the most part entertainment events are distractions that take you away from business, that make the mention of business an intrusion. To claim that business is the main purpose of an entertainment event raises doubts in the mind of an IRS auditor.

And although there may be time during hunting or fishing trips or while relaxing on a yacht to talk business, the IRS has no reason to believe that business is the main purpose of such excursions.

Furthermore, if the attendees at your entertainment event include people who are not business associates the IRS strongly doubts that the main purpose was business – especially if the wining and dining took place at a country club, cabaret, brew pub, vacation resort or the like.

***B. Entertainment is associated with the active conduct of your business:*** If business is not the main purpose of the social event then you must show that the event is associated with your trade or business. This simply means that you must be able to show a clear business purpose for the entertainment. The purpose may be to get a new client or to encourage the continuation of an existing business relationship. Think about what I said in **CHAPTER 6:** Anything you do that relates to your work, that stimulates or enhances your business, nurtures your professional creativity, improves your skills, wins you recognition, or increases your chances of making a sale may be a business expense and therefore deductible.

---

### REALITY √ CHECK

Raina Realtor's lunch with a potential home seller to discuss the sale price for the property clearly has "business as the main purpose."

However, if an existing client is offended by an experience with Raina's assistant and if Raina takes the client to a dinner at La Elegante not to discuss business but to smooth her ruffled feathers, then that dinner is "associated with" Raina's business. The purpose was not to discuss business, but to keep a client. Dinner is a deductible expense.

---

***C. Engage in business while entertaining:*** It's not the length of the discussion but its aim. If during the meal or entertainment you actively discuss business then the business portion of the meeting doesn't have to be of any specified length. It is not necessary to devote more time to business than to entertainment. If you're a woman of few words, you will not be penalized for getting your point across quickly.

***D. Engage in business before or after the entertainment:*** Enjoy whatever you're doing or watching – an evening out at a restaurant, play or sporting event – because it is not necessary to discuss business during the entertainment as long as the entertainment takes place just prior to or immediately after a business discussion.

Entertainment that occurs on the same day as the business discussion is considered to directly precede or follow business.

Time can be stretched when stuff happens. If the entertainment and the business discussion don't occur on the same day, you can still claim a deduction based on the particular circumstances. Perhaps there was a sudden change in schedule because of travel problems, someone fell ill, connections were missed. As even the IRS has to acknowledge, life is full of unforeseen events.

The rules about time sequence are not cast in concrete, as long as the full scenario – which includes the dimensions of the business discussion, the traveling schedule of the participants and the time of the entertainment – makes sense. You can turn an expensive lunch check, or a dinner for eight at home, into a deductible business meeting – if you have a good sense of timing.

---

### REALITY √ CHECK

Heavenly Happenin, a special events planner, invites a group of business associates from out of town to her place of business to present the wares of her Holiday Happy Happenings exhibit. If she entertains those business guests on the evening before the presentation, or on the evening of the day following the presentation, the entertainment is considered to be held directly before or after the discussion.

---

### REALITY √ CHECK

Harry Hardseat owns a custom-made furniture business in Tacoma, Washington. Over the years he has selected furniture for homes designed and constructed by Frank Boyd White, an architect-builder for the rich and famous, and the two have become friends. Frank and his wife are in Tacoma for several days, and on Tuesday, Frank and Harry talked business while looking over plans and discussing furnishings for a new home Frank is building. On the day after their meeting, Mr. and Mrs. White dined at the Hardseat home. Harry can deduct the cost of entertaining the Whites at home as a MEALS & ENTERTAINMENT expense.

---

***E. Great Expectations:*** You don't have to seal the deal. You do not have to show that business income actually resulted from each entertainment expense but you must show that some benefit had reasonably been expected. It's all right if the business discussion turned out to be fruitless, but you must be able to show some hoped-for specific business payoff, not just a vague expectation of gain.

By the way, building goodwill is not considered a specific business benefit.

---

### REALITY √ CHECK

Pat Personal Trainer invited another fitness professional to lunch to talk about jointly operating a fitness center at the mall. But his lunch guest, weighed down with problems, talked about nothing but his impending divorce and quarrels with his teen-age daughter. They never did get to talk business. Can Pat take the lunch as a business deduction? Yes. It is not Pat's fault that, for reasons beyond his control, he did not get to talk business at a lunch that was arranged for that purpose.

---

***F. Something of Substance:*** What's substantial to one may be trifling to another, so use your noggin. What is a substantial business discussion? The answer: it's up to you. The IRS says that a business discussion will not be considered substantial unless you can show that you engaged in it in order to win a specific business benefit.

Be careful if business is discussed only in passing, that is, "incidentally."

---

### REALITY √ CHECK

Hilda Headhunter's sister-in-law Selma gave her a piece of incidental business information when she told Hilda about a company looking for a human resources consultant. That piece of information alone was not enough to make the opera tickets deductible. But Hilda could deduct the tickets if Selma had sketched out a brochure and reviewed Hilda's marketing plan prior to the performance.

---

The IRS considers that dining and fun activities that take place at a convention, trade show, or similar event are always associated with business, since the independent professional is there to further his entrepreneurial goals. But how much business do you think gets discussed in the schvitz, at the gym, at poolside, on a hike, or playing roulette? Nevertheless, if it's a tax break, we'll take it. And, if it takes place at a conference or convention, it's allowed.

---

**REALITY √ CHECK**

If Tessie Tripp, at a trade show for travel agents, buys lift tickets as well as drinks and dinner for one of the speakers, or for one of her associates, the expense qualifies as deductible entertainment.

---

## Don't Get Personal: Stick to Business

Be careful with events that include both business and personal elements. The following situations need your attention. You'll have to allocate expenses between those for business and those that are personal.

*Mixed Groups:* If you entertain business associates as well as people not connected with business at the same event, you cannot deduct the entire cost as a business ENTERTAINMENT expense; you must separate the business expenses from the nonbusiness, or personal, expenses. If you cannot establish the exact expense for each person participating, allocate the expense on a per person basis.

---

**REALITY √ CHECK**

Miles Mingus invites fellow musicians, promoters and music critics to a party to promote his new song. In addition to the 20 professionals attending, his immediate family of 10 people also come to help him celebrate. Only two-thirds (20 out of 30 people) of the expense qualifies as a business entertainment expense. Miles cannot deduct the expenses for the ten family guests because those costs are nonbusiness expenses. But if his entire family were connected to the music business – hey, maybe.

---

*Home Entertaining, Sign in Please:* You may entertain at home, or if your office is in your home you may have business associates to your home for meetings during lunch, discussions over cocktails, or working dinners. You can deduct your costs for entertaining at your home the same as you can in any other setting. Be creative and clever in your substantiation. If you've sent written invitations be sure to keep one along with your guest list or have the attendees drop their business cards into the micaceous clay bowl at the entrance. Better yet, make sure the invitation states the business purpose for the event.

> ## REALITY √ CHECK
> Gary Geekery has many colleagues who spend most of their time in front of computer screens. Going against the digital grain, he thought they all needed a little face-time with their fellow IT and design people in their small city as an aid to better business communications and networking. Success! There are now 67 dues-paying members. Gary held a party to mark the first anniversary of his organization. The attendees at his home include members and their guests. Gary kept a list of invited guests as well as a sign-in guest book. He has also invited his parents (who doubted this venture would be a success) along with a few other friends. The portion of the cost that applies to family and friends is not deductible.

***Expenses For Spouses, Bring The Husband:*** You generally cannot deduct the cost of entertainment for your spouse or for the spouse of a business associate. However, you can deduct these costs if you can show that you had a clear business purpose, rather than a personal or social reason, for providing the entertainment for the spouses.

> ## REALITY √ CHECK
> Clarissa Clothier took an out-of-town client to dinner. Since the client's husband has made the long trip as well, it would be inappropriate for Clarissa to take the client and not include the client's husband. In such a case, the cost of taking the spouse to dinner, as well as the client, is ordinary and necessary. If Clarissa's husband joins the party because the client's husband will be at dinner, the cost of entertaining both husbands is deductible.

## Verboten! Prohibido! Not Allowed!
Watch out for these sensitive areas.

***Family Members As Potential Clients:*** You can no longer deduct the costs of a big party to which you invite people who might become your customers or clients. There has to be a more substantial basis for a deduction than the possibility of someone – and that includes your brother – becoming a client.

***Is it my turn?*** Expenses are not deductible when a group of business acquaintances take turns picking up each others' meal or entertainment checks without regard to whether any business purposes are served. The same applies if two genealogists, who happen to be friends, and sometimes talk business, meet every Tuesday for lunch. A this-week-you-pay-next-week-I-pay plan is not allowed. As with other tax matters: Be cool. Don't overdo it.

***Let Me Entertain Me:*** Regular meals while working, but not traveling, are not deductible. If Raina Realtor is always on the run from one showing or appointment to another, and rarely eats at home but instead grabs a bite on the road or in her office, she cannot deduct the cost of those meals. Perhaps the IRS reasoning: She'd have to eat lunch anyway. It's her poor organization skills, not a business reason that cause her to eat while working.

***Don't Go Over The Top:*** MEALS & ENTERTAINMENT expenses that the IRS considers to be lavish or extravagant will be reduced if the taxpayer is audited. But expenses will not be considered lavish or extravagant just because they take place at deluxe restaurants, hotels, nightclubs, or resorts if the expenses reasonably fit the circumstances. In some cases a drive through at Fast Finger Chicken might be suitable while in others, if the deal is big enough, a $200 bottle of wine might be perfectly appropriate.

## 50% Limit on Expenses

All right, you've figured out how to write off just about everything you eat and every place you play. Not so fast with the restaurant reservations. It is not a dollar for dollar deduction.

***You can deduct only 50% of your business-related*** MEALS & ENTERTAINMENT ***expenses.***

It doesn't matter if you are eating and playing, as long as you are also:
- Entertaining customers at your place of business, a restaurant, at home, or some other location
- Attending a business convention or reception, business meeting, or business luncheon at a club
- Traveling for business (whether eating alone or with others)

Meal or entertainment costs include:
- Taxes and tips relating to a business meal or entertainment activity
- Cover charges for admission to a nightclub
- Rent paid for a room in which you hold a dinner or cocktail party
- Parking at a sports arena

Let me restate, because this is one of those rules you do not want to believe and so conveniently forget: ***All of the above expenses are subject to the 50% limit. That means you get to deduct only one-half (1/2) of the expense.***

OK. Think you've got it. Now here are a couple doozers.

The cost of transportation, that is going to and from a business meal or a business-related entertainment activity, including parking, is 100% deductible as a TRANSPORTATION or AUTO or PARKING expense.

Except that parking at a sports arena it is only 50% deductible. Does that make sense? If you are looking for consistency, you are searching in vain, for the IRS tax code does not often make sense. It's a patchwork quilt that's been sewn together, misaligned and mismatched.

***Don't Mix Eating with Sleeping:*** MEALS & ENTERTAINMENT are the only business expenses deducted at 50 percent. Therefore, when traveling, as you track or record your MEALS & ENTERTAINMENT expenses, keep meal expenses separate from lodging. I'll explain more on this in the TRAVEL expenses section. For now, here's an example.

---

### REALITY √ CHECK

Stella Sellit stayed several days at the Hilton, saw a number of clients and took them out to dinner and to a jazz session in the hotel lounge.

Some of her business expenses are 100% deductible – the room charge, laundry and wireless service.

But the dinners and the lounge bill, which are MEALS & ENTERTAINMENT expenses, are 50% deductible.

Although all the expenses are on a single hotel bill, she has to keep the categories separate for tax purposes.

---

I suggest not putting MEALS & ENTERTAINMENT expenses on the room charge but paying for them separately with your credit card. This simplifies recordkeeping for some indies.

***No 50% Limit on Expenses If You Feed The Masses:*** You are not subject to the 50% limit – that means you get to deduct your entire cost – if you provide meals, entertainment or recreational facilities to the general public as a means of advertising or promotion.

- Raina Realtor provides hors d' oeuvres and wine at an open house.
- Attila Atelier serves champagne at the opening reception for one of her artists.
- Heavenly Happenin has a "Come-See-How-It's-Done" event at her main office. The public is invited to taste, test and view the inner workings of planning a gala. All food, drinks, supplies and any other expense of the event are 100% deductible for Heavenly.
- Stan's Steam Train, a local amusement ride, offers free rides on Halloween for all children under 5 years old. Stan gives the kids chocolate pumpkins and candy corn. All his costs are 100% deductible.

## Travel Meals & Entertainment

The deduction for MEALS & ENTERTAINMENT while traveling confuses a lot of people. All the information you need to get it straight is contained in CHAPTER 10: GETTING AROUND, but here's a brief summary:

Meals for yourself while traveling for business are all deductible – at 50% – be it breakfast, lunch, dinner, or a snack.

Meals or entertaining for business associates while traveling are the same as for non-travel. Whether you and your business associate are dining in London or in your home office, the same regulations apply.

## Entertainment Is Not Entertainment When Entertainment Is Your Business

Your type of indie business may determine whether an activity is entertainment and thus only 50% deductible or some other category of business expense and thereby 100% deductible.

- Theobald Theater Critic is paid for his drama reviews. When he attends a theatrical performance in his professional capacity, it is not a 50% deductible entertainment expense; it is a 100% deductible research expense.
- Nadine Novella is writing a short story, "Headed for The Big Time," about a player on a minor league baseball team. She has attended a number of games. Her cost of tickets for these entertainment events is fully deductible.

IRS regulation under Section 274 says that Theobald and Nadine may take 100% of the cost of the theater and baseball game tickets, typically an ENTERTAINMENT expense for others.

The IRS has not given the same provision for MEALS. Although there are no rulings or litigated cases on that point, freelance professional food tasters or restaurant critics, for example, in my opinion, have a reasonably solid case for deducting the full cost of a meal.

Don't get the idea that just because you call something by another name you'll get to deduct the entire expense. If you take a realtor out to dinner to promote your new territorial design homes, don't think that because you call it "promotion" it isn't really an entertainment expense. Yes, it is. And it's only 50% deductible.

See the reference table that summarizes what we discussed in this chapter.

## BUSINESS MEALS & ENTERTAINMENT EXPENSES
### When are they deductible?

| | | |
|---|---|---|
| **WHY** | For a business purpose. | • Present your idea, product or service<br>• Seek advice<br>• Review a proposal, contract, prototype<br>• Interview |
| **WITH WHOM** | Business Associate | • Client, customer<br>• Potential client, customer<br>• Professional advisors<br>• Supplier<br>• Employee<br>• Agent<br>• Collaborator<br>• Colleague |
| **WHEN**<br><br>Directly Related<br><br>Associated With | Business took place during the meal or entertainment<br><br>Business took place directly before or after the meal or entertainment | |
| **KINDS OF EXPENSES** | Typical of your indie business. | • Meals<br>• Tickets to entertainment events<br>• Tickets to sporting events<br>• Accommodations<br>• Transportation |

## CHAPTER 9: STAYING IN TOUCH
## Communication Expenses

In this chapter we'll look at expenses incurred when communicating with your clients, suppliers, colleagues, and other business associates. Typical means of communication are:

- Email
- Cell phone
- Telephone
- Personal Digital Assistant (PDA)
- Answering Service
- Social Networking
- Internet Service Provider (ISP)

If you've been reading **THE CONFIDENT INDIE** straight through this will be your first encounter with allocating expenses. Allocation becomes necessary when the same gadget (telephone or iPad) or service (your ISP), are used for both for personal and business purposes. The IRS calls these gadgets **listed property** and looks with a squinty eye at expenses that could have arisen from either personal or business use, citing them as "high-abuse items." "High-abuse items" include most means of communication as well as some other expense categories such as MEALS & ENTERTAINMENT and AUTO.

In order to take deductions for COMMUNICATIONS expenses you are required to keep a record to show how much you use the gadget or service in the conduct of your business or present an allocation that you could substantiate. It's an exasperating and irksome process. There are several ways to determine business use versus personal use and we will look at some of them in this chapter.

First, some very good news! The Small Business Jobs Act of 2010 removes from the category of **listed property** cell phones and other similar telecommunications equipment used primarily for business. After much research I confirmed that this new regulation includes not only the equipment, that is, the cost of the phone, but also the monthly service charge. *__Halleluiah! This means no more recordkeeping of business use versus personal use for such devices.__*

Do we really think that people – both indies and W-2 people – have been keeping a log of personal and business calls and text messages? No way. But now it's OK if you don't, if you follow some guidelines.

This new IRS regulation (It is section 2043 of the Small Business Jobs Act of 2010 and IRS code sections 274 and 162, in case your tax pro wants to know) is spelled out for, you guessed it, employers and employees. So we again need to extrapolate for the self-employed world.

You are self-employed and so you are both employer and employee. The new IRS regulation says that the employer may provide and deduct the cost of communication devices and service he provides for the business use of his employee. In other words, you, an indie, may provide for yourself and deduct as a business expense a cell phone used primarily for business. Don't try to finagle. Make sure you are getting that iPhone for business. And if you need to call home from a client meeting to check on the kids, that's OK. It does not reduce your deduction.

*__For 100% business deduction the primary purpose of the cell phone or other communication device must be for business.__*

Think about that. It means that your cell cannot then be your only phone. Even if you have no friends to call or text you must have another phone. Perhaps there's a landline in your kitchen, or another cell number you use for personal.

Since 1989, no business deduction has been allowed for basic local telephone service for the first telephone line in a residence. The IRS assumes that every American family has a telephone and uses it for personal communication. A family or even a single person living alone would not have a phone for solely business purposes. Therefore an indie who works out of her home and has only one telephone line – be it land or cell – cannot claim a business deduction for the basic local monthly telephone service charge even if she claims that that line is used for business purposes only and even if the phone is listed as a business line in the name of her business.

Nevertheless, even if you have only one line, after you exclude the basic service – be sure to get that cost in writing from your service provider – you can still deduct as a business expense additional costs and optional service costs. But you must keep a record. You must allocate. It may be easier, and with the 100% deduction of cell expenses, may even cost less, to have a second phone line.

What does the IRS mean by "other communication devices" that are also 100% business deductions? Well, we know that whatever is meant by that today will likely mean something else several months from now. I think of them as iPhones, iPads, cable hook up and service, Palms, and other PDAs.

Telephone expense for business can amount to thousands of dollars per month. Whether using a designated cell solely for business or allocating a mixed-use line, if in an audit you cannot substantiate your business use your deduction can be disallowed.

# HOW TO ALLOCATE BETWEEN BUSINESS AND PERSONAL USE

First off, know that the IRS:
- Requires substantiation of business use.
- Says it wants each date of qualified use and time documented.
- Says you can divide the number of hours of business use over the total hours actually used.
- Does not give a specific method.
- Without a log the IRS can and has completely denied any business usage.

If you have a mixed-use item, then allocate you must. Set up a method that works for you. The IRS wants a clear and specific designation of phone use, other communication devices and services, and, yes, computer use, for business purposes versus those for personal use.

I know no one who keeps a phone log. Most people can't even decipher their phone bills. In our household I do the taxes. My husband lost the coin toss and he is stuck dealing with insurance and the phone bills.

### Let's Get Practical
Whether keeping a record of personal use versus business use of the phone or time on your computer, it is best to use a method that you can credibly present to the IRS should your expense be questioned in an audit.

Here is one that I use often. If you and your teenage son are the only ones sending email from your computer you might calculate business use of your ISP this way:

- 2 parts for you: 1 part personal use; 1 part business use
- 4 parts for your son (he's on line twice as much as you)
- 6 is the total number of parts

In this example your business use is one-sixth. (Your one part business use divided by six parts total.) So if the monthly ISP expense is $60, then $10.00 is your monthly business expense.

Here are some other allocation methods that indies have used with varying degrees of success:

- Keep two months of a use-log – one month of the busy season and one month of the slow season. Use either time on the phone, or calls, or text messages. Once you determine business use and personal use, calculate the average business use of those two months then take that percent of the entire phone bill (after excluding the monthly cost of the basic household line if this is your only phone.) This method has been accepted in audits – it's highly accurate.

- Make all calls and send all emails through the computer's database and use the database program's recording method as your record of business use to calculate percent of business use.

- Guesstimate a percent of use and hope for the best.

I find recordkeeping for allocating the business/personal use of digital devices to be the most annoying and cumbersome of all the recordkeeping required by the IRS. My guess is that you feel the same as I do, so, somewhere along the way you will need to make a decision. Is it worth your time and effort to record time used for each activity? What would it cost you if the IRS questioned your return and you couldn't back up your claims for business use? Does your business involve a lot of time on the Internet? How much recordkeeping – and what method – makes sense for your business? The answers to these questions may depend on the nature of your business, how many phone lines and cell phones you use, and the total amount of various communications expenses you have in relation to your total self-employed income or to your other expenses.

Ask your tax preparer's advice on how best to handle these expenses in your unique situation. It has been argued by taxpayers that this requirement can be cumbersome and sometimes even costly. Courts have upheld the IRS stating that this is an irrelevant argument. So there!

Your tax pro should make suggestions suited to your circumstances in the context of all your other expenses and the accuracy of your records in general. Do be careful. The new regulation allowing for no allocation if the device's primary use is business warrants an A+ to the IRS. However, this is not carte blanche to deduct 100% of every gadget you have. In this, too, you will need to show proof of the primarily business purpose for the device.

## HOW DO YOU CATEGORIZE COMMUNICATION EXPENSES?

There is no specific line on a tax return for communication expenses; different types of communication fall into different expense categories. Usually the IRS looks at business telephone expense as a UTILITIES expense. It will be up to your tax preparer as to how she categorizes it. She may combine it with the costs of your answering service as TELEPHONE expense and list it under *other expenses* on your tax return.

Depending upon how you use the Internet your ISP costs can be a UTILITIES expense or perhaps a RESEARCH-STUDY-EDUCATION expense. The costs of setting up and maintaining your website is an ADVERTISING expense. The device, if it costs more than $100 I treat as EQUIPMENT. Less than that it's an OFFICE SUPPLY.

Some of the above expenses are explained from a different perspective in coming chapters. Keep in mind: It is not necessary for you to know the category or classification of an expense. What you need to know is that these are all business expenses and you want to take advantage of the deduction for every one of them.

## COMMUNICATION CHATTER

- If you're calling, texting or emailing someone who is a friend and a business associate, if she is primarily a business associate and you discuss business it's a deductible business COMMUNICATION expense.
- If you share a phone or ISP with another person pay your portion by check, preferably directly to the phone or ISP company. If that is not practical then pay your phone or ISP partner with a check made out to your partner. Note in the memo what the check is for. And keep a copy of the bill.
- A phone line does not have to be listed as a business line with the phone company in order to be deducted as a business expense.
- Don't buy a stack of phone cards for your kids and then deduct them as a business expense. If the size of the deduction doesn't fit what the IRS has set as a "market guideline" for your profession an auditor can disallow them in the absence of phone records.

- Telephone expense is not directly related to OFFICE-IN-THE-HOME expense. You may deduct for a phone used in your residence even if you do not have an office or studio in your home. If you do claim an OFFICE-IN-THE-HOME deduction don't think that somehow office size and phone use need to match. They don't. Your home office may take up 10% of your residence but you may use 80% of your landline for business. No correlation, no problem.

## CHAPTER 10: GETTING AROUND
## Travel, Transportation and Auto Expenses

Travel expenses, transportation expenses, vehicle expenses – aren't they all more or less the same thing? No more so than trudging by mule pack in the Andes, taxiing through city traffic, or jetting to LA. Let's look at them all.

## BUSINESS TRAVEL EXPENSES

Over the river and through the woods to Grandmother's house goes Pat Personal Trainer. Gram just bought a color laser and it's the cheapest way for Pat to print his new brochures. He leaves Friday afternoon. The bus gets him there in time for dinner. He works at the computer all the next day until the wee hours. (He's sure these new brochures will get him lots of customers.) Very early the next morning he kisses Grandma goodbye and heads back on the bus. Pat was **away from his home, for business, overnight.** It was business travel. Therefore he may deduct TRAVEL expenses.

Before I get into the rules and regulations of TRAVEL expenses, let me put your mind at ease. Travel rules are complicated. Don't expect to store them all in your memory for instant recall. ***This is a reference chapter.*** You'll need to refer to it often, whether you make trips bi-weekly to Florence or biennially to Philadelphia.

---

**THE IRS SAYS ABOUT BUSINESS TRAVEL ...**

If you temporarily travel away from your tax home for business you may deduct ordinary and necessary TRAVEL expenses. You may not write off "lavish or extravagant" expenses.

---

The IRS, you remember, says that an "ordinary expense is one that is common to your profession; a necessary one is one that is helpful and appropriate."

The IRS has written thousands of words on business TRAVEL. Here are the most important. Your trip is business TRAVEL if your business duties require you to be away from the general area of your tax home longer than an ordinary day's work so that you need to get some sleep or rest.

What is a **tax home?** Think of your tax home as your main or regular place of business. It doesn't matter where you maintain your family home. Thus, if you stay away from your tax home overnight, you'd need some rest while on that business trip, and so your costs would qualify as TRAVEL expense.

But, be careful: don't go around telling people that you ordinarily work 20 hours a day or you'll miss out on deducting your business trips!

Simply stated, we can define business travel this way: **If you are away from your place of business, overnight, for a purpose that benefits your business then you have been on a business trip and your costs are deductible TRAVEL expenses.**

---

### REALITY √ CHECK

What! You're an itinerant jester, who doesn't have a regular or main place of business? Then you don't have a tax home. Sorry, no TRAVEL expenses allowed.

---

### REALITY √ CHECK

Dalton Deliverance leaves the warehouse at five in the morning. Two hundred miles later he's at the turnaround. While his truck is being unloaded he has a big lunch and then dozes off outside the diner while waiting for the guys to finish up. He then heads back to the warehouse. He's home by ten that night. Dalton's lunch break nap was just that, "a nap." It was not enough time to get adequate sleep. His trip is not considered travel. Therefore he cannot deduct TRAVEL expenses.

---

### Travel Or Transportation

*Think of it this way: If it's overnight, it's travel.* A trip classified as business TRAVEL will get you a lot more deductions than will one classified as business TRANSPORTATION (see the next section). TRANSPORTATION expenses are solely the costs of getting from one business event location to another.

> ## REALITY √ CHECK
>
> Albuquerque is about 70 miles from my office in Santa Fe. If I drive to Albuquerque in the morning to meet with a client, have lunch alone at a restaurant, then drive to a second meeting, then drive back to Santa Fe, my only deductible costs are my auto mileage there and back and parking.
>
> Here's a different scenario. I drive to Albuquerque and in the morning I meet with a client, have lunch on my own. Since my other client is not available to meet with me until 8 PM I do some shopping, have dinner with a friend at a restaurant, and then meet with the second client. The meeting runs much later than expected and I'm too tired to drive back to Santa Fe. I stay in an Albuquerque hotel and drive back to my Santa Fe home office in the morning. Because I was there substantially longer than an ordinary day's work I can deduct my TRAVEL expenses that include my drive to, from and around Albuquerque, my lunch and my dinner (not my friend's dinner) and the cost of the hotel.

## Business Travel Expenses Are The Costs of The Trip

Business TRAVEL expenses can get tangled up in IRS jargon, so for easier understanding, think of them as falling into the following groups:

1. Transport
   This includes the costs of transporting you and your stuff, by any means, to, from, and while at your destination.
   - Airfare
   - Travel insurance
   - Auto rentals
   - Taxis, buses, subway
   - Baggage charges
   - Costs for separately sending your things, like mock-ups, samples, books

2. Lodging
   - Hotel
   - Campsite fee

3. Other travel-necessitated expenses

- Wireless fees
- Passport

4. Incidental expenses
   - Laundry, cleaning, pressing of clothes
   - Tips
   - Fees for services such as secretarial services

5. Meals for yourself while you're away. When you are traveling for business you may deduct the costs for all of your own meals – breakfast, lunch, dinner, snacks.

6. Meals & Entertainment for business associates
   You may deduct the expenses for MEALS & ENTERTAINMENT for business associates using the same guidelines explained in CHAPTER 8. The rules for MEALS & ENTERTAINMENT are the same whether you and your business associate are dining in Paris or next door to your home office.

If you are certain that your trip is entirely for a business purpose, then you may deduct all your TRAVEL expenses. It can be as simple as that. Or it may be as baffling as cashing a traveler's check in Gabon. Some of the complications are:

- Taking another person with you on the trip
- A trip that is part business and part personal
- A trip outside the continental United States
- A trip both within the USA and outside the USA

If none of the above complications applies to you, then skip the rest of the travel section. But do refer to it before the next trip if any of the above situations may apply.

### Arrangements That Complicate Business Travel

Just as a Midwestern storm that freezes up the national air traffic system can change a simple trip into a complex travel expedition so too can certain situations befuddle your understanding of business travel deductions. Let's look at a few complications.

***Taking Another Person with You on The Trip:*** You may deduct TRAVEL expenses for your companion if that person fits ***all*** of the following three conditions:

- Is a customer, client, supplier, agent, business partner, or professional advisor with whom you conduct or expect to conduct business, or your employee
  and

- Has a business purpose for the travel
  and

- Would otherwise be allowed to deduct TRAVEL expenses.

Bringing your best friend along because she'll type up your notes at the end of the day or help you charm the oldsters you're trying to sign up for your next senior cruise does not constitute a business purpose.

Old tax law allowed you to deduct expenses for your spouse if he served a business purpose. No more. If your husband is not your employee it doesn't matter how much help he is on the trip. No deduction for him.

---

**REALITY √ CHECK**

Mary Motivate flies to Atlanta to give her biggest motivational presentation yet. She had a two-for-the-price-of-one airline airfare coupon so she brought along her husband who makes sure the handouts, speaker system, PowerPoint and lighting go without a hitch. Mary's husband is not her employee.

Mary may deduct the entire cost of the airline ticket because she would have paid for one full fare anyway.

She does not have to divide the cost of the hotel room in half. If her double room at the hotel cost $200 per night and would have cost $170 for a single, she may deduct $170.

The expense for the car rental may be deducted in full even though her husband rides in the auto with her. She may not deduct any of her husband's expenses.

---

*A Trip That Is Part Business And Part Personal:* If you mix business and pleasure on a trip, deductions may depend upon whether you are traveling within the United States or outside the United States. The **BUSINESS TRAVEL EXPENSES** chart coming up on page 102 will help you quickly determine if your costs are deductible business TRAVEL expenses.

*Special Rule for Travel Outside The USA*: If you meet one of the exceptions below you may treat foreign travel in the same manner as travel within the United States.

- You were out of the country seven consecutive days or less (don't count the day you left the USA).

  or

- You were out of the USA for more than seven days (count the day you left & the day of your return) but you spent at least 75% of your time on business activities.

---

### REALITY √ CHECK

Warren Wordsmith leaves Albuquerque on Monday (This travel day does not count.). Arrives in Frankfurt, Germany on Tuesday (day #1). Attends the Frankfurt Book Fair for two days (days #2 & #3) then spends the rest of the time with his grandchildren; even visits Strasbourg, France with them. He leaves Frankfurt to fly back home on the following Monday (the 7th day, not counting the first travel day). Warren may not write off personal expenses, but he may write off all business expenses including all the airfare.

---

**Watch Those Waves:** If you have enough money to do your business traveling by luxury ocean liner (the IRS calls it "water transport") I'm sure you'll be talking to your accountant on how to write it off. But since different rules apply to that kind of travel do warn your friend Tracy Travel Agent that there are restrictions on the amount she can deduct for her New York to London business cruise and she'd better check with her tax advisor.

Also, check with a tax advisor if you're heading to a convention outside the North America area.

### Help with Travel Recordkeeping

**How to Use Alternative Travel Records:** For most of your travel expenses you will have receipts of some sort – cancelled checks, credit cards slips, printouts, or cash receipts. Well, after its own fashion the IRS has tried to make recordkeeping for travel easier. Yet, as is ever the case with IRS regulations, it is not self-employeds for whom easier recordkeeping was set up but for employers and employees; the self-employed just happen to benefit from the crumbs that fall from the table.

The IRS has issued per diem (per day) charts for domestic travel.

These charts list the maximum amounts allowed to be deducted without receipts for "LODGING" and for "MEALS + INCIDENTALS (M&I)." The self-employed may use the amounts listed for MEALS + INCIDENTALS only.

For domestic trips, go to the Government Services Administration (GSA) Per Diem Rates page[11]. Choose the year and city where you traveled, then go to the last column, labeled: "Meals & Inc Exp" and find the amount allowed for that city's cost of meals and incidentals for the day. Easiest tally is to multiply that amount by the number of **nights** you were in that city. Why nights, not days? Way too complicated to explain here.

If the city is not listed or you can't be bothered to check all the places you've traveled to, then use the standard M&I rate of $46. By the way, you can even get a per diem app at the GSA website[12].

For foreign travel, go to the U.S. Department of State Foreign Per Diem site[13].

Then go to the fourth from right column, labeled: "M&IE Rate" and find the amount allowed for that city's cost of meals and incidentals for the day. There is no standard foreign per diem rate.

If you choose to use per diem rates for one trip then you must use them for all trips that year. No mix and match allowed. This could be a tax and time-saver.

*Grouping Travel Expenses:* When travel expenses are deducted on your tax return they are not listed separately as lodging or airfare or incidentals. All travel costs fall into one of two business expense categories. One is MEALS & ENTERTAINMENT. This includes all travel meals plus any expenses for business entertainment while traveling. The other category is TRAVEL expense which includes everything except MEALS & ENTERTAINMENT while traveling.

There is a reason for the bifurcation. TRAVEL expenses get deducted at 100% of your outlay while MEALS & ENTERTAINMENT are deducted at 50%. MEALS & ENTERTAINMENT are fully explained here.

*Making Travel Arrangements, A Few Scenarios:* A business trip does not have to show a profit.

> ### REALITY √ CHECK
>
> Cindy Set Designer was very happy to land the contract for designing the sets for the Long Wharf Community Theatre. Even though it would be 11 straight hours of driving to get to Connecticut at least she wouldn't have to rent a car while there. Her work would last for three weeks, the pay wasn't good and she'd have to foot all her own expenses. But it would be a good career step. Renting two rooms from a local was cheaper than staying at a hotel and eating out. There was no refrigerator in the place so she rented one.
>
> She figured that by the time she was done her expenses about broke even with what she was paid or perhaps would exceed her income. But she knew that adding this prestigious theatre to her resume would get her more work. All her expenses were deductible – including rental of the refrigerator – even though this job may end up costing her money.

You must establish a business intent when you travel if you want to deduct business TRAVEL expenses. Plan your business trips carefully and well in advance.

> ### REALITY √ CHECK
>
> Sarah Sculptor is going from her studio in Ghent, New York to Boston, for five days of art study. Because she will not be enrolled in a formal course, she needs to establish her business intent. She prints out her online research of museums and their schedules. She writes and emails gallery directors, curators and art professors planning her many meetings and makes appointments to show her portfolio. Of course, she has easily accessible copies of all her letters and emails, all saved in her BOSTON TRIP – 2013 file. While in Boston she collects literature and business cards from at each appointment. Any sketches done on the trip Sarah dated & placed, for example "Boston Common, Sept 6, 2013."
>
> She also kept copies of all the follow-up correspondence and thank you notes that she sent to the directors – if not for meeting with her then for at least taking the time to read her request and respond. These she also keeps in her BOSTON TRIP – 2013 file. If Sarah stays an extra day because she ran into an old college friend – who is not in the arts and has no business connection to her – she cannot deduct the costs of that day but she does not have to prorate her travel to and from Boston.

---

## REALITY √ CHECK

Travel as a form of education is not a business expense. Jack Japanese Instructor may deduct a trip to Japan to take courses in Japanese and Japanese culture or history. He may not deduct the costs of a trip to Japan wherein he just travels around the country soaking up the culture.

---

## REALITY √ CHECK

If the trip is primarily a vacation, there is no deduction for travel costs to and from the foreign location. Just because Jack Japanese Instructor took a one-day Haiku course during his ten days in Japan does not make the airfare or any of his other expenses deductible. Only the cost of the Haiku course is deductible.

---

Be careful how much time you play when you could be working. If you play at least 25% of the time you'll need to allocate costs.

---

## REALITY √ CHECK

Shane Scriptwrite travels from New York to London ($1,000 one way) (day 1) to attend a three day course in scene blocking for theatre in the round (days 2, 3, and 4).

Before returning to New York he flies to France ($250) for a four-day vacation in Paris (days 5, 6, 7, & 8) .

He flies back (day 9) to New York from Paris ($1,300).

Shane may deduct all his London expenses. He cannot deduct any of his Paris expenses. Shane was on a personal trip for four of the nine days. He must deduct from his total airfare (New York to London to Paris to New York) of $2,550, 4/9 of the expense he would have had in flying directly from New York to Paris and back. He needs from his travel agent or as a Web printout the round-trip airfare for New York to Paris. Of course, the lower the New York to Paris round-trip airfare the better for his write-off.

---

I know. It makes little sense. You'd think that Shane could deduct whatever the round-trip fare to London would have been. Or at worst that he could take 5/9 (five business days out of nine days total) of that fare. But what the IRS says to do is from his total fare deduct 4/9 of the cost of a roundtrip trip to Paris.

Total paid airfare $1,000 + $250 + $1,300     = $2,550

NY / Paris round trip would have been $495 times 4/9  = (   220 )

Allowed airfare deduction   =   $2,330

It defies logic, but it's the IRS rule.

Are you supposed to know how to figure this out? No. So why am I telling you? Because with a little planning and consultation with your tax pro – **_before you take a business trip_** – you may be able to get a bigger deduction. Also, I thought you might like another example of crazy IRS logic.

## REALITY √ CHECK

P. R. Bernays mixes business and pleasure on his convention trip to Mexico. The industry convention is held in Puerto Vallarta. He has two travel days – there and back. He spends five days at the convention and spends the following three days sailing and scuba diving at a resort.

P. R. was out of the USA for a total of ten days. The allocation rules on foreign business travel apply. P. R.'s trip was primarily for business, he was outside the United States for more than one week.

The two travel days – the day the trip began and the day it ended – are counted as business days. Plus five days at the convention, for a total of seven business day out ten. P. R. spent less than 75% of his time on business (seven business days out of ten is 70% on business).

Therefore, he must allocate his transportation expenses. He can deduct only $700 of his $1,000 airfare because only 70% of his days were related to business activities.

# REALITY √ CHECK

Samantha Semblance went to the same convention in Mexico as did P. R. But she limited her scuba diving to two days.

Her foreign trip lasted longer than one week: 5 convention + 2 travel + 2 scuba = 9 days.

However, less than 25% of the time outside the United States was spent on personal matters (2/9 = 22%). Samantha may deduct her entire round trip airfare of $1,000.

## Things to Know before You Go

- While on a Vermont business trip you buy maple syrup for your kid sister who lives in Texas? No business gift deduction there.
- Pat Personal Trainer, while at Grandma's doing his printing, ran out for lunch. Yes, a TRAVEL MEAL expense.
- Pat gave Grandma a family tree software program as thanks for the use of her printer? Yes, a deductible BUSINESS GIFT expense.
- Any expenses you incur while on a fun side trip while away on business? Nondeductible.

Whether you are traveling alone or with a group of friends, whether the trip is mandatory (your client insists that you supervise the equipment installation) or not (a chance to study with a 98-year-old master who may not be around next year), the matter of business travel shows how complicated and difficult it is for an independent professional to distinguish between personal life and business life.

- Choose your business travel wisely. Plan ahead.
- Save all correspondence relating to your trip. Put it in a file folder labeled with the place and date of travel or some other label – April Convention – that makes sense to you.
- Keep a diary or log while on your business trip. Entries should show whom you met, and why.

Be sure to use the Business Travel Expenses chart on the following page when planning your next trip.

## BUSINESS TRAVEL EXPENSES

### PRIMARILY, but not solely, FOR BUSINESS PURPOSE

| WHERE? | MAY DEDUCT | MAY NOT DEDUCT | MUST PRORATE ON DAY-TO-DAY BASIS |
|---|---|---|---|
| All In the USA (includes 50 states & DC) | • All business related expenses that you would have incurred had you not taken any personal days <br> • Cost of transportation to & from | • Personal expenses | |
| All outside the USA* <br><br> *See the special rule for business travel outside the USA. | • All business related expenses that you would have incurred had you not taken any personal days | • Personal expenses | • Cost of transportation to & from |

### PRIMARILY, but not solely, FOR PERSONAL PURPOSE

| WHERE? | MAY DEDUCT | MAY NOT DEDUCT | MUST PRORATE ON DAY-TO-DAY BASIS |
|---|---|---|---|
| Whether in USA <br> or <br> Outside USA | • Only directly related business expenses incurred while at your destination | • Any other costs of the trip <br> • Cost of transportation to & from | |

### SPECIAL RULE FOR BUSINESS TRAVEL OUTSIDE USA

| HOW LONG? | MAY DEDUCT | MAY NOT DEDUCT | MUST PRORATE ON DAY-TO-DAY BASIS |
|---|---|---|---|
| 7 consecutive days or less (do not include day left USA) <br><br> or <br><br> More than 7 consecutive days (include day left USA) with at least 75% of time on business | • All business related expenses that you would have incurred had you not taken any personal days <br> • Cost of transportation to & from | • Personal expenses | |

# BUSINESS TRANSPORTATION EXPENSES

What if you sally forth on business and return without an overnight stay or a need for rest?

Had Pat Personal Trainer simply spent the afternoon using Grandma's laser and then hightailed it back to his home office in the same day he would not have had any TRAVEL expenses. However, he would have had TRANSPORTATION expenses. The distinction between TRAVEL and TRANSPORTATION is important because that distinction determines which of your costs are deductible.

Before looking at the specifics of TRANSPORTATION expenses, let's, once again, review the distinction: **If you stay overnight or long enough to need some rest, then it's travel. If not, then it's transportation.**

If you've accepted the useful and tax saving way of thinking like an indie business then you're already aware that anything you do that is related to your work or makes you better at doing what you're doing is a likely business expense, therefore, going to or getting back from whatever you are doing for business is also a likely business expense.

Although there are no limitations on **what** mode of transportation is used, there are rules regarding **when** transportation is a deductible expense. In the following cases of Anton and Syd you may be surprised to learn that you can't always deduct what you think of as business transportation – it depends on the situation. After you look at the two following circumstances I'll thoroughly explain TRANSPORTATION expenses.

---

### REALITY √ CHECK

Whether Anton Antique starts the day by taking a taxi, the trolley, or his own car from his apartment to his antique shop in town, he cannot deduct the cost of his transportation from home to work.

Even if Anton drove to his shop in his old – but not antique – Ford, laden with business papers and flash drives, used coffee cups, an iPad charger all tangled with his phone charger (his car looks like a messy office) and even if Anton made business calls on his cell phone all the way, he cannot claim the drive from home to work as a business trip.

Why not? The IRS says his drive is a **commute**.

---

┌─────────────────────────────────────────────────────────────┐

### REALITY √ CHECK

After Syd System gets his youngsters off to school he takes his coffee into his home office. He checks his email then heads into town to meet with a client. Whether Syd takes a taxi, the bus, or his own car, his transportation costs from his home office to the meeting are deductible.

└─────────────────────────────────────────────────────────────┘

It wouldn't matter that Syd's trip was a $2.00 subway ride and Anton's was a two-hour commute into the city. Anton was commuting, Syd was not.

## Commuting Expenses

The IRS does not allow a deduction for commuting to and from home and work. Whether you're Emma Employee or Indira Independent you cannot take your first trip – your movement from a personal place to a business place – or your last trip – your movement from a business place to a personal place – as a business expense.

Anton's first trip was from home to his shop: no TRANSPORTATION expense. All of Anton's expenses for his additional business treks through the day are deductible except the one from his last appointment in town to his home. That is his home commute.

Syd's commute is from his kitchen to his home office several yards down the hall. From his home office to his client's is not a commute but is business transportation and so he gets to deduct his expense. All Syd's business trekking for the rest of the day until he gets back to his home office qualifies as TRANSPORTATION expense.

***Work at Home to Increase Transportation Deductions:*** Let's take a look at how, by thinking like an indie business, Anton could increase his transportation deductions and perhaps save some money on taxes.

A major reason – possibly more important than the home office tax deduction itself – for establishing a home office is that it increases the possibilities for deducting transportation costs.

The IRS does not allow a deduction for commuting costs – from home to work and back. But it does allow a deduction for getting from one workplace to another. No office-in-the-home means no deduction for the miles from your home to your first work stop. However, if your commute is from your kitchen to your home office where you perform administrative tasks like calls, emails, billing and then drive to your other office, you are now driving "from one workplace to another." Without increasing any of your out-of-pocket costs, you have increased your business TRANSPORTATION deduction.

For just that reason the IRS fought long and hard to disallow using an office-in-the-home for "administrative" (that means emailing, billing, phone calls) purposes only. But, having lost the battle, the IRS has liberalized the rules on deducting OFFICE-IN-THE-HOME expense. You can have an office or studio elsewhere and still deduct costs for the area of your home used exclusively and regularly for administrative or management activities for your business. (Be sure to read CHAPTER 12 on home office deductions.)

## Getting Around The "Commuting" Limitation

Circumstances that allow part or all of your daily drives as legitimate deductions:

*The Temporary Work Site:* If you have a regular work place, you may deduct the cost of getting to a temporary worksite even if it is your first or last trip of the day.

---

### REALITY √ CHECK

Anton Antique's shop is his regular work place. Occasionally a client requires that Anton come to his site, let's say for a design consultation. Anton can deduct the cost of going from his home to the client's and back home . The client's home is considered a temporary work site.

---

*Transportation Away from Your Tax Home:* If you must leave your tax home you may deduct the cost of transportation even if it is your first or last trip of the day.

One morning Anton began his workday by driving all the way from his home in Worcester, MA, to a little farmhouse just beyond Providence, RI. He took the 50-mile drive to look at a large cache of 19th Century silver spoons up for sale. Although he has no office-in-the-home, he's entitled to deduct the mileage.

Had those spoons been in a home on the other side of Worcester, and had he started his day by driving there to see them, instead of driving to Providence to see them, Anton would not have been able to deduct his drive.

**Tax home** is another item in the quirky IRS jargon, and it has never been exactly measured in terms of distance. Some tax pros say your tax home is the 40-mile radius around your business. The IRS defines it as the "entire city or general area in which your business or work is located." In either case, Providence lies outside Anton's tax home, while the other side of Worcester does not.

In defining your own tax home, much depends on the geography and layout of your location. If your business requires these kinds of trips on a recurring basis, discuss your situation with your tax pro.

When considering TRANSPORTATION expenses expand your indie power mindset as you look for business events and destinations. They include:

- Meeting with clients, customers or colleagues
- Going from one worksite to another
- Getting to and from a business entertainment event
- Attending seminars or study courses
- Doing errands or shopping for business supplies

## BUSINESS USE OF YOUR AUTO OR OTHER VEHICLE

For many indies an automobile is the chief means of business transportation. Unless you live in Manhattan or some other major city everyone you know owns a car. Maybe two. For most Americans cars represent their second largest purchase (the first is a home). And, after mortgage payments, car expenses usually take the biggest bite out of income. With this in mind it makes complete sense for a solo entrepreneur to look toward taking every possible deduction for business use of her car.

Police habitually speak of "vehicles" instead of "cars" or "autos" – a practice that also makes sense when discussing business AUTO expense. Everything in this chapter – except for some differences in depreciation which I'll explain later – that pertains to "cars" also applies to vans, SUVs, trucks, motorcycles and other road vehicles. (An aside from the IRS: These rules do not apply to airplanes, boats or snowmobiles). So I'm going to use "car," "auto," and "vehicle" interchangeably.

Now mark the following carefully, because it's an exception to what I've been telling you in the last two sections about travel and transportation.

Let's say that in a given week you drive your car to numerous business appointments around town, for a total of 100 miles. In the same week you drive from Pennsylvania to Ohio for an overnight business trip, a total of 300 miles. We combine these for a total of 400 business use miles for the week. I know, I just got finished stressing the difference between TRANSPORTATION expenses and TRAVEL expenses. The reason for this seeming contradiction lies, as is so often the case, with the IRS. TRANSPORTATION is one category in IRS expenses, TRAVEL is a different expense category, and business use miles for your vehicle is a third.

Please, hang in here with me. It will all make sense shortly.

If you took a taxi for your business appointments around town, the cost would be listed as TRANSPORTATION expense on your tax return. If you took a bus for your overnight stay in Ohio, the busfare is listed as TRAVEL expense. But if you drove your car to all these appointments, the expenses are listed under business use miles for your vehicle.

## Calculating Auto Expense: Two Methods

Business AUTO expense can be figured in one of two ways. The first, the **standard mileage method**, simply multiplies your total business miles by a per mile rate set by the government. The rate changes yearly. For 2012 the rate is 55.5 cents per mile. For 2013 the rate is 56.5 cents per mile.

The other way, the **actual expenses method**, multiplies your total auto expenses by the percent of business use, and adds to that an amount for depreciation of the business portion of the cost of the auto. (Depreciation is explained in CHAPTER 13.)

Add to the total, with either of these methods, the business portion of auto finance charges, as well as all business tolls and parking.

---

### REALITY √ CHECK

Lily Legal purchased a $20,000 auto four years ago. This year she put 6,000 business miles on her car, out of a total of 10,000 miles. Her total expenses for maintaining the car were $4,200, which includes $500 in finance charges. Here's two methods of calculating Lily's AUTO expense:

**The Standard Mileage Method**: Business miles for the year are multiplied by the per mile rate for that year.

The rate for 2012 is 55½ cents per mile.

| | |
|---|---|
| 6, 000 business miles times 55 ½ cents per mile | = $3,330. |
| 60% of finance charges of $500 | = 300. |
| Total expense | = $3,630. |

---

**The Actual Method**: Business miles are divided by total mileage for the year to arrive at a percentage of business use.

Business miles      =  6,000.

Total miles         =  10,000.

                  =  60% Business Use

Total auto expenses are multiplied by business use percentage.

$4,200 times 60%   =  $2,520.

Depreciation       =  <u>1,065.</u>
Total Expense     =  $3,585.

In Lily's case, the **Standard Method** produced a higher deduction.

At the end of this section there is a completed BUSINESS USE OF AUTO, TRUCK OR OTHER VEHICLE worksheet, using the 60% figures in the above example.

When using the **actual method**, you will need information on the purchase date and price of your auto. If the first year you use your car for business is later than the year you purchased it you will need the fair market value of the car on the first day of business use. Think of it as what you could have sold it for on the day you started to use your car for business. You will also need a tally of all the expenses for your car, such as:

- Gas & Oil
- Repairs & Maintenance
- Tires
- Insurance (Remember AAA or other road service coverage, too.)
- Registration & License
- Car wash
- Garage rental
- Loan interest
- Lease costs

Tickets and fines for illegal parking or speeding are not deductible business expenses.

*Which is better, standard or actual?* The shocking answer: It depends. High mileage on a car that's cheap to run may get a better write-off using the standard cents-per-mile method. Low business mileage on an old vehicle with lots of expensive repair bills may get a better write-off using actual expenses. Let your tax preparer decide for you. She will calculate both ways and can switch from year to year to get the best advantage. There are some restrictions on switching which your preparer will take into consideration.

Of course, if for one reason or another you do not have good records of all your car expenses – say your forgetful brother borrows the car a lot and he simply cannot remember to get receipts when he buys gas – then you must use the standard mileage method. Another bothersome deduction problem for an indie occurs when several cars are used for business purposes. One of my clients has five cars in his family and although he, his wife, and children each has his or her own car, for various reasons they often must switch cars. It is impossible for him to keep track of expenses separately for each individual car. He may use his car 85% for business but his sons' cars only 10% for business. So he simply keeps a record of his total business miles and we use the standard method.

## How to Keep A Record of Business Miles

Regardless of which method you use to calculate AUTO expense you will need to know the total business use miles for the year.

If you use the actual method you will need to do a little more work. In this case you'll also need to know the total mileage for the year for the vehicle. And, if you use more than one car for business, you will need these figures for each car used for business.

If you have any questions about what constitutes business use of your car review the previous sections on travel and transportation.

*A Look at Several Quick Ways to Record Mileage:* Let's start on New Year's Eve! A little assignment before you head out to the party: Get the mileage reading on your car from the odometer and log or write it in your calendar.

Next assignment: On the following New Year's Eve, once again before you go out (because you'll never remember in the morning) write that mileage reading in your calendar.

Completing those two assignments gives you a beginning and ending mileage reading for the year so you know how many miles you put on your car for the year. Now let's see what you do between parties.

As long as accuracy is your goal, the method used is not important. Choose the routine that suits you and your business. Patti Partyplanner, who runs all over the state checking party and convention sites and prices of supplies, and listening to bands, will have a very different method of calculating business mileage than will Rob Rolf who rarely needs to leave his massage studio. Let's look at the different ways that they, and Lily Legal, figure out business miles.

---

### REALITY √ CHECK

Patti Partyplanner spends much of her day in what she calls her "business" car. She was distraught at the cumbersome way her former tax preparer told her to calculate business miles. Sammy Segar told her to write down the odometer reading every morning – 79,814.5 – and then at the end of the day write down the new reading – 80,013.6 – and then subtract. 199.1 miles. What a bother! By day's end she was so tired that she often made mistakes in arithmetic.

Patti has another car – bigger, with a childseat, devoid of the clutter of her business car. She uses that one for just about all the family errands. Patti came up with a much easier way of calculating business miles. She does her New Year's Eve notations in the calendar. But then instead of writing down all her business miles she just notes in her calendar the few occasions she uses the business car for personal errands. She deducts her personal miles from her total miles to come up with a business use figure.

---

### REALITY √ CHECK

Rob Rolf uses his car for business only once a month to buy supplies. All he has to do is to check the mileage from studio to supply house and back and multiply it by 12 and he's got his total business miles for the year.

---

---

**REALITY √ CHECK**

Lily Legal goes to the court house twice a week. She has an occasional trip to a client's office. Like Rob Rolf she does the multiplication thing to figure her court house appearances – two trips times 48 weeks (she takes off four weeks a year to go to Aruba). And she uses her appointment calendar to determine which clients she met with at their offices. Around early December she has her clerk figure the miles from her office to each client. He logs the mileage in her appointment book and tallies them up. He adds that to her court appearance mileage for total business use mileage.

---

As you can see from the above examples, there is no set way to keep a mileage record. Use a method that suits you.

***Using A Calendar to Record Miles:*** Here's an easy, straightforward way to record business miles. I assume every indie uses a calendar or scheduling software to note activities, appointments and, possibly, errands. Maybe you use two, one on your iPad, the other on the kitchen wall. They clearly – but not necessarily neatly – show events such as printer on Monday; Tuesday, Town Library; Thursday at 1, lunch with Clyde Client; Saturday, marketing workshop; PTA meeting the second Monday of every month; Wednesday, client presentation.

After a business appointment – driving to the printer's and back – upon returning to your office or home studio or workshop, you jot down or log the mileage on the calendar. Anyway, that's how it's supposed to work, but you know how it goes: at times it has slipped your mind, or you hadn't time because you had to get somewhere else. So in a week or a month or at year's end with your appointment software open or calendar in front of you you'll see that you met with the printer on that day. If you don't know the mileage to the print shop out comes MapQuest or ask your wife, who knows the mileage to every place in the county. Then note the mileage in your calendar.

Any kind of calendar, appointment book, or computer date book will do. Whatever you are comfortable with. Do not use a mileage log separate from your other calendar. That's just another thing to keep track of and it's double work to jot down your appointment in your calendar and a second time in your mileage log. Forget it! Enter your mileage on the calendar that you use for all the other events and meetings going on in your life – that way you won't miss any business mileage.

At the end of the year add up – using a calculator that has a tape – the business miles that you noted or logged in your calendar. By the way, if you know that at least once a month you run to the office supply store or the Quick-Send postal drop once a week but don't write these errands in your calendar then multiply the trip mileage by the appropriate number of trips to come up with more miles to add to your calendar-logged totals. Many solos who work at home cheat themselves in business mileage. They forget that before picking up the kids at daycare they went five miles in the other direction to pick up new business cards at the printer.

If your New Year's numbers showed a total of 20,000 miles and your calendar totals 15,000 business miles then you know that 75% (15,000 divided by 20,000) of your car was used for business. That enables you to deduct 75% of your entire year's worth of car expenses and will also get you a 75% write-off of the cost of your car.

---

### ALERT!

A word of caution whether you keep a paper or software calendar: If your date book is stolen, mislaid forever or dropped on the tile floor, you've lost your entire year-to-date records. If you must carry it with you or you like to keep it in your car, then at the end of each month backup, backup, backup. If a paper calendar then tear out each month as it's complete and leave it back at the office or in your desk at home.

In this way if it disappears you've lost only the current month.

---

In the event of an audit the IRS will want to see your appointment calendar. For psychologists, reporters and other professions where confidentiality is a concern, should you be audited: photocopy your calendar and black out all confidential information on the copy you show to the IRS.

***What if you missed New Year's Eve?*** How does the IRS check the mileage figures you use? Well, in an audit they'll ask for auto repair receipts. Most repair receipts have the odometer reading at the time of the repair written on the receipt. If you forget to check your mileage reading on New Year's Eve check a recent repair slip and make a guesstimate.

***More Than One Vehicle Used for Business:*** If you use more than one car for business, and you use the actual expenses method to calculate your business auto deduction then you must segregate the expenses and mileage for each vehicle. If for instance you use the van as your business vehicle but on rare occasions you use your husband's car you must keep the same records on your husband's car as on your van. Tally his expenses at year-end and, though it may be tiny, take your business percent.

***Tired of The Same Old Wheels:*** Spreading your business driving between both (all) your cars will increase your AUTO expense deduction.

If your policy has been to use only the old clunker to cart around your supplies and drive from your office to your workshop, change your ways and put some business miles on the new Volvo as well. For instance, if 3,000 of the Volvo's 10,000 miles per year were for business you will get a deduction of 30% of all Volvo costs. That means a deduction of 30% of the $40,000 purchase price as well as things like insurance, gas, etc.

And this is in addition to the deduction for 90% or 95% of the costs of the old clunker.

***Using A Borrowed Car:*** No matter. Keep records just as you would for any other vehicle you use for business.

***Lease or Rent A Car:*** Same thing. Keep the same records as you would for a car you owned.

Have your lease or rental agreement available for your tax preparer because you are required to reduce the amount of AUTO expense deduction by a small percentage of the fair market value of the leased car. Your preparer will need to get that figure from your lease agreement.

If you rent a car while on a business trip the entire cost of the car rental is a TRAVEL expense. If, however, your trip is mixed business and personal you'll have to keep a mileage record.

---

### WHATTA CONCEPT!
#### Lease Versus Own

Should you lease?

If your business requires you to wow clients with glitter, a new car every two years is imperative, and leasing is probably the better way for you. Leasing versus owning, however, is generally based on how good a deal you can get, with tax considerations secondary.

If tax savings is a key factor in your purchasing decision then run it by your tax pro. (Try to time your purchase so that you're not questioning her at the height of the tax return season.) Any savings in tax deductions must of course be balanced against purchase price, operating expenses and other considerations.

---

## TO SUM UP GETTING AROUND

- TRAVEL is overnight.
- TRANSPORTATION takes place in the same day.
- Your means of getting from one place to another whether for TRAVEL or TRANSPORTATION may be the same.

On the following page is the completed **BUSINESS USE OF AUTO, TRUCK OR OTHER VEHICLE** worksheet, using the 60% figures in the Lily Legal PREVIOUS example.

# BUSINESS USE OF AUTO, TRUCK OR OTHER VEHICLE: 2012

| | Vehicle #1 or Self | Vehicle #2 or Spouse | Vehicle #3 |
|---|---|---|---|
| Description of Vehicle and Date Purchased | Lily's blue car 1/1/08 | | |
| Cost, or, If 1st year of business use Then value on 1st day of business use | 20,000 | | |
| Mileage @ January 1 | 29450 | | |
| Mileage @ December 31 | 39450 | | |
| Total miles for the year | 10000 | | |
| Total business miles for the year | 6000 | | |
| Business % | 60 | | |
| Business miles times 55 1/2 cents per mile | 3,330 | | |
| Loan interest paid this year times business % | 300 | | |
| **Total Standard Auto Expenses** | **3,630** | | |
| Actual Expenses | | | |
| Loan Interest Paid This Year | 500 | | |
| Gas | 1,900 | | |
| Repairs / Maintenance | 450 | | |
| Insurance (Include AAA, etc.) | 1,350 | | |
| Registration / License | | | |
| Car Wash | | | |
| Garage Rental | | | |
| Sub-Total Expenses | 4,200 | | |
| Rental r Lease Costs | | | |
| Total Expenses | 4,200 | | |
| Business Percent | 60 | | |
| Total Actual Expenses | 2,520 | | |
| Depreciation (calculated by tax preparer) | 1,065 | | |
| **Total Actual Auto Expenses** | **3,585** | | |

## CHAPTER 11: LEARNING THE ROPES
### Education And Research Expenses

Learning can be fun, useful, profitable – and tax-deductible. In this chapter I'll show you how to reduce your taxes while learning, whether learning takes place in a classroom, at a workshop, online, in the field, at the theatre, or using the most ancient of learning tools, the book.

## BUSINESS EDUCATION EXPENSES

After almost a decade in business, Caitlin Caterer is prospering. Never having specialized in any specific type of food, her catering service has always done its best to fill requests for all sorts of cuisine. She has noticed that many of the young professionals moving into her neighborhood are vegetarians. They are prosperous and entertain frequently. She doesn't understand how they can pass up veau orloff but for the sake of her business she wants to be ready, willing and able to cater to their tastes, and has concluded that it would benefit her business to be more versed in the art of vegetarian cooking. A chef who accepts very few students has been recommended to her, but his course in meatless cookery is a big-ticket item. After checking with her tax advisor Caitlin decides to take the course. She has learned that she can deduct the course, the materials required for the course, as well as her transportation there and back. So her out-of-pocket costs will be less than she thought.

---

**THE IRS SAYS ABOUT BUSINESS EDUCATION EXPENSE ...**
You can deduct your education expenses (including certain related travel expenses) if you can show that the education maintains or improves skills required in your trade or business, or the education is required by law or regulations for keeping your pay, status, or job.

---

You cannot deduct education expenses you incur to meet the minimum requirements of your present trade or business, or those that qualify you for a new trade or business.

Let's look at the IRS language from the viewpoint of self-employment. In order for an indie to deduct EDUCATION expenses he must determine the following:

**Part One:** Does the course qualify as business education?

**Part Two:** Which of the costs of education are deductible as business expenses?

## Part One: DOES IT QUALIFY AS BUSINESS EDUCATION?

As we've just seen, the indie's first step is to determine whether the course, seminar, convention, workshop, or webinar qualifies as business education.

Can Harvey Housesitter deduct the expenses of a course on how to care for indoor plants?

Can Syd System (who works in his home office and whose misbehaving dog is driving him crazy) deduct the cost of dog obedience training, so that he can work without interruption in peace and quiet?

### Qualifying Education

Not all courses qualify as business EDUCATION expense. According to the IRS, courses must meet at least one of the following tests in order to qualify:

1. The education must be ***required by law*** in order to keep your present income, status, or job.
   or

2. The education must be ***required by your employer*** to keep your present income, status, or job.
   or

3. The education must ***maintain or improve skills*** needed in your present work.

Let's look at each of these requirements.

### *1. Education Required by The Law*

Once you have met the minimum educational requirements for your business, you may be legally required to get more education in order for you to hold on to your present position or status.

---

### REALITY √ CHECK

Stacy Stockbroker works out of her home office. She has satisfied the minimum requirements for a series seven license. In order to maintain her licensed status she has to take continuing education courses required by the Securities and Exchange Commission and the National Association of Securities Dealers. Stacy may deduct the cost of the continuing ed courses.

---

## 2. Education Required by Your Employer

The IRS also allows deductions for education required by your employer. Since you are a self-employed and thus your own employer, you have to decide for yourself (and with the help of your tax consultant) whether the deduction will meet the criteria.

Furthermore, many self-employed professions and businesses are not licensed and for many no certification is necessary, which means that the education you require of yourself is even more of a judgment call.

So what do we have to go by? For one thing, the IRS admonition, "in order to be deductible a business expense must be ordinary and necessary to your profession." What you require of yourself as your own employer is determined by the criterion in the third requirement below.

## 3. Education to Maintain Or Improve Your Skills

Education not required by laws or regulations may qualify for deduction if the education maintains or improves skills or knowledge required in your present work.

It doesn't matter whether a course or workshop is academic or vocational in nature; and refresher courses, seminars on current developments, and correspondence courses can be included.

---

### REALITY √ CHECK

Sally Shrink, a practicing psychiatrist, is studying at a fully accredited institute to become a psychoanalyst. Since the study maintains and improves skills required in her profession, Sally can deduct the cost of her studies.

---

> **REALITY √ CHECK**
>
> Rebecca Repair fixes old appliances, not only because she's a green activist but she also loves the aesthetics of pre-digital design. Being one of the few with her skills, she makes a good deal of money as well. She's hooked up with Anton Antique to service anything he's picked up at an estate sale that's in need of a fix.
>
> She has subscribed to an online service that keeps her up to date on parts, paint, and inner workings of her vintage appliances. She also attends a four-times-a-year hands-on workshop where she learns new techniques for finishes, wiring, etc. The email service and the workshops maintain and improve skills required in her work.

> **REALITY √ CHECK**
>
> Angelo Automend has been fixing cars – radiators, mufflers, electrical systems and fuel systems – for several years, but he has always sent potential customers elsewhere for accident collision repair. Now Angelo has decided to expand into collision work, but has to take a course on it at the community college. Would Angelo shock his friends by announcing that he's going to straighten out bent fenders and twisted frames? Of course not – it's a logical development of his business, and he can deduct the cost of the course.

You can see that Dr. Sally Shrink and Angelo Automend were able to deduct the cost of their education because it was closely tied to or an expansion of their present work. Even if a freelancer attends a workshop because his business has changed its focus, as long as he's not going into a new trade or business and if the new focus involves the same general work as he's been doing, then the cost of the workshop is deductible.

Caitlin Caterer can deduct the cost of her course in vegetarian cookery, and Harvey Housesitter can deduct the course in indoor plants, but Syd System cannot deduct the cost of sending his rambunctious dog to obedience school.

You are also allowed to deduct the cost of education to maintain your skills while you are temporarily absent or on leave from your business.

The IRS defines *temporary leave of absence to be a year or less*. In order for the deduction to qualify, however, you must return to the same general type of business.

---

### REALITY √ CHECK

Nyssa Nutritionist likes children and wants to add more day care centers to her client list. She leaves her nutrition counseling business to become a full-time graduate student in children's nutrition for two semesters – less than a year. Then she'll pick up her business where she left off.  She can deduct the costs of her education.

---

### REALITY √ CHECK

Eddie Electronic worked as an employee for TV Quick Fix, Inc. where he was assigned to fixing TV sets, though he was qualified to do a lot more. He left the job, took a month-long course, "21st Century Electronics." Shortly after that he started his own business.

He may deduct the costs of the course because it was related to his present work, and he returned to work in the same field. Since the IRS has no problem with a switch of employers, Ed's becoming his own boss was OK too.

---

If you are absent from your work longer than a year you cannot deduct the expense of any work-related education.

---

### REALITY √ CHECK

Nat Newdad loved his work as advisor to small corporations on how to avoid hostile takeovers. As an independent consultant he enjoyed total flexibility in his work schedule. He wanted to be a full-time father when his first child was born, and was successful enough to have the wherewithal to take off a year. He finished up his contract with Innovative Ideas Corporation just before Christmas, only days before his daughter was born. He is planning to return to his consulting business after her first birthday.

While on this sabbatical Nat took two expensive online courses on mergers, acquisitions and other restructuring activity. But, because the IRS defines temporary absence as one year or less, any seminars that Nat attended to keep current with the corporate community would not be deductible because he was away from his business for more than a year -from a few days before his daughter's birth until a few days after her first birthday.

---

## Nonqualifying Education

Certain education costs do not qualify for deductions even though they meet some of the criteria we have examined. For example, even if the education is required by law or needed to maintain or improve skills you cannot deduct the costs if:

1. The education is needed to meet minimum education requirements.

    or

2. The education qualifies you for a new trade or business.

Let's look at each of these disallowed education expenses.

### *1. Education to Meet Minimum Professional Requirements: No Deduction*

You cannot deduct the costs of pursuing the minimum requirements necessary for your profession, trade or business. It doesn't matter whether these minimum requirements are mandatory because of laws, regulations, or industry standards. Watch out for the definition of minimum. Just because you are doing the work does not mean that you have met the minimum educational requirements of your trade or business.

---

### REALITY √ CHECK

Annabelle Architect is attending college with the intention of becoming an architect. To help pay her college expenses Annabelle freelances for several local architectural firms. She prepares architectural drawings and researches the cost and availability of new materials. Although her college courses in architecture improve the skills she uses in her freelancing, she has not met the minimum job requirements of an architect. Her college education does not qualify for a business expense deduction.

---

### REALITY √ CHECK

Raina Realtor quit a dead-end no-future job. She took the six-week real estate course required to get a realtor's license. The costs of the course are not deductible.

---

Also, courses to prepare for a bar examination or a certified public accountant examination cannot be taken as educational deductions.

### Two Exceptions to The Minimum Requirements Exclusion

The first: If the minimum requirements change while you're in the field any education costs incurred to meet the new standards are deductible.

---

**REALITY √ CHECK**

If state law changed and required all realtors to take an additional course on mortgage financing Raina would have to take the course before she could get her license renewed.

Because she had already met the minimum requirements when she originally got her license the cost of the course would qualify for deduction.

However, a new applicant for a realtor's license would have to satisfy the new minimum requirements and could not deduct any of the schooling.

---

The second exception to the minimum requirements exclusion: Once minimum educational requirements have been met, an indie can deduct the costs of education if he transfers the business to another state where additional testing or more education is necessary for certification.

---

**REALITY √ CHECK**

Dr. Endie Naturopath's practice was in Connecticut. When she moved to Hawaii she had to take an exam in order to get licensed in that state.

Because Hawaii's exam included a test on homeopathy, an area in which Endie had not concentrated while a doctor in Connecticut, she had to take a refresher course before she took the exam.

Endie can deduct the costs of the course. The IRS considers that once you have met minimum educational requirements in any state in which you practice, any courses you might have to take upon being certified in a new state qualify for deductions.

---

### 2. Education to Qualify for A New Trade or Business: No Deduction

Education expenses not related to your present trade or business are not deductible.

**REALITY √ CHECK**

Thomas Twocareers, a real estate agent, has decided to become a massage therapist, so he enrolls in an intensive – and expensive – six-month course in his new chosen field. The cost of the course does not qualify for deduction. His career has veered off in an entirely new direction.

***Bones of Contention.*** Whether certain courses or workshops qualify for deduction can be a judgment call.

**REALITY √ CHECK**

After becoming a psychoanalyst Dr. Shrink decides that the key to understanding the mind lies in computer theory. She takes an intensive course in cybernetics to discover the sources of reason. Dr. Shrink decides that mind and body are so closely linked that she wants to combine and incorporate both in her work, so she undergoes training in Rolfing, a form of physical therapy that attempts to explore manifestations of neurosis that show up in physical problems.

After the training in Rolfing she also takes a course in nutrition and its effect on behavior psychology.

In all these instances Dr. Shrink and the IRS might have cause to argue about whether such courses qualify for deduction. My vote goes for a deduction in all three situations.

## TO SUM UP QUALIFYING EDUCATION

To the IRS deductible education expenses are "qualifying" education expenses. What I hope you have gleaned from this extensive look at what qualifies as business EDUCATION is that in order to deduct education costs as a business expense:

- The education must get beyond the minimum requirements of your professional field.
- You must be actively engaged in your indie endeavor or must be returning to it. (See Temporary leave of absence.)
- The education must be demonstrably related to your field of endeavor.

## Part Two: WHICH EDUCATION COSTS ARE DEDUCTIBLE?

OK, you've determined that your course, seminar, convention, workshop, or webinar does qualify as business education. But which of the costs related to the education are deductible as business EDUCATION expenses?

The IRS says that if the education qualifies as a deduction, then the following educational expenses are generally deductible as business expenses as well:

- Tuition, books, supplies, lab fees, and similar items
- Other educational expenses such as costs of research
- Transportation and travel costs

Tuition and supplies, other direct costs such as paying someone to type your term paper, or admission fees to a presentation where attendance was required by your instructor, are all unquestionable EDUCATION expenses. However, expenses for transportation and travel can get complex.

TRANSPORTATION costs related to EDUCATION expenses include:

- Bus, subway, cab, or other fares
- Use of your own car (See CHAPTER 10.)

TRANSPORTATION expenses do not include amounts spent for travel, meals, or lodging while away from home overnight. Those are TRAVEL expenses.

If you haven't read CHAPTER 10, which explains the difference between travel and transportation and travel for educational purposes, be sure to do so.

The following explains what you can deduct as business transportation when getting to and from classes. If the class you're attending is a mile away you may not want to be bothered with these complicated rules. But if you drive 40 miles each way or your train fare is $40 round-trip to attend class, you might be interested. You decide how well versed you want to be in this area.

What the IRS allows for local transportation costs depends on whether your education is on a temporary or regular basis.

For education on a temporary basis – to the IRS that's one year or less – you can deduct the round-trip costs of transportation – that is, from your place of business or from your home to school and then back. You can deduct the entire round-trip cost regardless of the location of the school, distance traveled, or whether you attend on work or non-work days.

Here are a few scenarios:
Let's say that your pet-grooming service is your full-time occupation and that you go directly home from your shop every evening. If after arriving home you attend poodle-cutting class nightly for three weeks you can deduct your daily round-trip transportation expenses between home and school.

If on some nights, or every night, you go directly from your shop to school and then home, you can deduct your transportation expenses from the shop to school and then home.

If the course were given on six consecutive Mondays, a day that your shop is closed, you can still deduct your round-trip transportation expenses in going between home and class.

If you attend class on a regular basis rather than on a temporary basis – that means for more than a year – then the IRS will not let you deduct your round-trip transportation expenses.

Instead you may only deduct one-way transportation expenses from your shop to school. If you return home after work and then go to school, your transportation expenses cannot be more than if you had gone directly from your place of business to school.

The same one-way versus round-trip rules apply if you drive your car to class. Be sure to see the previous chapter on business use of auto.

Go ahead. Say it. ***These regulations are crazy.*** I agree with you. You are not going to remember the specifics. I often don't remember them. Just know that they are here for easy reference should you need them.

Keep in mind the difference between TRANSPORTATION and TRAVEL. If it's overnight it is TRAVEL.

Travel expenses for qualifying education are treated the same as travel expenses for other business purposes. Many rules and regulations apply to business travel deductions, so once again I urge you to read CHAPTER 10 for the specifics on TRAVEL deductions. For some general rules keep in mind that:

- You cannot deduct expenses for personal activities, such as sightseeing, visiting, or entertaining.
- If you mix business with pleasure you will have to prorate or exclude certain expenses depending upon where you traveled and for how long.

TRAVEL costs related to EDUCATION expenses include:

- Getting to and from the location of the course, seminar, or workshop
- Lodging while going to, coming from, or while at the location
- Meals (subject to the 50% limit) while going to and from and while attending the course

The following examples illustrate how and to what extent business travel is deductible when it is mixed with personal travel on the same trip.

---

### REALITY √ CHECK

Patti Partyplanner's business is in Boston. She traveled to Philadelphia to take a deductible one-week course on security measures for large events. While there, she entertained friends and took a one-day trip to Valley Forge. Since the trip to Philadelphia was mainly for business, she can deduct her round-trip airfare, the transportation related to the course, and meals and lodging for the days of the course.

Patti cannot deduct the transportation or other expenses of her visits with friends or her trip to Valley Forge.

---

### REALITY √ CHECK

Estelle has really made a go of her estate sales business in Seattle. She flew to San Francisco for a two-week seminar on new trends in tracking down and marketing antiques. While there, she spent an additional four weeks visiting her mother. Given these facts, her main purpose was clearly not business. Therefore she cannot deduct her airfare or any other expenses during her four-week visit with her mother. She can deduct only her expenses for meals and lodging for the two weeks she attended the seminar and any other seminar-related expenses.

---

---

**ALERT!**

Heed not the siren call of certain cruises and conventions which offer seminars or courses as part of their itinerary. Even if these are work-related, your deduction for travel may be limited if the travel is by ocean liner, cruise ship, or is held outside the North American area.

---

**ALERT!**

You may no longer treat travel as a form of education even if it is directly related to your business.

---

In CHAPTER 10 I explained that Jack Japanese Instructor may deduct a trip to Japan to take courses in Japanese and Japanese culture or history. He may not deduct the costs of a trip to Japan if he just travels around the country soaking up the culture.

If the trip is primarily a vacation, there is no deduction for travel costs to and from the foreign location. Just because Jack Japanese Instructor took a one-day Haiku course during his ten days in Japan does not make the airfare or any of his other expenses deductible. Only the cost of the one-day course is a business expense.

## WHICH EDUCATION RECORDS TO KEEP

You may at some time be called upon to prove that your education expenses are legitimate business deductions. In addition to credit card receipts, checks and online payment records that show your expenses you may also need to prove that the course or workshop itself was a valid business deduction. Therefore, you should also keep papers such as:

- College transcripts
- Seminar agenda
- Catalogues or brochures
- Course descriptions
- Workshop speaker lists
- Scholarship information

If you have attended a workshop that you believe qualifies for EDUCATION expenses, keep – in addition to records of the expenses – evidence of the workshop's connection with your business, especially if the connection is a bit wacky or sounds just a trifle too imaginative. If at a later date you can show how that course figured in your business, also put that information in your tax file of the year that you took the expense. For instance, if Dr. Shrink is written about in the local paper as an innovative psychiatrist who incorporated Rolfing into her diagnostic technique, the clipping should be saved for the IRS.

## TAKING CREDIT WHERE CREDIT IS DUE AND OTHER TAX BENEFITS FOR THE GET-SMART FREELANCER

The recent economic malaise has spawned a lot of talk about retraining and re-educating for the 21st century. New skills are needed to train, to educate, to teach old dogs new tricks – and the self-employed are included. If you are a more-action-than-talk kind of indie and are honing up on your skills know that there are many tax benefits for higher education or vocational school expenses for those who qualify – for the most part, lower- and middle-income Americans. You may not claim more than one type of tax benefit from the same expense. Therefore you are not allowed to deduct your education costs as a business expense and then use the same expenses for another tax benefit. This is where the knowledge of a tax professional is direly needed because many calculations may need to be done to determine which tax treatment does you the most good.

Many education incentives are in the form of **tax credits**. Even though your tax preparer will advise you on and calculate which benefit suits you best it is important for you to have a grasp of the difference between a business expense deduction and a tax credit and how each may save you some tax money.

---

### WHATTA CONCEPT!
#### Deductions Versus Tax Credits

There is a big difference between a **tax deduction** and a **tax credit**.

A **deduction** is subtracted from your income, a benefit to you because your tax is calculated on the amount of your income. A $1,000 deduction reduces your income by $1,000 and depending upon your tax bracket and state taxes could save you from zero up to $500 in taxes.

A **tax credit** is an amount subtracted directly from your tax. A $300 tax credit reduces your tax by $300; a $1,000 tax credit saves you $1,000 in taxes.

---

When you have deductible business education expenses your tax preparer will compare the tax savings of a deduction against the tax savings of a credit. There are often income limitations on tax credits. That means if your income is over a certain amount you are not eligible for the tax credit.

Be sure to categorize your EDUCATION expenses carefully so that your tax pro can get you the best tax savings for your educational dollar.

| EDUCATION COSTS: ARE THEY DEDUCTIBLE BUSINESS EXPENSES? | | |
| --- | --- | --- |
| Is the education needed to meet the minimum educational requirements of your trade or business? | **YES** | Your education does not qualify. |
| | **NO** | Your education qualifies. |
| Is the education part of a study program that can qualify you in a new trade or business? | **YES** | Your education does not qualify |
| | **NO** | Your education qualifies. |
| Is the education required by law, to keep your present income, status, or job? | **YES** | Your education qualifies. |
| Does the education maintain or improve skills required in doing your present work? | **YES** | Your education qualifies. |

# RESEARCH OR NOT, IT'S DEDUCTIBLE

When you become involved in any dealings with the IRS, keep in mind that the agency is a self-contained and distant realm, with its own special terminology and its very own arcane definitions for everyday words. Take for instance the meaning that the IRS attaches to the word *research*.

In ordinary English, research is the common element in these four examples of valid business expenses. In the MEALS & ENTERTAINMENT section of CHAPTER 8, page 83, I used the following two examples:

- Nadine Novella is writing a short story, "Headed for The Big Time." All expenses associated with her *research* at the baseball games are fully deductible.
- Theobald Theater Critic is paid for his drama reviews. When he attends a theatrical performance in his professional capacity, it is not a 50% deductible ENTERTAINMENT expense; it is a 100% deductible *research* expense.

And in CHAPTER 6: INDIE POWER MINDSET I gave you two other examples:
- A structural engineer drives through Millionaire's Mile looking at the period architecture of the houses. Stops to sketch and take notes. Since this is *research* for him the drive is a business event and the mileage there and back is a business AUTO expense.
- Ivan Inventor – of computer games that is – shouldn't assume that buying someone else's computer game can't be a business expense. Even if he stayed up half the night fighting invaders from another galaxy, he was *researching* the competition. The purchase of the game is a business deduction.

In each of these examples my use of the word "research" describes quite clearly the activity that has led to a business expense deduction. But the IRS attaches its own particular meaning to *research*. It speaks in a special language that classifies expenses in its own way – and as far as that agency is concerned, only one of these examples (Ivan Inventor) is categorized as a RESEARCH expense. All the other expenses are deductible business expenses, but, by IRS definition, they are not RESEARCH expenses.

---

**THE IRS SAYS ABOUT RESEARCH AND EXPERIMENTAL COSTS ...**

They are the reasonable costs you incur for activities intended to provide information that would eliminate uncertainty about the development or improvement of a product.

The term "product" includes the following as well as items similar to these:
- Formula
- Invention
- Patent
- Pilot model
- Process
- Technique

---

But in the IRS realm, RESEARCH & EXPERIMENTAL costs do not include expenses for any of the following activities:

- Consumer surveys
- Efficiency surveys
- Management studies
- The acquisition of another's patent, model, or process.
- Research in connection with literary, historical, or similar projects.

The IRS does consider the costs of developing computer software to be a RESEARCH & EXPERIMENTAL cost. Therefore, in our above examples only Ivan Inventor can call his expense RESEARCH. That doesn't mean, however, that the expenses of Nadine Novella, Theobald Theatre Critic and the engineer who took a drive through Millionaire's Mile cannot be deducted. They are perfectly legitimate deductions – but to the IRS, they are not RESEARCH deductions.

If all these other expenses are deductible does it really matter what we call them? Well, here's an answer you won't like: Sometimes.

For instance, there's a big difference for Theobald Theater Critic. Because, were he in a different line of work going to the theatre for business would be an ENTERTAINMENT expense and so only 50% deductible.

And, if something by IRS definition is a RESEARCH expense then your tax preparer will have several ways by which she can deduct that expense. Her choice would be determined by your tax situation. This choice of tax treatment is not available for other kinds of expenses.

The IRS provides no guideline as to what to call those other expenses that we call "research." The drive through Millionaire's Mile will show up as an AUTO expense deduction when the mileage is added to the rest of the business miles. But, what about the others? Over the years I have called them a number of different things and they've never been disallowed for being misnamed. Nadine's baseball ticket expenses I label as RESEARCH and Theobald's theater ticket I comfortably call PERFORMANCE ADMISSIONS. It really doesn't matter what we call them – your tax preparer will make her own choice – the important point here is for you to know that they are legitimate business expenses and be sure that your preparer understands what may be your unique situation in incurring that expense. Be sure they make it to your tax return, uncut.

Because RESEARCH expenses (in the IRS terminology) have a special character, they can be treated in a variety of ways on your tax return. Your tax preparer will want them set apart from other expenses so that she can get you the best deal possible – that is, the biggest tax write-off – on your return. You might be able to claim a **research tax credit.** Remember tax credits? A direct write-off against your taxes! If you think you will have RESEARCH expenses it's smart to contact your tax pro before you start spending money. She may have some tax-saving advice that works only if you do your spending in a certain way.

## CHAPTER 12: WHERE YOU HANG YOUR HAT OR DO YOUR DIGITAL
### The Tax Implications of Where You Work

As an indie business you may work anywhere you want. You may rent an office or studio, purchase an entire building in which to set up shop, or work out of your home – whatever suits your situation. As you'll learn in this chapter you may also work out of all these locations and deduct expenses for all of them.

## RENTING WORK SPACE

Renting an office or studio or workshop gives you clear and unchallengeable deductions. Rent, utilities, cleaning service, parking lot snow removal, repairs, et al are 100% deductible business expenses.

Deducting INSURANCE payments may be a little tricky, and you'll want to have your insurance bill available to show your tax preparer. This is because you can deduct only the portion of your insurance payment that is for the current year. If your payment covers part of next year the deduction will have to be prorated, part for this year and part for next year. Also, you may not deduct your rent security payment. (It's not an expense because you're going to get it back. But it is an expense if you don't get it back.) Except for insurance payments and security deposits the deductions for a rented office, studio, or workshop are clear-cut.

## OWNING A BUSINESS BUILDING

If you purchase a building for your business the deduction is more complicated. You get to deduct all the typical expenses such as UTILITIES, REPAIRS and REAL ESTATE TAXES. And you also get to write off the cost of the building. – but not all at once. A commercial building is a capital asset and its cost must be depreciated over 39 years. Let's say you purchased a $39,000 building in an office park (no land came with the purchase) and you gave the seller a check for $39,000; your deduction for the year of purchase and for the next 38 years would be $1,000 per year. That deduction is called a **depreciation** expense and your tax pro will calculate the amount for you based upon the purchase information that you provide to her.

If you purchased an old ranch, with a large isolated shed that you could use for a workshop and great fields where you could roam while sweeping the cobwebs out of your brain, it would work like this: You cannot deduct the cost of the land as a business expense. Assume you paid $104,000 for the ranch. And a real estate tax bill shows that 25% of the cost is for the fields and meadows and 75% is for the building – the shed. Because you can deduct only the cost of the shed, and not the cost of the land, the cost of the building must be calculated. In this case the cost of the building, 75% of $104,000, is $78,000. Depreciating that over 39 years – you can think of it as dividing the cost by 39 – gets you a whopping $2,000 per year depreciation deduction.

Whether you pay for the entire building when purchased, which is highly unlikely, or, more typically, you obtain a mortgage to finance your purchase, you still get the same $1/39^{th}$ of the cost of the building as a depreciation deduction. When you have a mortgage you also get a deduction for the mortgage interest paid for the year. That gives you a two-part deduction: One part is the $1/39^{th}$ cost of the building, the other part is the mortgage interest paid. These two parts do not – unless coincidentally – equal your monthly mortgage payment. Many indies mistakenly think that the mortgage payment is the deductible amount.

## WHATTA CONCEPT!
### The Impact of Taxes on a Mortgage Rate

Deducting mortgage interest as a business expense reduces the cost of a mortgage. Here's some arithmetic on a 6% and a 4% mortgage to show the tax savings:

| Mortgage Rate | 6% | 4% |
|---|---|---|
| Mortgage balance | $100,000 | $100,000 |
| Finance charge for the year | $6,000 | $4,000 |
| Combined tax rate (federal + SE tax + state) | 30% | 30% |
| Tax savings from mortgage deduction<br>30% x $6,000<br>30% x $4,000 | $1,800 | $1,200 |
| **Actual Mortgage Rate Paid**<br>$6,000 - $1,800 = $4,200<br><br>$4,000 - $1,200 = $2,800 | 4.2%<br>instead of 6% | 2.8%<br>instead of 4% |

# UNCONVENTIONAL WORKSPACE ARRANGEMENTS

- A speech therapist gets to use his mother-in-law's casita in exchange for taking care of the grounds.
- Nancy, of Nancy's Nuts, uses a local bakery's oven to roast nuts at night, in exchange for providing the bakery with little bags of nuts to sell as point-of-purchase items at the register.
- A photography designer has the use of a business's studio and lights over the weekend in exchange for recommending clients.

Many indies make creative arrangements to obtain workspace for no outlay of money. For others, there may be a cost – Nancy pays for the nuts and spices that she gives to the bakery. But she has no deductible RENT or LEASE expense. These are all legitimate workspace arrangements.

# OFFICE OR STUDIO OR WORKSHOP IN THE HOME

Here we run smack into one of the most persistent old husbands' tales: Don't take office-in-the-home, it's a red flag and the IRS will be at your door.

---

**THE IRS SAYS ABOUT OFFICE-IN-THE-HOME ...**
In recent years the IRS "has uncovered a number of abusive home-based business tax schemes that erroneously assert that individuals can operate any type of unprofitable 'business' out of their homes, and then claim personal expenses as business expenses." The IRS "will continue to focus ... enforcement efforts in this area."

---

So what's an indie to do? I'll tell you what to do: If you use your home for your self-employed business, then, by golly, don't be afraid to take the deduction. By deducting expenses for your home workspace you'll pay less tax. The only caveat: Play by the rules.

The IRS has relaxed the rules on home office and they are simpler than you may have been led to believe. There are now only three home office rules. And your workplace at home must meet all three requirements.

They are:
## Rule 1: Exclusive Use

## Rule 2. Used on A Regular Basis

## Rule 3. Principal Place of Business

Each will be explained below. Rule 1 has a few exceptions. The other two are iron-clad.

### Rule 1: Exclusive Use
The part of your home used for business must be used exclusively for business.

| Reality √ Check |
|---|
| Lily Legal writes her briefs at the dining room table but also has dinner parties there. She has to forgo any deduction for the dining room. |

### Rule #2. Used on A Regular Basis
The part of your home used for business must be used on a regular basis for business.

| Reality √ Check |
|---|
| Clement Creator has a rented studio in town. He also has great light in a back room of his house. The room is always locked and seldom used. Once in a while he brings a potential buyer to his home to look at a painting and he uses the back room for the viewing. This is not regular use and so he cannot deduct the use of that room as a business expense. |

### Rule #3. Principal Place of Business
Your home office or studio or workshop must be your principal place of business. If your home office is your ***only place of business*** then no explanation is needed.

| Reality √ Check |
|---|
| Bulky Benjamin runs his watch repair business out of his basement and only out of his basement. There's no question that the basement is his principal place of business. It's his only place of business. |

But for many indies who have **_more than one place of business_**, the IRS term **principal place of business** is misleading. If you have more than one place of business, and one of them is in your home it qualifies for home office status if it fits **_any_** of the following three criteria:

- It is where you perform substantial **_administrative tasks_** or management activities.
- It is a place where you **_meet clients, or patients, or customers._**
- It is a **_separate structure._**

Note the word substantial. It connotes activities like bookkeeping, phone calls, emailing, ordering supplies, or setting up appointments. Not a phone call now and then, or every once in a while bringing your laptop into the den to do some emailing.

---

### Reality √ Check

Dr. Endie Naturopath runs a successful holistic health practice. Bob, her bookkeeper does all the recordkeeping at his home office. Endie often sets up patient appointments on her cell phone while on the road. She does minimal paperwork at her rented office in the city where she meets with patients and presents a "professional face."

She has three children and likes to spend as much time as possible around the house, so she does most of her administrative and management chores at her home office, including patient callbacks, supplement supplies ordering, patient chart reviews and notes. Endie can deduct her home office.

---

The other IRS definition of principal place of business is a place where you meet clients, or patients, or customers.

---

### Reality √ Check

Celia Ceramist rents a neighbor's garage as her work studio. It's always a mess. She has set up the small sunroom in her home as her showcase studio. Potential buyers come there by appointment to view her work.

Although her works also show at a number of galleries throughout the United States Sally can deduct the sunroom as a home office.

---

The final definition of a workspace that qualifies as a principal place of business is a separate structure.

---

### Reality √ Check

Kyla Chiropractor shares an office with an acupuncturist. They alternate days. Kyla does not keep patient records at the office. Each morning she brings from home that day's patient folders. She keeps all her patient records, and her professional library, in a small barn on her farmland home.

Kyla can deduct the barn.

---

There are a few exceptions to RULE 1. Remember, Rule 1 requires that the workspace be devoted **exclusively** to business.

An indie who needs a **place to store inventory or product samples** and whose home is the only fixed location of her business can deduct that storage space even if it is also used for other purposes.

---

### Reality √ Check

Betty Bestow sells most of her gift baskets at Christmas, Easter and Mother's Day, often at flea markets, home parties, and via her website. Just before the holidays her inventory is very high. She stores it all in her basement. But Betty has two teenagers and a lot of their personal items end up in that part of the basement.

That's OK. Although the kids throw their stuff in there, Betty can deduct the portion of the basement used for storage as long as she has no other storage facility.

---

**Entrepreneurs who run daycare centers** are also exempt from the exclusive use rule. If the area is used as a service business involving the care of children, the elderly, or the sick, it can also be used for personal purposes without forfeiting a deduction. However, the deduction is allocated based on how many hours out of a 24-hour day the area is used for these business purposes.

---

### ALERT!

If required in your state, you must have obtained a license or other certification, or you cannot deduct home expenses.

---

---

### Reality √ Check

Sophie Soccermom watches her neighbor's children in her home and charges the going daycare rate. She's saving the money she makes for her daughter's college costs. Although Sophie is a bona fide self-employed she does not, alas, have the required license approval by her state and so she cannot deduct any home office expense for her daycare business.

She may deduct all her other daycare business expenses.

---

What do we do when a husband and wife, in two different indie businesses, share a home office or studio and neither has exclusive use? A typical example would be Victor Visual, a graphic designer and his wife Faye Fabrique, a textile designer. There is good news here. The United States tax court ruled that a taxpayer running two business from one home office may deduct the expenses of that home office[14] as long as the use meets the regulations – rules one through three – for each business. The expenses of the home office or studio then must be split proportionately between the businesses. It then follows, as the night the day, that a proportionate split between the husband's business and the wife's business is an allowed home office deduction.

That means that Victor and Faye may tally hours of use by each, or perhaps measure the private as well as communal space, and come up with an arguable proportionate split of the home studio and each take deductions for his or her share.

## OFFICE-IN-THE-HOME DEDUCTIONS: WHAT, HOW AND WHEN

Let's look at the various aspects of an actual home office deduction.

### What's a home?

Your home may be any kind of residence: House; apartment; condominium; cooperative; houseboat; mobile home.

### What portion of your home and which expenses can you deduct?

All expenses for the portion of your residence used for business are deductible. That includes rent, repairs, utilities, security system, and upkeep expenses. If you own the home, deductions include mortgage interest and real estate taxes. If for instance 20% of your home is used for business then you can deduct 20% of all these expenses.

### How do you calculate the business-use portion of your home?

There are two ways to calculate the business space as a portion of your home.

*First: Method: Measure square feet.* What is the square footage of the area or areas used for business? You calculate square feet by multiplying the width of the room or business-use area by the length of the room. A 15-foot by 20-foot room is a 300-square-foot room. You calculate the percentage of business-use by dividing the business square feet by the total square footage of your home. If the office space is 300 square feet and the entire apartment is 1500 square feet the business use is 20% (300/1500 = 20%). If the attic, basement and garage are heated and used as general living or storage quarters then you must include them in your calculation of total square feet.

*Second Method: Count the rooms.* If rooms are of approximately the same size then you can divide the rooms used for business by the total number of rooms. One room out of four would be 25%. Even if rooms are not the same size you can still use this method. For instance, two bathrooms may equal one regular-sized room, or a large living room may count for two rooms. Remember the attic and basement in this method, too.

A business area doesn't have to be an entire room. A part of a room can be taken as a deduction, if it is used only for business. In your calculations remember to include closet space where you store office supplies or the shelves in the living room that stack only your business books. A 12-inch-deep shelf that runs for six feet is another six square feet of space. (1 foot times 12 feet = 12 square feet.)

If you take an OFFICE-IN-THE-HOME deduction, I recommend to you as I do to my clients: Take photos of the business area. The space you use this year may be different than the space you use next year after the baby arrives or Grandma moves out. If your tax return is questioned, your photos will provide proof of business use for the year in dispute. A calendar or newspaper in the photo showing the date adds to your evidence. Keep the photos in your tax file for that year.

## What costs can you deduct?

Expenses are broken into three groups. The first I call *entire* (the IRS calls them **indirect expenses**). These are costs that pertain to the entire residence: rent, or mortgage interest; real estate tax; utilities such as heat and water; repair of a roof. The next group is for expenses related to the ***business area only*** (the IRS calls these **direct expenses**). They include the repair of a window in the studio, or a lock for the office door. The last group includes ***personal*** expenses you cannot deduct such as plumbing repairs in the master bathroom; a chimney sweeping of the family room fireplace.

You cannot deduct lawn care unless there is an area that is for the exclusive use of your business. The housekeeper that you have agreed to pay "off the books" – the one who takes cash only – cannot be deducted as an expense. You can deduct the costs for a legitimate cleaning service or a housekeeper for whom you pay all payroll taxes. Which, by the way, is the law and I advise you to follow the law.

## What about the price of the residence itself?

Just as you may deduct the cost of a commercial building that you own for your business you may also deduct the cost of the business portion of your residence. First the cost basis of the entire home must be established and then the business portion of that basis must be calculated. This would be a good time to go back to CHAPTER 7: UP AND RUNNING and re-read **WHATTA CONCEPT! Capital Expense and Basis**, page 46.

A home purchase includes more than the price of the house. The other charges, often called closing costs, add to the cost – also known as basis – of the house. These include things like attorney fees, inspection costs, title insurance, etc.

Your tax preparer will need to calculate the total basis of your house in order to determine the basis of the business portion of your residence.

Every capital improvement also increases the home's basis. A capital improvement is something new, something beyond a repair, something that becomes part of the structure. A new roof, a new bathroom, adding windows in the attic – these are capital improvements. Repair of a broken attic window or a bathroom faucet is not a capital improvement.

As a tax deduction REPAIRS are more beneficial. The entire cost of a repair is deductible in the year paid. The business-use portion of a roof repair is an immediate deduction whereas the business portion of a new roof must be written off over 39 years.

> ## Reality √ Check
>
> Miles Mingus' new recording hit 100,000 downloads on iTunes. He got a sizable recording contract. He decided to spend the contract money rather than send it to Uncle Sam.
>
> Boy, was he sorely disappointed upon finding out that the $20,000 studio remodeling job wasn't going to get him a big tax write-off.

> ## Reality √ Check
>
> Karen Coolcuts spent her summer patching plaster and sanding floors – part of the overhaul of what was once a bedroom and master bathroom that would soon serve as her new hair styling salon. Just because some of the work was more repair-the-old than install-the-new doesn't make it a REPAIRS expense.
>
> That Karen also installed new wiring and plumbing and gave **new use** to what was once part of a residence makes the entire remodeling job a CAPITAL IMPROVEMENT. The $80,000 cost will have to be depreciated over 39 years.

## TO SUM UP HOME OFFICE EXPENSE

Forget the old husbands' tale. Engage your indie power mindset. Yours is an honest, serious business and it is your obligation to take every deduction you can. Whether you rent, own, or use a home office for your independent venture, take the deduction.

# 13

## CHAPTER 13: HERE TO STAY OR GONE TOMORROW
### Equipment, Inventory And Supplies

*Things* used in your business: This is an area that often stumps an indie. Is it an office supply? Or is it equipment? And what's this thing called COGS? The stapler you bought will last more than a year. Does that make it "equipment?" And your brother said you'd better have a year-end inventory amount before you go see your accountant, but you're not sure what inventory is?

Well, don't fret. All you must know is this: If you use it in your business it's a deductible business expense. The tricky part is how the expense gets written off on your tax return – right away, all in one year; over a period of years, or perhaps when you sell the business. But you won't be making those calls; leave the fretting to your tax professional.

Nevertheless, the better you understand the distinctions the better will be your records and the easier will be your tax return preparation (thus reducing your tax prep fee) and the likelier that you will not miss any deductions. So let's take a look at how to group the *things* you use in your business.

## EQUIPMENT

I start with EQUIPMENT because it may be the easiest to understand.

If you purchase a tangible item (that means something you can touch and very likely, that you, or you and some friends, can actually pick up) and if this tangible item will last longer than a year, it's probably a piece of EQUIPMENT. When is it not EQUIPMENT? A desk, a copier, a massage table, a drafting board, a display case, a computer, a high-powered drill, are all considered EQUIPMENT. If the tangible item lasts longer than a year and costs more than $100 it is EQUIPMENT. By that definition, a stapler is not EQUIPMENT; it's a SUPPLY.

EQUIPMENT is also called a "business asset." It's an asset because it adds value to the worth of your business. If you are a public relations consultant let's say your business is you, on the phone. That's all there is. When you buy a desk on which to lean your elbows you now have some tangible thing of value that is part of your business. The desk is a business asset and adds to the value, the worth, of your business. Using my definition of EQUIPMENT, if you bought the desk at a garage sale for $70 it's not EQUIPMENT it's a SUPPLY.

EQUIPMENT, unlike SUPPLIES, gets deducted over a period of years. This is called ***depreciating the asset***. The number of years for depreciating is called the asset's useful life and is determined by IRS classification on the type of equipment. For instance, a computer gets written off over five years because that's how long the IRS says it will be used in a typical business setting. Yeah right, five years. Do we know any solo who has used the same computer in his business for five years if he could afford to buy a new one? A desk is depreciated over seven years.

Depreciation is complicated, arbitrary, and not a good conversation starter at a cocktail party. Do not try to figure it out unless mastering it is part of your total career plan. Here are the main points you need to know about EQUIPMENT and depreciation:

- If it lasts more than a year and costs more than $100, it's EQUIPMENT and is depreciated.
- Be prepared to give your tax preparer the date of purchase.
- If you use the EQUIPMENT for personal as well as business use you can deduct as a business expense only the portion used for business. You will need to present your preparer with a personal-versus-business use breakdown. (I explain mixed-use in CHAPTER 9, page 87.)
- Even though EQUIPMENT gets depreciated over a specified number of years, there are special allowances that permit greater deductions in the year of purchase. This can be a huge tax savings! These allowances change almost as fast as the weather in Santa Fe and the start and cut-off dates vary. If you plan to purchase EQUIPMENT in any one year, discuss your purchase with your tax pro ***before*** your purchase.

Sometimes a REPAIR to a piece of equipment or business asset is classified not as a REPAIR expense but as EQUIPMENT. If the repair is not ordinary maintenance but is an improvement to the equipment and adds to the value of it or prolongs its useful life then the cost of the repair will have to be depreciated. If you took the $70 desk that you bought at the garage sale and had it re-glued and refinished and set off with a custom cut glass top for a cost of $800 then the entire $870 would be depreciated as the cost of the desk.

## Both Business And Personal Use

You may want to check out, in CHAPTER 9: STAYING IN TOUCH, page 87, the details on how to handle something you use both in your business and personally. Typical mixed-use expenses are telephone, Internet service, car, camera, and computer. If you split between business and personal use, or share with someone else the use of a business service or piece of EQUIPMENT, the purchase cost and/or service fees will have to be allocated. If you get to use the family computer for business only after the kids are asleep and that amounts to three of the computer's nine-hour work day then your business use is only one-third (3/9). If the computer cost $900 then your EQUIPMENT expense will be $300 (1/3 of $900). In situations like this the IRS expects a log of computer use, for instance, a pad next to the computer showing date and time used for business or use your computer's timer to keep a record. This is a very difficult, or let's be frank, just about impossible, procedure to follow. If you cannot have a computer for business use only – which is the easiest solution – then you'll have to make prorating calculations. You can try tracking use for one day a week for a couple of weeks, then use that percent for the entire year. Or maybe just clock in and out when you use the computer for business and take that percent of an 18-hour day. That assumes the entire family sleeps a minimum of six hours. If there are four users then maybe you'll want to simply take one fourth as business use.

And what if you have a *business* computer? There's little doubt that at some time it will be used for a personal reason. Whether it's finding an old schoolmate or researching the price of a refrigerator, or keeping your bookkeeping – both business and personal – on computer, you will need to come up with some arguable – to the IRS that is – percent of business use. If you decide five percent personal use, well then, other than throwing the I Ching or the dice, you need to be able to show how you came up with that figure.

And, while we're on personal and business use, there are many typically personal or household items you might not think of as business equipment. Think again.

---

### Reality √ Check

Rob Rolf washes and dries all the sheets and towels that he uses in his massage business in his home appliances. That means a percent of the cost of his washer and dryer is a business EQUIPMENT expense.

---

> ## Reality √ Check
> Musician Miles Mingus has a superb music system set up for listening and recording. Of course, a business deduction.

> ## Reality √ Check
> Tessie Tripp bought an HD camcorder. She records and views travel events and some of her tours. If she also uses the camcorder to tape family events she'll have to allocate some of the cost of the EQUIPMENT to personal use.

## Converting from Personal to Business Use

Many independent professionals migrate to self-employment from the joys of hobbyland or from work as an employee. Caitlin Caterer came to her profession when her kids entered school and by turning her joy of cooking for friends into a profitable business. Eddie Electronic went from selling himself short while working for someone else to selling his service for himself and keeping all the profit. Both these indies started their sole proprietorships with equipment and supplies that they had purchased for private use. Caitlin had a significant culinary library that she began accumulating before she went into the catering business. Eddie had more electronic testing equipment and software than many who had been in business for years. Both Caitlin and Eddie used these things in their new business venture. And they could write off the costs of their personal-to-business-use equipment and supplies. Here's how:

They need to look at each item as if they were they buying it used from a thrift shop or on the Web. If Eddie, over the years, paid thousands of dollars for his equipment and software but could now sell it all at a flea market for $900, then he treats these items as a $900 purchase of used equipment and supplies for his business. If Caitlin, over the years, paid $2,000 for her book collection but now, because many of the books are out of print, could sell her culinary library online for $2,800, she would get a library deduction for her new business in the amount of $2,000. Why less than it's worth? Because you get as a deduction, either your cost or the fair market value at the time the item was put into business use, whichever is lower.

If you are moving your equipment from the family room to your new office, to help you with the conversion, you might want to check out the easy to use **EQUIPMENT WORKSHEET** in my companion publication, **Five Easy Steps**.

# INVENTORY and COST-OF-GOODS-SOLD

The word "inventory" is often used when what is really meant is "cost of goods sold." COST OF GOODS SOLD or COGS, is just that: Your cost for the items or materials – the goods – that went into the items that you sold? **An inventory is a record or accounting of things**. If you're having a picnic and want to know if there's enough soda or paper plates you might check the pantry for how many plates, and the number of cans and flavors of soda. This list would be an INVENTORY of picnic supplies.

---

### Reality √ Check

Wooly Weaver buys all the wool that goes into his rugs from a local shepherd. He may buy $2,000 worth of wool and although his sales ran around $10,000 he still had about half the wool he'd purchased stored in the bin. Wooly's COGS for that year was $1,000 (½ of $2,000).

---

### Reality √ Check

Anton Antique frequents estate sales where he buys much of what he later sells. If he pays $200 for a vase which he then sells for $450, his COGS is $200.

---

### Reality √ Check

Clarissa Clothier purchases 100 fuzzy bunnies at two dollars each to give away with each pair of children's pajamas she sells. The $200 purchase (100 fuzzy bunnies times $2) becomes part of her INVENTORY. If she gives away 25 bunnies then her COST-OF-GOODS-SOLD is $50 (25 fuzzies times $2).

---

INVENTORY is an accounting of the cost of supplies on hand. In Wooly's case it was zero at the beginning of the year, he then added to his inventory by a purchase of $2,000 worth of wool. And at year-end his inventory balance was $1,000.

Anton keeps an accurate list of all purchases. As he sells each piece he notes it as sold on his "in-house" list. At the end of the year he adds up the cost of all the pieces sold to come up with his yearly COGS.

The only items that become part of INVENTORY are those items that will eventually be sold as a typical function of your business. Sometimes packaging is included.

---

**THE IRS SAYS ABOUT INVENTORY ...**

An inventory is a thoroughly detailed and itemized list of all material goods you have on hand to sell, or what will become part of the merchandise you will sell, with the values indicated.

---

There are several to calculate INVENTORY. It depends on your kind of business, the amount of your gross receipts, whether you are a cash basis or an accrual basis taxpayer (see **WHATTA CONCEPT!** Cash vs. Accrual Recordkeeping in the next chapter), and what type of recordkeeping suits your style. This is an area that you must discuss with your tax professional. If you will have items that go into the making of your product, or you will purchase many items to sell, then you need to get guidance on this from the very beginning.

## SUPPLIES

So, if it's not EQUIPMENT and not part of your COST OF GOODS SOLD, the only things left are SUPPLIES. There are OFFICE SUPPLIES and then there are just plain business SUPPLIES. Don't get hung up on the distinction between these two because they get deducted in the same way on your tax return.

OFFICE SUPPLIES are those items that typical offices use: paper; toner; pens; staplers. Business SUPPLIES are those items specific to your business: sheets to a masseur; tissues to a psychologist; maps to a tour director; seed and fertilizer to a landscaper.

## CHAPTER 14: WRITE-OFF WRAP-UP
## Business Expenses with A Twist

Thus far in **PART II** we have examined a broad range of business expenses. In this chapter we look somewhat more briefly at other expenses not previously covered. There are also guidelines for distinguishing between a few valid and invalid deductions.

On Federal Schedule C: Profit or Loss From Business in Part II: Expenses, the IRS lists a number of expenses that it regards as typical of sole proprietors. The final line in that section is labeled "Other expenses." Among my clients – and my guess is that for you as well – many business expenses fit nowhere else.

Of the expenses I haven't yet presented, I want first to go over those specifically listed on Schedule C. Then we'll look at the ones that end up on the ***Other expenses*** lines of the tax return.

Expenses specifically listed on Schedule C:
- Insurance (does not include medical insurance)
- Interest Or Finance Charges
- Legal & Professional Fees
- Repairs & Maintenance
- Taxes As An Expense

Other expenses:
- Bad Debts
- Business Bank Account Fees & Merchant Fees & Credit Card Fees
- Clothing/Uniforms/Costumes & Their Care & Hair & Make-Up
- Dues & Memberships & Admissions & Fees
- Publications

Taboo expenses – with a rare exception:
- Penalties, Fines, Bribes & Kickbacks
- Contributions

# SCHEDULE C EXPENSES

### Insurance Premiums

You cannot deduct personal insurance, such as life insurance on yourself. Nor can you deduct the premiums for insurance that pays you for lost earnings due to sickness or disability. This is usually called disability insurance. Sometimes a disability policy will include as part of the premium a portion for business overhead expenses such as rent, utilities, etc., that continue during a period of illness or injury. That portion of the premium is a deductible business expense.

All **business** insurance is deductible and includes the following:
- Fire and theft
- Liability
- Malpractice
- Business interruption
- Coverage for a business vehicle
- All insurance for employees

Even if you are a cash basis business you cannot deduct the cost of insurance premiums paid for a future year. Such prepayment can be deducted only in the year to which the premiums apply. When tallying your insurance costs be sure to keep a note on such payments so that you can alert your preparer.

The deduction for health insurance premiums is confusing to many indies. To be clear, I am speaking of insurance premiums for medical, dental and long term care for the self-employed and their families that are paid by the self-employed and not paid through an employer's plan (for instance, via a spouse's job).

Health insurance premiums are not business expenses. Yes, you may deduct 100% of the cost of health insurance (there is a limitation on long term care premiums) paid by you but you may not deduct them as a business expense. Premiums are deducted as an adjustment to income. An *adjustment to income* provides a smaller tax advantage than a direct deduction against business income.

## Interest Or Finance Charges

*Credit Card Interest:* You may deduct as INTEREST expense all finance charges on business loans, or personal loans if used for a business purpose. You will need to show that the loan was used for business and not for a vacation in the Bahamas.

Likewise the business portion of credit card interest is deductible. You must be able to substantiate that the card was used for business for the portion of business interest that you are deducting. Unless you enjoy numbers puzzles this will be a burdensome chore. You'll need to decide whether the amount of work calculating the business expense is worth the small tax benefit. If you are going to make many expensive business purchases on a credit card that you will not pay off each month then using one card for just those purchases may make sense. This goes against my recommendation of using only one credit card, but makes sense if you must buy for business on credit.

*Home Equity Interest:* Home equity or line-of-credit finance charges are deductible as business INTEREST expense, but again, you must be able to show that the loan was used for business purposes.

*Mortgage Interest:* The mortgage finance charge on a business building is of course a business deduction.

Mortgage interest on the business portion of your home office is part of your home office expense. The finance charge for the business-use portion of your auto will be part of your auto expense deduction.

In the old days I had to purchase expensive books to do my tax research. Now I do much of my research online via IRS websites, university websites, tax information services and by direct phone contact with the IRS. The IRS Small Business and Self-employed Center[15] online or via phone at 800.829-4933 can be very helpful. I expect you'll find the people friendly and personable. Various people specialize in varied areas depending on the topic and the complexity or unusual nature of the question. Often the person you ask won't be able to answer your question but will have someone else get an answer back to you. Sometimes the answers aren't a straightforward yes or no. Here's an example:

Until a few years ago *student loan interest* was not a deductible personal expense. Now it is, as an *adjustment to income*. So, my logic works this way. If an EDUCATION expense meets the criteria for a deductible business expense, then any student loan interest acquainted with that specific EDUCATION expense is a deductible business INTEREST expense. I ran my idea by the "tax law specialist" at the IRS Small Business department. This was his conclusion: "I see your logic, but I don't know if it's deductible." I asked him how to find out. His response; "Through an audit." I said that if my client borrowed money from his brother to take a business course and he paid back his brother with interest that the interest was a business INTEREST expense. Right? "Right," he says. So then I'm going to tell my clients and readers that the student loan interest is a deductible business INTEREST expense. He suggested I do that. So I have been taking that deduction for my clients. So far there hasn't been an audit of a return that includes this deduction. Will let you know what happens if there is one.

## Legal And Professional Fees

Legal and professional fees for attorneys and accountants that directly relate to the operation of your business are deductible as business expenses.

Whether the fees come out of a zoning case, a lawsuit with a client, or a dispute with the government about business taxes owed – all are business deductions. Fees in a business-related lawsuit – win, lose or draw – are deductible. Professional fees incurred in negotiating a business contract or in registering a copyright are deductible business expenses. In some instances legal fees become part of the basis of the item to which they relate. For instance, legal fees you pay regarding the purchase of a business building become part of the cost of the building. Here's a reliable test of whether professional fees are deductible: Will the outcome affect the bottom line of your business? If the answer is yes or maybe, you can be pretty sure the legal fees are a business expense or capital cost. With that in mind, what about the fee you paid a lawyer for your will? Clearly, it's not a business deduction but a personal expense. (By the way, it's not a personal tax deduction either.)

Perhaps the most obvious deductions are bookkeeping and tax preparation fees. You cannot deduct the cost of the preparation of your entire tax return. Your preparer will allocate a portion to the business part of your return.

Your tax preparer will scrutinize any legal fees you pay to acquire or set up your business, or to acquire a business asset, to determine how the fees must be treated on your return. Indies often assume that if they paid several thousand dollars to an attorney to help set up a business, the entire amount can be deducted in the first year. No way. Check out CHAPTER 7 to get a grasp of how these fees are deducted as START-UP COSTS.

## Repairs And Maintenance

This one seems like a straightforward deduction. Your computer crashes; you take it to be fixed; the expense is a REPAIR deduction. You purchase a one-year service contract on your new Giclee printer, it's a REPAIR expense. You hire a rug shampoo service to get your office looking spic and span, that's a MAINTENANCE expense.

Any upkeep that keeps your business premises, property, or equipment in a normal efficient operating condition is a deductible REPAIRS & MAINTENANCE expense. However, if such care adds to the value or usefulness of the property or equipment, for instance, if a business item is refurbished, the expense may have to be written off over a number of years. This is a judgment call made by your tax preparer.

## Taxes As An Expense

In PART V you will read about the taxes you must pay as a sole proprietor, here we'll look at the kinds of taxes that are deductible business expenses.

Various kinds of taxes incurred in operating your business are generally deductible. How and when to deduct taxes in your business depends on the type of tax.

Any sales tax you pay on things used in your business is treated the same as the item purchased. For instance, sales tax or gross receipts tax on office supplies is deducted as part of SUPPLIES expense. The same goes for a tax on a computer purchase; it becomes part of the EQUIPMENT expense.

If you collect sales or gross receipts tax on services or products that you sell you have a choice on how to handle that inflow of money. IRS publications tell you not to include it as income and not to deduct it as an expense. But for many indies it is much easier to include it as income and then tally up their checks to the local government to determine their sales tax expense. How you handle this is up to you as long as you are consistent. If you do not claim the sales tax as income be sure that you do not deduct the amount you forward, or pay, to the state or city as an expense.

Here are some other taxes that may be deducted as business expense:
- Excise taxes
- Local occupational taxes
- Personal property tax on property used in your business
- Payroll taxes paid for your employees
- Real estate tax on business-use property

*You cannot deduct federal or state income taxes as business expenses*. However city or state business taxes, such as the New York City Unincorporated Business Tax, is a deductible business expense. If your local government requires a commercial rent tax, that too is deductible.

In **PART V** you will see that you get to deduct one-half of the self-employment (SE) tax that you pay, however, it is not a business expense. It is deducted as an *adjustment to income* and helps lower your taxable income but not your business income.

## OTHER EXPENSES

The preceding expense categories are all specifically named on your Schedule C. Now for some of the items that go on the *Other expenses* lines of your Schedule C.

### Business Bad Debts

This one is confusing. Most sole proprietors think that if they get stiffed by a client or customer they can write off the bill as a business expense. Unfortunately that's not how it works. You can deduct an unpaid fee as an expense only if you've already claimed it as income. And in the cash method for recording income, which most sole proprietors use, an unpaid fee from a client was never recorded as income in the first place – in which case there's no deduction when you give up on the "friendly reminders," call off your collection attorney, and throw in the towel.

---

### WHATTA CONCEPT!
#### Cash vs. Accrual Recordkeeping

As a self-employed in business you get to choose when to report your income and expenses. Don't get too excited it's not as liberal a choice as it sounds. You may opt for a **cash basis** method of bookkeeping. This is one that claims income when it is received and deducts an expense when it is paid.

Or you may choose an **accrual basis**. This bookkeeping method claims income when the client is billed, regardless of when the client pays you. An expense is claimed when you receive the invoice – when you become liable for it – regardless of when you pay it. You must use the same method for both income and expenses. The cash method is simpler and is used by most self-employed people.

---

You may, of course, deduct any expenses incurred for that in-the-red client, such as TELEPHONE and TRAVEL, but you cannot deduct the value of your time and your services as a business expense.

---

### Reality √ Check

Woody Awlwood put a lot of time and materials into a new railing for Shifty Scofflaw's beach house. He billed Shifty $5,000, sent a half-dozen "friendly reminders," and tried a collection attorney, but Shifty hasn't responded and Awlwood knows he'll never get a dime. Since Woody is a cash basis taxpayer he never claimed as income the never-received $5,000. Therefore, he cannot deduct it as a BAD DEBT.

---

### Reality √ Check

Frank Boyd White runs his architectural business using the accrual method. He billed Diners Delight $7,500 for preliminary design drawings two years ago. That's also when he claimed the $7,500 as income. Construction on the highway fronting the diner caused so much traffic congestion that business for the entire strip mall plummeted. Diners Delight went out of business. Mr. White can write off the $7,500 as a business BAD DEBT.

---

## Business Bank Account Fees And Credit Card Fees

Yes, they are deductible business expenses if – but only if – they are for your business. If you have only one checking account for both business and personal you will have to prorate the fees. A bounced check fee charged for a client's bad check is, of course, a business expense.

The same holds for a safe deposit box fee. If the box contains only business papers and documents and password lists then deduct the whole thing. If your Mom's turquoise necklace is stashed in there too, prorate you must.

Be careful about credit card "fees." Often a credit card company will call a finance charge a "fee." It's trying to trick you into thinking that you're paying less interest that you actually are. Interest charges belong in the INTEREST expense category, not in OTHER.

## Work Clothes & Uniforms and Their Care; Hair and Make-up

Uniforms are deductible. But what about the only three-piece suit that you own, which you wear only to meetings with important clients? No, it is not a business WORK CLOTHES deduction. Although you may feel like you're in uniform, the IRS considers it street clothing. Buying a whole new wardrobe to replace your jeans and tee-shirts so that you can look the part of a prosperous business owner won't get you a deduction either. Streetwear-type business clothing must have your business name on it – and not held on by a safety pin or Velcro – in order to be deductible.

Clothing not considered typical streetwear such as a tuxedo or an evening dress purchased for a presentation are business WORK CLOTHES expenses, as long as you don't wear them to your weekly block parties with friends and neighbors.

If you are a performer the same rules apply. If you can wear the clothing as ordinary streetwear it is not a business expense. So toe shoes are deductible. But tights? You see them every day on the street. The amount of income you make as a performer and what kind of backup you have proving your professionalism will influence which and how much performance-wear you can deduct. Do you have posters showing you arabesquing in pink tights? Is there a photo of you in your oversize business suit and orange wig doing clown tricks for the school assembly? This is something you will need to discuss with your tax preparer.

Required PROTECTIVE CLOTHING – such as hard hats, safety shoes, work gloves, and rubber boots – is deductible.

If any clothing does fall into the narrow groove of special business attire then the care and upkeep of that clothing is also a business expense.

There is an exception. You may deduct the cost of DRY CLEANING AND LAUNDRY of all your clothes while on a business trip. You may deduct the first cleaning bill after your return for clothing used while traveling. But don't get too creative and save all your winter's dirty clothes for cleaning the day after you return from a three-day business trip.

Hair styling and HAIR CARE costs and MAKE-UP purchased solely for use on specific business occasions – not for everyday business wear – are deductible business expenses. So, a brunette who had her hair dyed black so that she could play Lady Macbeth would get a deduction but 55-year-old Raina Realtor, who gets a weekly facial because she believes it keeps her looking younger and so gives her more confidence, cannot deduct the weekly expense.

## Dues, Memberships And Admissions Fees

Before reading here about which DUES are deductible as a business expense be sure to read about DUES in the MEALS & ENTERTAINMENT and the LOBBYING sections of CHAPTER 8.

If it's a social club, country club, or athletic club, forget about it – you cannot deduct the cost of membership even if you belong only to further your business.

The IRS states flatly: "no deduction (is) allowed for business clubs operated to provide meals under circumstances generally considered to be conducive to business discussions." If you take a business associate to lunch at the club you can deduct the cost of the meal – but not the club dues.

So what DUES & MEMBERSHIPS can you deduct? Well, first, the group must not be organized for fun or entertainment purposes. And, of course it must be related to and useful to your profession. So an artist could deduct membership in a museum, a non-fiction writer could deduct dues to the historical society. In general the following kinds of organizations (with a typical example) are looked upon favorably by the IRS:

- Trade boards & associations: Greater Washington Board of Trade
- Business leagues: United Agribusiness League
- Chambers of commerce: San Diego Regional Chamber of Commerce
- Civic or public service organizations: Rotary Club of Portsmouth, NH
- Professional organizations: New York Bar Association
- Real estate boards: Honolulu Board of Realtors
- Professional unions and guilds: Authors Guild

## Publications

Depending upon your business, some or all reading material may or may not be considered a business expense.

A writer; well, he can pretty much write off everything he reads – books, online news subscriptions, magazines. If he's not reading it for content then he's reading it for style.

An indie who is a public relations consultant must keep abreast of politics, social and arts information and trends as well as technological advances that affect her business. Without a well-grounded awareness and knowledge of the world, how could she run a successful business? Developing a PR campaign for a teen product, for example, would require her to keep up with the music, fashion, and other interests of teen life.

A tour director must also be conversant in many fields. Her clientele are young, old, business executives or retired, couples and singles. She will be planning their trips and conversing with them on history, geography, art, social trends. She must have a wide knowledge base. I'd be hard pressed to say what reading material she could *not* deduct.

On the other hand, the only reading material that the security alarm system installer can legitimately write off are his professional journals, and maybe a local online crime news service since his knowledge of break-ins or theft may help him promote his business.

## TABOO EXPENSES

### Penalties & Fines and Bribes & Kickbacks

Most indies think that if they have to pay a parking fine because their client meeting ran late, the cost should be deductible. And that they should be able to deduct a penalty paid to the local tax authority because they misread the confusing sales tax form they had to fill out. I agree – but the IRS doesn't.

The IRS says you cannot deduct penalties or fines you pay to any government agency or instrumentality for any kind of violation. These include:

- Civil actions
- Criminal actions
- Housing code violations
- Late payments for taxes
- Traffic violations
- Trucker violations of state maximum highway weight laws and air quality laws

Anything you pay trying to beat a fine or penalty is a deductible business expense if the offense relates to business. You can deduct legal fees and related expenses to defend yourself. These costs would be a LEGAL & PROFESSIONAL FEES expense.

And there's an exception to the non-deductibility of penalties: The **nonconformance penalty**. You can deduct a nonconformance penalty assessed by the Environmental Protection Agency for failing to meet certain emission standards. That means if you couldn't move the repairman fast enough to get the emissions filter installed on your chimney and you are fined, you can deduct the cost of the fine on your tax return. I want to let you know that it's one of many IRS regs with which I disagree. Many of the big guys would rather pay the fine than fix the chimney! Hey, it's deductible.

When I visited Mexico a while back I met an American running an American business there. He told us many interesting stories of business dealings in Mexico, including how his company dealt with the notoriously corrupt Mexican police. He said that he always made sure that his truck drivers had five hundred dollars in cash hidden in the truck ready to pay off La Policia when his trucks were stopped on trumped-up charges. The payoffs were actually in his company budget. I never did get an answer to my question: "under what budget category?"

Bribes and kickbacks are not deductible expenses. (However, if you're on the receiving end, they are taxable income.) There are a few exceptions and if yours is a profession that engages in such practices then you need to consult with your tax preparer. Find out whether the illegal payment you are making violates a law that is "not generally enforced." That's in quotes because the IRS says that if the law is not generally enforced by a state government, then you get to deduct the payoff. Hmmm ...

## Charitable Contributions

A sole proprietor cannot deduct charitable contributions as a business expense.

If country doctor Emma MD pays for an ad in the Girls, Inc. newsletter announcing the new hours of her family clinic, even though the organization is a charitable organization, Emma may deduct the cost of the ad as an ADVERTISING expense. However, were Emma to write out a check to the organization as a charitable contribution in hope of promoting more women in medicine, she could not deduct the contribution as a business expense. She could deduct it only as a personal charitable donation on her Federal Schedule A: Itemized Deductions. Emma's medical practice is an LLC run as a sole proprietorship and so it is a pass-through entity, therefore, only she personally, not her business, may deduct any business-related charitable contributions.

## CHAPTER 15: DEDUCTIBLE BUSINESS EXPENSES
## A List

In the following list of deductible business expenses, you will find more than one hundred typical and not-so-typical business deductions. Some have been addressed previously and some have not. All expenses are listed so as to help you readily determine into which IRS business expense category they would likely fit.

IRS categories are of little concern at this point. The main thing is to have a grasp of legitimate business deductions. Keep in mind what I said in CHAPTER 6: INDIE POWER MINDSET, "anything you do that relates to your work, that stimulates or enhances your business, nurtures your professional creativity, improves your skills, wins you recognition, or increases your chances of making a sale may be a business expense and therefore deductible." If you maintain your indie power mindset you needn't worry about missing any potential business deduction.

If you *know* that an expense is deductible, don't concern yourself with which expense category it fits into. Simply stick it into the closest match you can find or give the expense its own category and deduct it. The IRS will not disallow the deduction for being in the wrong category as long as it is a legitimate expense.

Below is a list of typical and not-so-typical business expenses.

---

### EXAMPLES OF 100+ BUSINESS EXPENSES

---

**1. Advertising / Promotion**
- Business Cards
- Christmas / Holiday Cards
- Google Ads
- Mailing Lists
- Photo Production

- Posters
- Professional Registries
- Resumes
- Webinars - that promote you or your business
- Website Development & Hosting

2. **Auto / Truck / Motorcycle**: On the **AUTO** worksheet

3. **Commissions / Fees**
   - Agent Fees
   - Franchise Fees

4. **Subcontractor Fees**
   - Assistant
   - Business Coach
   - Models
   - Supervision for Psychologists
   - Voice Coach

5. **Equipment:** Costs more than $100 and lasts more than one year
   - Office Furniture / Lamps
   - Computer / Printer / Scanner / All Technical Hardware
   - Washer / Dryer: e.g. massage therapist business % for business linens
   - Alarm System
   - Camera & Accessories
   - File Cabinets
   - Music System
   - Rugs
   - SmartPhone
   - Stand Alone Shelves
   - TV & Video
   - iPad

6. **Business Insurance**
   - Business Interruption - for loss of profit due to fire, etc.
   - Credit Coverage - for unpaid debts
   - Disability for non-spousal employees only
   - Fire / Theft / Flood

- Liability & Malpractice
- Merchandise & Inventory
- Workers' Compensation for Employees

### 7. Business Loan Interest
- Mortgage on Business Property
- Business Loan
- Business Portion of Credit Card Finance Charges

### 8. Legal & Professional Services: for business only, e.g. not will preparation
- Accountant Fees
- Attorney Fees
- Bookkeeper Fees
- Lobbying Expenses with Restrictions
- Pension Administrator Fees for Employees

### 9. Office Supplies & Expense: General supplies used in your office or workplace; note, fine art is not an office décor expense
- Office Materials: e.g. paper, toner, light bulbs
- Cleaning Supplies & Paper Products: e.g. tissues; towels
- Coffee / Bottled Water / Candy for The Office
- Fire Extinguisher
- Flowers / Plants for The Office
- Plant Hangers
- Software

### 10. Postage
- US Mail / Fed Ex / UPS
- Freight / Shipping
- Messenger Service
- Post Office Box: Business % if also used for personal

### 11. Equipment Rental / Lease
- Chairs
- Tables
- Workshop Tools

### 12. Rent On Business Property
- Office
- Studio
- Rehearsal Space
- Warehouse

### 13. Repairs / Maintenance
- Of Equipment: e.g. piano tuning; service contract
- Of The Office: e.g. cleaning service; repair of a window
- Laundering of Linens Used in Your Practice
- Landscaping / Lawncare for Business Property

### 14. Supplies: Incidental supplies used in your specific business, not office supplies and not supplies used in the production of your product
- Animal Treats for A Dog Sitter
- Linens for A Massage Therapist
- Music Scores for A Music Teacher
- Props & Scripts for A Performing Artist

### 15. Business Taxes
- Employer's Share Of Payroll Taxes
- Federal Highway Use Tax
- Franchise Tax
- Gross Receipts / Sales Tax
- NY Commuter Tax
- NY Unincorporated Business Tax
- Personal Property Tax on Business Assets
- Real Estate Tax on Business Property

### 16. Licenses / Fees
- Yearly Business License
- Franchise Fees
- Regulatory Fees to State & Local Governments
- Zoning Permit

### 17. Travel: On the **TRAVEL** worksheet

## 18. Meals / Entertainment
- With Business Associates: e.g. clients, potential clients, colleagues, employees
- At Your Office
- At A Sporting Or Entertainment Event
- Parties for Business Associates
- For The General Public: e.g. for a grand opening or gallery show

## 19. Telephone & Other Communication Utilities
- Monthly Service + Accessories for Business Line
- Business % of Personal Line exclude base line charge
- Cell or SmartPhone Service
- Answering Service
- Internet Service Provider

## 20. Office Or Studio Utilities: Not home office
- Electricity / Heat / Water / Trash Pick-up
- Exterminator Service
- Security Company Monthly Fee

## 21. Wages To Employees

## 22. Bank Services Charges: Allocate if both business and personal use
- Business Bank Account Fees
- Check Printing Fees
- Client Returned Check Fee
- Safe Deposit Box

## 23. Copyright Fees / Royalties / Patents

## 24. Costumes / Cleaning / Make-up
- Clothing with Business Name Permanently Attached or Printed
- Tuxedo / Evening Dress
- Hair Done for Award Presentation
- Make-up for A Performer
- Uniforms

**25. Dues / Entrance Fees**
- Civic & Public Service Organizations: e.g. chambers of commerce
- Competition Fees
- Professional Societies: e.g. bar or medical associations; real estate boards

**26. Business Gifts**: Maximum, $25 per person, per year
- To Clients
- To Potential Clients
- To Business Associates
- Thank You to Mom for Fixing Your Computer
- Tips: e.g. for travel assistants; backstage help

**27. Studio / Office-In-The-Home**: On the **HOME OFFICE** worksheet

**28. Photocopies / Printing**

**29. Publications / Anything you read**
- Books
- Digital Subscriptions
- Kindle, Nook Downloads
- Online Research Services
- Newspapers & Magazines ... if they're still around in hardcopy

**30. Recording Costs**
- Master
- Packaging
- Production
- Recording Studio
- Studio Musicians
- Studio Techs

**31. Study / Education / Seminars / Research**
- Concerts
- Conventions
- ISP
- Lessons / Courses
- Library Fee
- Museums / Galleries

- Performances
- Tuition & Fees
- Video / Film / DVDs: attend / purchase / rental a la Netflix
- Webinars
- Workshops

## 32. Transportation

- Bus
- Subway / Train
- Taxi

## 33. Supplies Used in The Production of Your Product

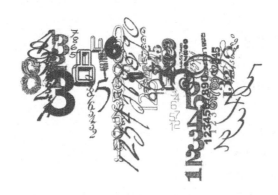

## PART III: INCOME

I introduced the concept of income in CHAPTER 1. If you haven't already read that chapter you need to do so before continuing.

As I explained in CHAPTER 1: **Earned income is payment for services performed**. It is money or goods that you receive in the form of salary, wages, professional fees, commissions, royalties, stipends, tips, etc. for work that you do.

Earned income is not money or things you receive for reasons other than work. For instance, earned income is not a gift from Grandma, nor unemployment compensation, nor dividend income, nor insurance proceeds.

There are only two types of earned income:

- W-2 earnings
  and
- Self-employed income

PART III explains the latter: Income earned by a self-employed.

## CHAPTER 16: CAMELS OR CASH

### What is self-employed income?

Self-employed income is compensation for a service you have performed or a product you have provided. Does the source of the income matter? No; it could be paid by your sister or the Government of Egypt. Does the form of payment matter? No; it could be cash, or check, or you could be paid in camels.

---

### THE IRS SAYS ABOUT SELF-EMPLOYED INCOME ...

If there is a connection between any payment you receive and your self-employed trade or business, the payment is self-employed income. A connection exists if it is clear that the payment would not have been made but for your conduct of the trade or business.

---

Let's look at a few indies and their sources of self-employed income.

CARPENTER: Woody Awlwood
- Building a porch
- Selling a desk he made
- Designing a layout for kitchen cabinets

WRITER: Nadine Novella
- Book advance
- Royalties (These royalties differ from the kind of royalties received from a copper mine in one's investment portfolio.)
- Kill fee for a magazine piece
- Speaking honorarium
- Gold bookmark received as a writing contest prize. (Its fair market value is determined and reported as income.)

REAL ESTATE BROKER: Raina Realtor
- Commission on a sale
- Referral fee from a fellow broker
- Fee for a real estate appraisal in a divorce case

SOFTWARE DEVELOPER / INFORMATION ARCHITECT: Syd System
- Hourly fee for database program upgrade
- Payment received for cost plus mark-up for hardware parts
- Two massages in exchange for setting up massage therapist's computer. (The fee generally charged by the masseur is the amount reported as income by the information architect.)
- Corporate payment for analysis of current system.
- "What to Look for in Buying a Computer" lecture fee at local men's club

Each of these transactions results in income for a self-employed person - even the bartering that took place between Syd and the massage therapist. I'll explain bartering in the next chapter. Don't be fooled into thinking that because the payment you receive is out of the normal course of your business or is not in good ol' American currency that it is non-income. However unorthodox, it is still self-employed income. Remember: The IRS says, "If there is a connection between your self-employed trade or business and the payment, then the payment is self-employed income."

## UNDERSTANDING INCOME LINGO

There are many terms used in connection with self-employed income. It is your responsibility to claim all your income and it is the responsibility of your tax pro to put the right income on the correct line of your tax return. Recall the example of Rick Reporter from CHAPTER 1. The two income terms you must know are **gross** and **net**. Rick received $1,000 self-employed income for a blog piece he wrote. That was his **gross self-employed income**. He had a $20 expense, which left him with $980 in **net self-employed income**. The $1,000 is also called his **gross receipts** or **gross sales** and the $980 can also be called his **profit,** or **net profit** or **net income** or his bottom line.

Rick's income situation was simple. Most self-employed income scenarios are more complex than Rick's and may call for additional income terminology. But don't worry – if you understand Rick's self-employed situation you understand the basics: **Gross self-employed income minus expenses leaves you with a net self-employed income.**

### Who's more savvy?

While we're on the subject of gross versus net income let's take a look at two entrepreneurs, Heavenly Happenin and her sister Eartha Happenin. Each is a special events planner. Last year each had a net income of $40,000. If you looked only at the bottom line you'd think they were equally savvy business people.

However, Heavenly's gross self-employed income was $60,000. Her staff costs and expenses totaled $20,000. A little arithmetic and you see that her costs were 33% of her gross (20,000 / 60,000). Her income formula looks like this: $60,000 - $20,000 = $40,000.

On the other hand, Eartha's gross self-employed income was $100,000. Her expenses were $60,000, that's 60% of her gross - almost ***double the rate*** of her sister. She probably had to work a lot harder and longer to bring in $100,000 than her sister did to bring in $60,000 and yet they both ended up with the same $40,000 net profit. Her income formula looks like this: $100,000 - $60,000 = $40,000.

Now which one do you think is the more savvy business person? Don't be fooled by the numbers. A very large gross income doesn't signify anything until it's compared to the bottom line, the net income.

## PAYING TAX ON INCOME

*On his net profit a self-employed pays self-employment (SE) tax* – and that's different than income tax.

On the tax return of a self-employed the amount of **net profit** is added to other kinds of income – interest, dividends, capital gains, alimony – to come up with total income. After various adjustments and personal deductions the result is **taxable income**. *Income tax is calculated on taxable income.*

A self-employed may have a net profit but have no taxable income. In that case he would pay self-employment (SE) tax but no income tax.

**Net profit** and **net income** are often interchangeable terms. Neither term means the same as **taxable income**.

---

### Reality √ Check

It must be overwork!'" That was the only explanation Woody Awlwood could come up with for the nonsensical thing his tax preparer told him. "Woody, good news, " said his preparer. 'With all your deductions your income tax is zero. You need to send the feds only another $1,239."

"No income tax but I have to pay more than a thousand to the feds! That's absurd. I already paid them $3,000. How could this be?" shouted Woody.

---

Here's how: Woody's net profit for the year was $30,000. He had no other income but he had a loss in the stock market, high mortgage interest, property taxes, and he donated used clothing to a local charity. He also supported his two children. This is how he got to zero taxable income.

| | |
|---|---|
| Net profit from business | $ 30,000. |
| Deduction for 1/2 SE tax | ( 2,119. ) |
| Property tax | ( 3,000. ) |
| Mortgage interest | ( 12,000. ) |
| Contributions to Goodwill | ( 1,500. ) |
| 3 exemptions: Woody + 2 kids | ( 11,400. ) |
| Taxable income | -0-. |

In the example above Woody's SE tax was just under 15% of his $30,000 net business profit and his income tax was zero. I'll explain more about taxes in PART V.

## YOU'RE THE BOSS. PAY YOURSELF WHATEVER YOU WANT

Many self-employed people have a misguided idea about their own business profits. They think that the weekly, monthly, or occasional checks they write to themselves – often called draw - is their income or their profit. They are wrong.

The checks a self-employed makes out to himself have no bearing whatsoever on his income, expenses, profit, or taxes. Whether you write yourself a $100 or $1,000 check every week you are doing nothing other than altering cash flow by moving money from one place to another. It's called draw because you are drawing money away from someplace.

Let's examine this concept by the example of Raina Realtor.

---

**Reality √ Check**

Raina thought she managed her business finances well last year. She brought in $130,000 and after subtracting $20,000 in expenses and the $60,000 she paid herself in $5,000 monthly checks she had $50,000 left in the bank. At the end of the year she "knew" she'd have to pay taxes on the $60,000 "income" she'd paid herself.

***Raina thought her income was $60,000:***

| | |
|---|---|
| Gross income | $ 130,000 |
| Less expenses | ( 20,000 ) |
| Raina paid herself | ( 60,000 ) |
| Money left in the bank | ( 50,000 ) |

---

---

*Raina's income is $110,000:*

| | |
|---|---|
| Gross income | $ 130,000. |
| Less expenses | ( 20,000 ) |
| Net profit | $ 110,000 |

You can see that Raina's profit on which she had to pay tax was much higher than the amount she had "paid" herself.

---

## TO SUM UP INCOME

- If it's related to your self-employed venture then it's self-employed income no matter how you're paid.

- Don't let the fine distinctions in the various terms for income confuse you. Keep in mind Rick Reporter and his same but very different W-2 income and self-employed income. Also, know the difference between **gross self-employed income** – everything you bring in – versus **net self-employed income** – what you're left with after subtracting business expenses.

- Self-employment tax and income tax are paid on two different income amounts.

# 17

## CHAPTER 17: WHAT DADDY'S ACCOUNTANT FORGOT TO TELL YOU ABOUT INCOME
### More When, Where And How of Self-employed Income

Sammy Segar CPA may be a whiz at retirement planning and may know just when your daddy should cash in his stock options, but Sammy lacks the know-how to advise an independent professional, whose business life – in every respect – is more complicated than that of the guy who receives a company paycheck. Here are some aspects of self-employed income that are often overlooked.

## SITUATIONS TOO TRICKY FOR SAMMY

### Take It – Don't Fake It: Constructive Receipt

If you can get at the money you are considered to have received it. As a result, as soon as money or property is available to you, or is credited to your account, or is in the hands of your agent, it becomes income to you. If you receive a check in November, even if you don't deposit it until January, it was income to you in the year that you received it.

If Nadine Novella's literary agent receives her royalty check, that's income to Nadine on that day even if her agent doesn't forward it to her for a month. This approach to when payment becomes income is called **constructive receipt**.

### Income after The Doors Close

P. R. Bernays closes up his solo shop as a public relations consultant to work as an employee in the PR department of Masdrogas Pharmaceuticals Inc. Months later he receives a late payment check from a client for whom he had developed a sales campaign back when he was an indie. Is it self-employed income? It sure is.

### Trading Products And Services

If your work is paid for with a product or a service instead of with money, that's called **bartering.** And, guess what! It's income. The fair market value of the item or service you receive is part of your gross income just the same as had you been paid in dollars.

The massage therapist in CHAPTER 16, page 168 whose computer was set up by Syd System in exchange for two massages, claimed $200 ($100 per massage) as part of his gross self-employed body-work income, and subtracted $200 in computer services, for a net income of zero. If there is no net income there is no SE tax nor income tax liability. You still need to show the transaction, however, because you must claim all income regardless of payment type. Also, some states require that sales tax, gross receipts tax or a general excise tax be paid on gross income; New Mexico for example would have required approximately $14 in gross receipts tax on the $200 bartering income. Hawaii would have required about $9.

Syd, on the other hand, had $200 of income for the work he did, but because the massages were not ordinary or necessary business expenses, he could not deduct them. He must include the barter income from the transaction.

A lot of bartering goes on that the IRS isn't aware of – but now you know the rule.

---

### WHATTA CONCEPT!
#### Income That Is Not Self-employed Income
As you read the following pages about what is and what is not self-employed income, keep in mind that, if it is not self-employed income then there is no SE tax liability. You learned in CHAPTER 4 that SE tax is the Social Security and Medicare tax of a self-employed. Although payment received may not be self-employment income it may still be taxable income subject to income tax.

---

## Grants, Awards And Prizes
When you receive money under a research grant or an award and you perform a service or produce a product for the use of the grantor, then the money you receive is self-employed income.

However, if you get a grant to go on retreat, think alone in a cabin, or converse with other thinkers, but do not have to present your thoughts to the grantor for his use, the grant money (although taxable) is not self-employed income.

## Reimbursement for Expenses

A client reimbursement for expenses is not income. There are two different bookkeeping methods for handling client reimbursements and they are explained in CHAPTER 21.

## Worldwide Income

No matter where your self-employed income comes from it is part of your gross self-employed income. If Miles Mingus sells 100 CDs while on his European tour, the sales are included in his US income. Same thing with the jewelry Trixy Trinkets sells internationally on the Web.

Special rules apply if you live outside the United States. If you spend all but the holidays virtually communicating with your clients from a beach in southern France, you'd better get advice from a tax professional who has experience with freelancers living out of the country.

## Loans

Short on cash? It's OK to borrow from yourself or someone else. It's not income. As a self-employed, if you borrow against an asset that you own the loan proceeds are not income.

---

### Reality √ Check

Anton Antique had a vast collection of first editions which his brother admired and envied. Big Brother loaned Anton $5,000 using the books as collateral. The $5,000 was not taxable to Anton. He used it to buy a computer which was a deductible business EQUIPMENT expense. The loan interest Anton paid his brother was a deductible business expense, too. (And taxable to Big Brother.)

The same treatment would apply had Anton borrowed the money from a bank or taken a cash advance on his credit card.

---

## Interest Income

If your business checking account, or other bank or investment account, earns interest or dividends that income is not self-employed income. It is personal investment income. But if you charge interest to clients on balances owed to you - often called a late fee or finance charge - then that interest is self-employed income.

## Sale of Business Property

A gain or loss from the sale of equipment, property or other assets used in your business but not held primarily for sale to customers is not self-employed income.

## Rental Income

Rental income that you receive from tenants, although taxable income, is not self-employed income unless your profession or business is that of a real estate dealer, or you provide services such as cleaning, linens, meals, etc. for your tenants.

You are a real estate dealer if your business is buying and selling real estate for yourself with the purpose of making a profit. You are not a dealer if you buy and hold real estate for investment or speculation.

---

### Reality √ Check

Mike Mobile had a sizeable piece of land near the lake. He let visitors park their campers there for a fee. He provided no services. The fees he received were rental income not self-employed income and so were not subject to SE tax. Within a few years the spot had become so popular that he added some amenities and raised the rent. He provided things like a laundry facility, wireless connection, fresh water, a coffee bar in the main building. Now he's receiving income as a self-employed.

---

### Reality √ Check

Billy Bridesnapper rents out a part of his photo studio space to Victor Visual. Billy's rent is $1,000 per month. Victor pays him $300 per month.. The easier way for Billy to treat the money from Victor is to include the $300 per month as income and then deduct the entire $1,000 per month that he pays for rent. (Careful of state gross receipts tax regulations with this method, though.)

The alternative method is to not include the $300 rental income in his gross income and deduct only $700 per month as his rent. In either case Billy must keep an comprehensible record of the transactions.
If Billy does not rent his studio but instead owns the building from which he runs his wedding photography business, then the rental income from Victor is taxable rental income and does not get included with his self-employed income.

---

## Hobbies

Any money you make on your hobby is not self-employed income. To refresh your thinking on what is a hobby see CHAPTER 3: FOR FUN OR PROFIT.

---

### Reality √ Check

Shane Scriptwrite earns his self-employed income as a scriptwriter, and his hobby is collecting comic books. His sales of comic books are not part of his self-employed income.

---

### A One-Shot Deal Does Not A Business Make

---

### Reality √ Check

Dennis Dubya-two retired at 65 from his job at Toys 'n' Things. He spent his summers playing golf and winters skiing.

His golf skills were so impressive that he was asked to give lessons to teens at the local youth club. Dennis was paid to give lessons to the young people over the course of the summer. The youth club sent him a Form 1099-MISC at the end of the year .

This was not self-employed income for Dennis because he was not in business as a golf instructor - that is, it was not a continuous or regular activity.

---

The IRS made a ruling on a case like this in 1992 regarding a non-business activity for a man named Batok. If you should have a similar situation be sure your tax pro is familiar with this case. She'll need to write "As per the Batok Case, TC Memo, 1992-727" next to the "Other Income" line in the personal section of your tax return. In this way you may avoid correspondence from the IRS as to why you haven't paid SE tax on the income. If you are wondering how this might apply to you, since you are a self-employed in business, here's a typical example:

> ## Reality √ Check
>
> Charlotte Salesrep runs a profitable solo enterprise representing several children's toymakers. Every once in a while she is paid to babysit for the neighbor's kids. Her babysitting earnings are not self-employed income.
>
> Charlotte's tax professional should know that her babysitting earnings are not subject to self-employment tax. Charlotte can help her tax pro make that distinction by keeping a complete record of all money received.

The tax situations illustrated in this chapter emphasize an indie's need to consult with a tax professional knowledgeable and experienced in advising independents.

## CHAPTER 18: GETTING PAID IN THE PARKING LOT
## Cheating by Hiding Income

Under the table. In the parking lot. Off the books.

Of course it's income; and yes you must report it on your tax return.

---

**Reality √ Check**

Miles Mingus plays a regular gig at Jazzy Jack's Pub. Jazzy Jack has a cash business; all his barflies pay for their drinks with hard currency – no plastic or checks, thank you.

And Jack pays Miles the same way – in cash, which he takes from an envelope in his desk in the back office.

Nobody's claiming a lot of the income and nobody's paying a lot of the taxes – until Jack gets audited. The IRS says that a review of Jack's sizeable purchases for liquor just don't match up with the tiny income he reports from bar sales. Whoops! Now the IRS checks out the waiters, the staff, and the tax returns of the musicians.

---

The IRS is not a morality agency, it is a monetary agency.

It doesn't care what you do for a living as long as you pay taxes on the income you make doing it. If you make your living as a hit man or a lady of the night or a drug dealer, be sure to pay the IRS its fair share. Remember the Chicago mobster, Al Capone? He wasn't sent to prison for murder, bootlegging or racketeering; he was convicted of tax evasion for not reporting the money he earned in his self-employed endeavors.

When the IRS calls for an audit its only purpose is to collect more tax money with some interest and penalty to boot. Criminal activity is not suspected. But if you are caught in outright cheating – particularly in deliberately failing to report a significant amount of income – the IRS will not hesitate to prosecute you.

## Getting Paid "Off the Books"

I've always understood "off the books" to mean that the worker doesn't claim the income and the person paying doesn't claim the expense of the worker, nor pay benefits, keep records nor send W-2s or 1099s to the government.

An attendee at one of my seminars told me that he thought it meant he was "not an employee on the employer's books." That is, he was an independent contractor – a self-employed. To me it was obvious from the nature of the job that he was an employee. Apparently the employer was trying to bamboozle the worker.

There is no legitimate "off the books" category of employment. If someone wants to pay you that way find out what he really means and don't agree to anything crooked. It's not worth it!

## Getting Paid in Cash

Clients and customers may ask you – or request – that if they pay you in cash could you lower the price? Their reason: "Oh, you know, cash means less paperwork." Yeah, right. Cash means it's off the books. They're offering you a chance to hide income. If you did it, you would be committing a crime. If you feel you really want to get or keep this client but feel you can only do so by lowering your price then tell them, "Cash is too troublesome for my recordkeeping, I much prefer a check. But I can give you a discount off my regular fee." Then give him a "new customer" discount or your "February" discount or a "friend" discount. If the client insists on paying cash then still give him a receipt.

On any receipt or invoice, always show the total fee and any discount you give.

Hiding income does not give a positive, professional image of your business. It raises questions, such as:

- Are you a legitimate business?
- Do you want your service or your product to be treated seriously?
- Do you want to be looked upon with respect in your business community?
- Do you want to get the best payment possible for your service or product?

We've all run across the trail of the underground economy, with its little hole-in-the-wall operations that seem to be running on cash and are probably not reporting their income. For the most part they are secretive and secluded little businesses that won't go anywhere and will never amount to anything. The people who use their services know that they can treat them and dismiss them in any way they wish. Illegal businesses are at a great disadvantage; they have no recourse because they can't come out of hiding. I've helped businesses go legit, they've come out of the closet and they've never regretted it. The owners sleep better, too.

You need to know that there is no limit on how long the IRS can come after you if you have intentionally failed to report income. If you're claiming a HYUNDAI income you better not be leading a LEXUS life. The IRS might make you take the "economic reality" test: Can you do the things you're doing on the income you reported?

Clearly, simply, bluntly: ***Don't hide income.***

If you get caught it's fraud. And if you're caught you can be sure the IRS (and the state as well) will scrutinize much of your other financial dealings.

If you are ever audited, and the IRS refuses to accept some of your deductions, you will have to pay the additional tax on the lost deductions as well as interest on that additional tax amount. You also may have to pay a late payment penalty of up to 25% of the tax owed. You'll be out some money, but you've simply had a legitimate disagreement with the IRS about a deduction. You will not be hit with criminal charges or fraud penalties for hiding income. A fraud penalty can be as high as 75% of the tax owed. That is in addition to the tax owed plus interest.

There are ways to cut your taxes that are not criminal. One way to get your taxes as low as possible is to consult a tax pro with experience in guiding the self-employed. Make sure you talk with her as soon as you consider going into business for yourself. There are ways to time income and treat deductions that can work most advantageously for you if discussed early and planned ahead of the transaction.

## TO SUM UP CHEATING

Knowledge, not cheating, is the key to paying the lowest possible tax.

Start by understanding the basic tax and financial concepts regarding your self-employed venture – be it about income, expenses, taxes or recordkeeping.

**PART IV** will continue to guide you in your quest for that know-how.

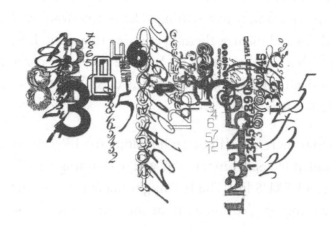

# PART IV : RECORDKEEPING BASICS

"Keep good records."

That's what you read in all the self-employed how-to books, that's what you hear from financial advisors, insurance agents and your father. As if everybody were born with recordkeeping skills but just needed an occasional prodding to stay up-to-date. Well, as you have probably learned, it's a skill that doesn't come with the first slap on the bottom the moment you're born. It is also a skill that, like cooking, can be done a myriad of ways, either in-house or send-out, using different flavors and different styles to please a lot of different palates but all satisfying a universal need: Everybody's got to eat.

It is important to remember that recordkeeping systems are as unique and different as the people using them. There is no "ideal system" that will work for everyone, but, as we all know: Everybody's got to keep records.

Your ideal recordkeeping method depends on *you*. It must suit your needs, your style and your time. Some indies clobber, others nuance, until they build a system that works for them. However, before you can build you need a foundation on which to build. Just as **The Confident Indie** provides the foundation for your understanding of income, expense, and tax basics of self-employment, so too does it provide the basics of keeping track of income and expenses.

Here you will build your foundation. Then, should you choose, you will be ready to develop your own recordkeeping method with the help of **Five Easy Steps**, the companion publication to this book. **Five Easy Steps** is a guide of step-by-step instructions on how to keep audit-proof tax records using my worksheets and my **Most Simple System**.

## CHAPTER 19: RECORDS AS RESOURCE
### Why Keep Records

Let's first look at a few reasons other than taxes and Uncle Sam why good records benefit *you*. I will also answer that pressing question in space-strapped households: How long should I keep which tax records?

As a self-employed it is important that you keep business records not only because of your dealings with the government – its requirements and your wish to pay as little tax as possible – but important also because of other likely events and circumstances in your life.

Independent professionals grumble about the detailed records that a meddling Uncle Sam requires them to keep. Yet many indies, once they start keeping records, realize that they have a resource in their hands that helps them monitor their businesses. Records can tell a self-employed person not only how his business is doing but can also help predict how it may do next year. Perhaps Astrid Astrologer doesn't need records to look into the future but the rest of us do.

There are non-tax reasons why a self-employed might need business information at his fingertips. The examples that follow, by no means an exhaustive list, should get you thinking about the ways that business records may benefit your financial situation – whether professional or personal.

## GETTING A LOAN

Whether you apply for a business loan, a personal loan, a mortgage for a new home or to refinance your present home, the lender will want to see your business records. If you don't want to show business records, but have substantial assets, you may be able to get a "no-doc" loan (no income verification documents required) but it's going to saddle you with a higher interest rate.

The financial meltdown of 2008 has made lending institutions – you and I call them banks – even more demanding in their loan application document requirements. And, even though mortgage companies have adopted new criteria that give the self-employed a more level playing field, it's still standard practice that, all things being equal, Emma Employee has a better shot at any kind of loan than does Indira Independent. Even all things not being equal, even if Ms Employee makes less money, the lending institutions tend to think of her salary as more dependable. I know, the benefits of self-employment due to financial crises and downsizing have not yet reached the psyches of loan officers. In the twentieth-century thinking of these guys Emma's pay is more predictable than is Indira's. Lenders tend to get nervous thinking that Ms Independent is more likely to run into hard times when the cash flows out instead of in, and then she might fall behind in the repayment schedule.

In most instances in which Emma Employee would have to show a W-2, Indira Independent would have to confirm her income via a federal Schedule C, Profit or Loss From Business (a part of her tax return). If the loan were applied for in mid-year Emma would have to show a pay stub with year-to-date earnings, and Indira would have to show a year-to-date profit and loss statement, often required on an accountant's letterhead. Emma's source for her information is the payroll department where she works. Indira's source is her own recordkeeping.

## COLLEGE FINANCIAL AID

When applying for student aid for yourself or your child you will be required to complete financial aid forms. You must have records that will provide you with the correct information in order to fill out these forms accurately. You cannot guess. If you estimate because your records are incomplete then you may be asked to submit a revised application when your records are complete. Often you will be required to submit documents to substantiate the information you provided. False or misleading information on a federal request for college aid can subject you to a $20,000 fine or prison or both[16].

## GRANTS

When applying for a grant for any kind of project you may need to show your project expenses to date as well as expected research and other costs necessary to completing the work.

## COURT CASES

Records are the very lifeblood of litigation.

In a divorce, proof of income – or lack of it – is often required whether debating a division of assets, amount of alimony or child support. Just as an ex-spouse-in-waiting must prove the $70,000 assistant manager salary via a W-2, an independent professional must show by means of accurate records that, even though the project sold for $70,000, the net income was only $10,000.

If you are a plaintiff in a negligence case in which you were injured, and your suit includes reimbursement for lost income, your business records are essential. You'll need them to show your income over past years and that you expected to earn even more this year had you not been laid up in traction for many months.

## INSURANCE

Without sufficient records there is no way to substantiate a loss for insurance purposes whether it's a home that went up in flames or a burglarized storage unit. Without proof of the cost or value of a computer or a camera, how are you going to get your insurance company to reimburse you for those items? You'll have trouble enough even with the records.

When you do record your possessions – whether via computer, camcorder, or still camera – keep a copy of your records in a safe place off premises such as a friend's house or a safe deposit box.

CHAPTER 20: WHAT TO CAST AND WHEN will guide you vis-à-vis the time periods that various *tax* records need to be kept, but here's a note on insurance policies: If you have umbrella coverage or liability insurance for your business or home, keep the old policy records for past years, in case someone files against you claiming injury in a past year. The records ought to be kept for as long as your state's statute of limitations is in effect. The same goes for the auto insurance.

# WARRANTIES

Most warranty agreements are inflexible about expiration dates. Whether it's the laser printer or the washing machine that dies a week before the warranty runs out, it helps mightily to be able to prove the purchase date to the seller or manufacturer.

# EQUIPMENT, INVESTMENTS AND OTHER ASSETS

Not only for your own tax preparation do you need to know the cost-basis of assets, stocks and other investments sold, but also, if you gift an asset to someone, you need to provide basis information to the recipient of the gift.

# OTHER IMPORTANT STUFF

A note on some personal records: Don't throw away your birth certificate, marriage certificate (even if the marriage is long gone), will, divorce decree, Social Security card, passport, various licenses, title to your automobile, insurance policies, college records. And, although it's best if all these records are organized in a filing system of your own devising, if you lack any sense of organization, at least keep them all in one place – a file box labeled *"Important Stuff"* – not divided among a kitchen drawer, summer home, attic, bedroom closet, car, and office desk. That's called the "sloppy spouse system" and is hazardous to your mental health.

Recordkeeping is a lot like exercising at the gym. It's really hard to get started. You have to want to get better at it. You have to make an effort. And you have to do it consistently. If you take time off it takes three times as long to catch up. An indie power mindset along with the **Most Simple System** will get you to the treadmill with the right attitude and the right gear. There's no telling how high or fast you can go after that.

# 20

## CHAPTER 20: WHAT TO CAST AND WHEN
## How Long to Keep Which Records

### A Sad Tale

Since she first started out, Lisa Locksmith had her taxes prepared by Cousin Careless. But Careless retired and Lisa had to find a new preparer. She asked other independent professionals for suggestions and that's how she came to use Fanny Flawless.

To her initial consultation Fanny asked Lisa to bring copies of all tax returns since the start of her business. Lisa searched her garage and behind the winter tires in a box marked "KEEP" she found returns for 2007, 2008, 2009, 2010 and 2011.

"Why, Lisa," says Fanny after reviewing the five previous years' tax returns, "you've never deducted any costs for use of your car. Don't you use your car in your business?"

"Of course I do," says Lisa. " I put about 10,000 miles a year on my car just going to lockouts from my home office."

"Well, there are no auto deductions on any of these returns," says Fanny. "And 10,000 miles could save you about $2,000 a year in taxes."

"Good grief!," says Lisa. "Can't I go back and fix those returns or something and get my money back?"

"That's called amending your return and you can amend for only three years after you filed your return. Let's see. Today is March tenth 2013, so you lost out on amending 2007 which you filed in August 2008. The same with 2008 which you filed in September 2009. But we can re-file for 2009, 2010, and 2011. You could recoup a substantial amount of tax already paid to the feds and your state. Can you review your records and get an accurate tally of your auto miles for those three years?" asks Fanny.

"Are you kidding?! Careless told me I didn't need to keep anything but a copy of my tax return. I threw all that stuff out ages ago."

### The End

Yes, it is a sad tale with a cost to Lisa of about $6,000. Most folks, when they think or ask about record retention are concerned about an audit and how far back can the IRS go in requiring substantiation for deductions. They rarely consider that they might need old records to claim a tax refund or credit. The rules are clear-cut when looked at from the taxpayer's side of the fence. You have three years from the due date of your return, with extension, to change – that is, amend – your tax return and claim a credit or refund. If you were an energetic early bird and filed before the due date you still have three years from the due date.

## TO CAST OR TO KEEP

Contrary to popular opinion people don't usually get into trouble for not saving records but for saving the wrong ones or outdated ones, or not knowing where the right ones are. The huge stack of papers in the attic is often a monument to inertia complicated by not knowing which records need to be kept and which can be tossed. Here's a general rule of thumb.

This chapter about ***the basics of record retention*** is the starting point. You will take a big step forward in your organization proficiency once you know which tax records to keep and for how long.

### WHATTA CONCEPT!
### Record Retention Simply Stated

Keep tax returns (not records, but actual returns) forever. Label a box "My Tax Returns" and put them in there. Keep every year-end summary of your pension forever. Label a box "Pensions" and make a folder for each plan you have. Put that plan's year-end statement in the folder and close the box.

Keep everything else for seven years from the last time it had any impact on your financial life. Label a box "2012 Tax Records: OK to throw out 12/31/2019."
The chart **How Long To Keep Records** can be found near the end of this chapter.

# YOUR TAX RETURNS

Your tax returns are historical information – save them forever. They can be a source of horror or amusement.

---

### Reality √ Check

I was working with a graphic designer who had been a client for some time whose income had made giant leaps in the last few years but he was struggling to make ends meet. He had trouble managing his money and he didn't know where to start. I pulled out his tax return of five years earlier and showed him that his income at that time was the same amount as his current yearly credit card finance charges. That got his attention!

---

### Reality √ Check

Really old returns proved useful in a divorce case. The father told the judge he expected his daughters to work part-time while in college and contribute toward the expense of school. The ex-wife thought that this would be too much to expect from the children.

To show that his expectations were reasonable, the father found his tax returns from his college days showing his income earned while attending college. He graduated with honors. The judge decided for the father.

---

### Reality √ Check

Another client, let's call her Dr. Endie Naturopath, was stopped at a light in Seattle, not far from Bastyr University, her alma mater, when her car was struck from behind. Serious neck injury prevented her from working for the next year and severely limited her future practice. It was the fault of the sweet young thing driving the Smart Car – thank goodness it wasn't a Lincoln. In preparing for the court case, Endie's lawyer told her to present proof of her income since the start of her practice to show how her income had been reduced by not being able to work after the accident. Unlike the traditional medical professions, there is scarce statistical information on typical income and growth of income for naturopathic doctors. Endie's tax returns were crucial to a fair settlement of the case.

---

More routine but also very useful is using the previous year's tax return as reference when gathering material for the current year's return.

You can obtain back-year tax returns from the IRS but this entails unnecessary time and expense, so be sure to save them.

# RECORDS SUBSTANTIATING YOUR TAX RETURN

The main reason to save tax records is to substantiate the items of income and deduction on your tax return in case of an audit. You should keep those records at least through the time when the IRS can question your return's accuracy. This time is called the statute of limitations.

**In general, the statute of limitations is either three years after the due date of your return, or three years after the date you filed – whichever is later.**

For example, if you filed your 2011 tax return on March 20, 2012, it could be called for an audit through April 15, 2015.

If you filed your 2011 return on October 15, 2012, the extension deadline, it could be questioned through October 15, 2015.

Easiest way to think about it: the IRS can come after you for questions about a transaction up to 4 years after the transaction. That is, 2011's records are vulnerable through 2015.

### There Are Exceptions to The Rule
*If You Paid Late:* If you filed your tax return but couldn't pay your tax right away, you are open for an audit until 2 years after you paid the tax, regardless of when you filed your return.

*If You Forgot Some Income:* If you filed a return in which you understated your income by 25% or more the IRS can come after you for six years, not just three. Six years after filing is usually seven years after the transaction. That's why the rule of thumb is to keep your records for seven years.

> **Reality √ Check**
>
> In all innocence, Prudence Pas de Deux, in the year her net profit was $10,000, didn't claim as income the $5,000 grant she received to choreograph the winter pageant for the School for the Deaf. That's more than 25% of her income that she didn't claim and the IRS has 6 years to come and get the tax and interest and penalty from her.
>
> Prudence's ignorance of tax regs shows us how susceptible we all are to oversights – our own and those of our financial advisors. Because the IRS can go back to overlooked income six years after you've filed, I urge that you keep records for seven years. For example, for events that took place in 2012 keep records through 2019.

*If You Committed Serious Tax Misconduct:* No limit! There is no statute of limitations if you intentionally fail to report income. The IRS can come after you anytime if you file a fraudulent return or fail to file a return. That's why you should permanently keep records for any year that you didn't need to file a return. Your records will provide evidence in case the IRS ever questions why you didn't file for that year.

*If You Voluntarily Extended The Deadline:* A taxpayer can agree to extend the statute of limitations if the IRS asks. This happens if some item on the return needs more time to be resolved. Check with your tax pro before signing on to this.

*If You Live Or Work in A State with A Different Statute of Limitations:* Be careful, some states may have a longer statute of limitations than the feds. For example, in California the statue of limitations is four years, not three.

## RECORDS FOR MULTI-YEAR DEDUCTIONS

Even if you filed everything on time and on the up-and-up, there are situations where records must be retained for a longer period.

If you have a business expense that you do not entirely deduct in the year you incur the expense, but instead spread the cost over a period of years, then you must retain the records at least long enough to meet the statute of limitations for the last return on which you deducted the final portion of that item.

This kind of expense deduction is called **depreciation** or **amortization**. It applies to things like business EQUIPMENT, VEHICLES, and BUILDINGS, as well as OFFICE-IN-THE-HOME and START-UP COSTS.

> ### Reality √ Check
> Clarissa Clothier purchased a computer in 2010. It will be deducted on her tax returns in 2010, 2011, 2012, 2013, 2014 and 2015. Were the IRS to suspect hidden income her 2015 return could be questioned through 2022. So the records for the 2010 purchase of her computer are open to question by the IRS 12 years from the date of purchase. This is seven years from the last year it appeared on her tax return (2015 + 7 = 2022).

Records for business equipment and property that must be written off over a period of years should be kept for as long as you own the property and then for seven additional years after you've disposed of it. EQUIPMENT and property are things such as:

- Office hardware
- Furniture
- Warehouse building
- Vehicles

> ### Reality √ Check
> Clarissa finished deducting the 1995 business truck on her tax return years ago but it still runs like a charm. If she sells it in 2010 and her 2010 tax return is audited in 2012 she may need to show records for the purchase of the truck, deductions for its use over the years, as well as for its sale in 2010.

The same applies to records relating to your residence. The larger tax exemption for gains on the sale of personal residence has prompted some homeowners to question whether they need to bother saving any of their home-related tax records. Well, you may be a homeowner today and a self-employed with an office-in-the-home tomorrow. And tomorrow you'll need all your home purchase and capital improvements records. When you deduct expenses for OFFICE-IN-THE-HOME the same record retention rules apply as for any other multi-year deduction. Keep records for seven years after you sell your residence.

## Segregating Multi-year Records

To simplify your future I suggest a file folder or box labeled "Equipment and Other Long-Lasting Things." This can be the place where you put receipts, bills of sale and instruction manuals for equipment, autos, office furniture, etc., and active warranties and service contracts on equipment. If you own a home, also have an "Ongoing Home" file. Two simple-to-set-up folders that will save you time down the road.

Although most audits take place within two years from the time you file your return, the IRS can wait as long as three years – and in some circumstances even longer. For instance, when Prudence Pas De Deux neglected to include at least 25% of her income on her return, the statute of limitations extended from three to six years after filing. That's seven years from the time of the transaction. The table below takes into consideration such circumstances.

| HOW LONG TO KEEP TAX RECORDS | | |
|---|---|---|
| **The Record** | **The Situation** | **Keep Records for How Long** |
| Tax Returns | Any | Forever |
| Records Substantiating Tax Return | Filed on time, including extensions | 7 years from the year of the transactions |
| | Filed late | 6 years from filing date |
| | Paid Late | 6 years from last payment |
| | Filed a fraudulent return | Forever |
| | Never filed a return | Forever |
| Receipts for A Multi-Year Deduction | Any | 7 years after the year you disposed of it |

# CASTING WITH ASSURANCE

As I said in the beginning of this chapter, people don't usually get into trouble by not saving records but by saving the wrong ones. Don't confuse keeping records with never throwing out a piece of paper. Use the table above – **HOW LONG TO KEEP TAX RECORDS** – as a guide for pitching to the round file, with assurance, but keep in mind that there are other non-tax records not included in this table.

Keep the records listed below, each in its own file folder, clearly labeled, in a safe place:

- Birth and death certificates
- Marriage and divorce papers
- Adoption papers
- Military service records (You'll need them when you file for Social Security.)
- Wills (Do not keep this in your safe deposit box.)
- Asset lists (so your estate can be properly administered)
- Medical records (one for each family member)
- Loan and lease agreements
- Personal and business insurance policies (See note in previous chapter, page 186.)
- Employment agreements
- Pension documents and pension tax returns (This is Form 5500 or 5500-EZ.)
- A complete record of pension contributions and withdrawals (found on the year-end statement)

# 21

## CHAPTER 21: AS IT EBBS AND SWELLS
### The Basics of Income Recordkeeping

Cash flow! I'm sure many of you have heard the term. There's all the goofy comments that it does anything but flow. Very often it just stops; for the lucky ones it's a tidal wave; for the unlucky ones it backs up. For most of us it doesn't flow evenly but surges once in a while and ebbs when we need it most.

It may help you to understand the term **cash flow** if you think of money coming in to you as *inflow* rather than **income**. Interest from your savings account is income; a birthday check for $500 from your great-uncle is not income; on a sale of stock some of what you get may be income but some of it is a return of your own money; health insurance reimbursements are generally not income. Some inflow is income while some is not. Inflow is any money you receive. Sometimes it is called cash receipts.

And think of any money you spend as outflow rather than as an expense. A utility bill is an expense; it might also be a business expense. Buying a vacation home is money out but not an expense because you are exchanging one asset –money in the bank – for another asset – real estate. A birthday check to your housesitter is money out but is it an expense? Outflow is money spent or disbursed and so it is often called cash disbursements.

In CHAPTER 19: RECORDS AS RESOURCE there were many reasons given for the benefits of general recordkeeping. Let's examine the importance of an accurate record of all money coming in to you – inflow.

---

**THE IRS SAYS ABOUT RECORDKEEPING ...**
Except in a few cases, the law does not require any special kind of records. You may choose any recordkeeping system suited to your business that clearly and accurately shows your income.

---

# INCOME VS. INFLOW

In order to tally your income you need to be able to distinguish income from all other inflow. Therefore, you need a record of the source of each and every deposit made to each and every one of your financial accounts – checking, savings, investment, retirement.

Only by being able to identify every cash receipt can you isolate that which is income, that which is not, and those that are transfers from other accounts.

In a simple audit of a self-employed the IRS will want to see monthly bank statements for that year, as well as the previous December and the following January for all accounts. They will add up every deposit. You must be able to explain any difference between the total deposits and the amount of income shown on your tax return. A written record of inflow may save you time and stress as well as untold amounts in taxes, penalty, and interest charges.

---

### Reality √ Check

If Syd System's tax return shows gross self-employed income of $30,000 and Syd's bank statements show $35,000 in deposits then Syd had better have a good explanation for the extra $5,000, and a note from Mom saying she loaned it to him will not do.

If Syd's bank statements show $25,000 in deposits but his tax return shows $30,000 gross self-employed income the likely assumption is that he had $25,000 income in checks and $5,000 cash income. If that is the case, it means he is not depositing all of his income into his checking account. This may lead the IRS to question how much more than the claimed $5,000 cash income he's not putting into his checking account. Many indies think that as long as they claim "some" cash income the IRS will be happy and not look to see how much other cash income is not claimed. The IRS knows this ploy.

---

Both situations – bank statements showing less in deposits than claimed as income and statements totaling more than was claimed as income – lead to more thorough scrutiny by the IRS.

And what if Mom did loan Syd $5,000? His written income log should show just that to the IRS. In a situation where money comes from a family member a copy of the check from Mom would be an invaluable addition to the inflow log.

# INCOME RECORDS AND ESTIMATED TAX PAYMENTS

The amount and timing of your estimated tax payments ("estimateds") may be based upon how much income you receive and when you receive it. **PART V** provides a complete discussion of taxes but here I'd like to give you a perspective on income records and paying tax on income. There is no need to pay tax on income not yet received. For instance, if Luisa Lifecoach received in January, her only income that year, a $40,000 project payment from her corporate sponsor, she would be required to make her first estimated payment the following April 15. If, however, she did not receive the payment until September then her first estimated payment would not be due until September 15. An income log, with backup, would enable her or her financial advisor to calculate estimated tax payments to her advantage.

If Luisa didn't consult with anyone about estimated tax payments but just paid them when she had the money, as an after-the-fact remedy, her income records could help her tax preparer show the IRS why a payment made in September instead of April was acceptable, thereby saving Luisa some interest and late payment penalties.

## Don't Rely on The Sleepy Bookkeeper

Perhaps the best reason to keep a record of your income is because someone else's error can make your life miserable.

Depending upon your business, you may receive a Form 1099 from every client you worked for during the year; or some may send a year-end payment summary; or each of your clients may have a bookkeeper you can call to get a tally. However ... you do not want to rely on the recordkeeping of others!

People to whom you sell your service or product make mistakes – their bookkeeper had a bad day, there was a glitch in the new computer program, someone was too lazy to double-check an entry.

Many first-time clients have come to me having no idea of their income. Their plan was to add up all the 1099s they received from clients and use that as their income amount. How foolish to rely on the accuracy and honesty of others for such an important part of your financial well-being! One typo can plunge you into a tax inferno!

## WHATTA CONCEPT!
### What to do about an incorrect Form 1099-MISC

The company or individual who pays you $600 or more in one year is required to send you a Form 1099-MISC stating your income. A copy also goes to the federal government and in some cases to the state as well. Compare your record of income to all Forms 1099-MISC that you receive.

You must claim the income you received whether correctly stated on a 1099 or not.

If a 1099 understates income, as long as you are satisfied with the explanation given you by the payer, there is no need to insist on a corrected Form 1099. But you must claim the correct amount as income.

If a 1099 overstates the amount paid to you contact the payer for an explanation and correction. For instance, if all your 1099s total $60,000 but you received only $50,000 in gross income – then you need to get the discrepancy corrected. Contact the issuing party quickly.

The rule is that 1099s must be sent to the recipient (that's you) by January 31 and to the governments by the end of February, so you have only one month – the month of February – to get the original 1099 changed before it is sent to the feds. But if the original erroneous 1099 has already been sent to the government more effort is required – the issuing party must file a corrected Form 1099.

If you receive an overstated 1099 and you have income from many sources it may not be necessary to have the 1099 corrected. You'll need to discuss this with your tax pro. Keep copies of any correspondence regarding incorrect 1099s.

### Reality √ Check

Raina Realtor kept an accurate record of her commissions for the year and so when the realty firm sent her a Form 1099 erroneously stating $5,000 more in income than she had received she could prove the correct amount. A copy of the incorrect Form 1099 went to the IRS so Raina must get the realty company to send a corrected form to her and to the IRS.

In a case such as Raina's I include a copy of the corrected 1099 with the tax return along with an explanation, just in case the realty firm didn't get around to sending the corrected one to the IRS.

Errors happen whether your income is from many sources or from only one. And it doesn't matter whether the source is some mom-and-pop shop or some by-the-book corporation. An indie who is a freelance head-hunter for the big and powerful accounting firms marvels at the inaccuracy of the income statements she receives from them every year. To our amusement, we compare her accurate amounts to their faulty 1099s and come up with thousands of dollars difference. And, financial recordkeeping is their business!

Writers across the country know that small – and not so small – publishing companies are notorious for their faulty recordkeeping. It is often a hassle and sometimes impossible to get accurate royalty statements from many of them. The least that should be done when receiving royalties is to record the income received and note the period of time that the royalties cover. Save the royalty statements for the life of the book.

If trying to collect from a delinquent client, accurate records are indispensable in arguing your point. For instance, if you've not received final payment because the company that owes you the money changed bookkeepers and your invoice has been put in the "paid-in-full" bin you should be able to show any partial payments received, when and for how much.

> ### Reality √ Check
> When Attila Atelier sold three of Clement Creator's paintings for a total of $20,000 Clement knew his 60% share should be $12,000. When he received three checks totaling only $10,900 he used his income record to show Attila's bookkeeper where the mistake had been made and that he was still owed $1,100.

Real estate sales persons paid by commission from one realty company, authors paid solely through a literary agent, musicians paid by numerous clubs and bandleaders, personal trainers paid by multi-million dollar corporations – all have run into serious problems when they have relied upon someone else's records. Be smart – rely on yourself.

---

### ALERT!

There's a new form out from the IRS – Form 1099-K[17]. You'll be receiving it in time for your 2012 tax return.

---

### THE IRS SAYS ABOUT FORM 1099-K ...

Form 1099-K states merchant card and third party network payments. A payment settlement entity (PSE) must file Form 1099-K for payments made in settlement of reportable payment transactions for each calendar year. A PSE makes a payment in settlement of a reportable payment transaction, that is, any payment card or third party network transaction, if the PSE submits the instruction to transfer funds to the account of the participating payee to settle the reportable payment transaction.

---

Sound like gobbledygook? *It simply means that if you sell anything on Amazon, craigslist, eBay, Etsy, or the like, or receive payments through Intuit or any other online service, you will receive a Form 1099-K stating the income you received.* That income amount now has its very own line on an indie's federal Schedule C.

## HOW TO RECORD INFLOW

Astrid Astrologer gets paid mostly in cash; Wally Windowasher mostly by check; Bulky Benjamin's customers pay for their watch repairs in cash or by check or credit card. What should each indie do with the income when it's received? Well, as I said before, most important: Don't hide it.

Next: Keep it simple. If you receive payment by check, deposit the entire check into your checking account. *Do not split the check*. That is, if you receive $500 and you need $100 cash, deposit $500 and then write out a check to yourself for $100.

You probably think that it would be simpler to deposit only $400 and keep the $100 cash. No way. Here's why.

The IRS is not interested in deductions alone. In an audit of a self-employed its expectation is that not all income is being claimed. Make it simple on yourself and the auditor by keeping a clear record of the flow of money. In financial circles that's called an **audit trail** and you want to keep the trail neat and tidy. To do that you must deposit all money initially into the same account. Whether it's a payment from a client, your spouse's paycheck, or a birthday present from Mom, deposit the entire amount into your primary account. Then – if you want to move some money into savings, or to an investment account – write out a check or have money electronically transferred from your primary account to another account. This way your audit trail will directly lead from one stepping stone to the next rather than zigzagging sideways and backwards. (Yes, I did say into the same account. I called it a ***primary checking account***. You will read more about personal and business checking accounts in the next chapter.)

***An example of a zigzag:*** You receive a $1,000 payment by check. You split the check and put $500 into checking, and $300 into a savings account and keep $200 cash. Then two days later – balance running low in your checking account – you transfer $300 from savings back to your checking account. When you look at your bank statements a year later will you be able to recall which deposits were income and which were transfers?

By depositing everything initially into your primary account it is easy to see that anything that went into a savings or investment account was not income but a transfer from your primary account and that only the deposits into the primary account are to be looked at as possible income. You can easily show a transfer ***out of*** the primary account matching a transfer ***into*** another account by the matching dates and amounts and "transfer" written on the deposit slip or in your electronic records. Should you need to prove your income to the IRS you can take them down a straight path rather than scrambling through a financial maze.

## The Simplicity of An Inflow Log

In **Five Easy Steps** I give instruction and examples of various kinds of inflow logs. Some call an inflow log a "receipts journal," "cash receipts ledger," or a "spreadsheet." How simple it is will depend upon the type of freelance endeavor you have, what else is happening in your financial life, how much information you want readily available, and whether you keep your records manually, digitally or a little of both.

An inflow log is easy. Although it must be accurate it can suit your business and your recordkeeping style. It must be configured in such a way that for all money received it will be evident how much you received, when you received it, from whom and for what.

## Reimbursements from Clients

Based on the frequency of questions I receive to my blog on this topic it appears that reimbursements from clients cause much confusion for indies.

When you receive reimbursement from your client for expenses (such as TELEPHONE, TRAVEL, or SUPPLIES) regardless of the recordkeeping method you use, log the reimbursement as inflow and classify it as a reimbursement.

Let's say you bill a client $5,000 for services and $800 as reimbursement for TELEPHONE expenses, for a total invoice of $5,800. There are two different bookkeeping methods for you to choose from when handling client reimbursements. We'll look at each.

I find Method One easier:
- When you get the check for $5,800 in the deposit note the $5,000 as *fee income* and the $800 reimbursement inflow as *reimbursement income*.
- Claim the entire $5,800 as gross income.
- At the end of the year, if your business phone bills total $12,000, you may deduct the entire amount because you have claimed the reimbursement as income.
- This way, your deposits match your income and your checks to the phone companies match your expenses.
- A variation on this method may be necessary in states where tax is levied on gross income. Since reimbursement is not income you will want to differentiate the fee from the reimbursement for state tax purposes.


The more standard is Method Two:
- When you get the check for $5,800 note in the deposit that the $5,000 is *fee income* and the $800 is *reimbursement inflow*.
- Claim only the $5,000 as income.
- Then, at year-end, instead of simply totaling and deducting your $12,000 in telephone expenses you'll have to remember to reduce the total telephone expense by the $800 reimbursement that you did not include as income. You will come up with a phone expense total of $11,200. ($12,000 phone expense less the $800 you were reimbursed).

I prefer Method One because it's easier to include the expense reimbursement payment in income and then deduct all expenses – reimbursed and not. The method works if you have no need to keep separate records of reimbursed expenses for client or state tax purposes.

The above example was for one client with one category of expense. More categories of reimbursed expenses for many clients may require Method Two. If you must keep records for specific clients and their expenses there is more information about how to do that in **Five Easy Steps** and on my blog http://junewalkeronline.com/blog/.

Whichever way you keep your books, it nets out to the same income in the end. See below for an example of a self-employed with $40,000 gross income and $27,000 in expenses, $11,000 of which were reimbursed by clients:

| | |
|---|---|
| Gross fees (does not include reimbursements) | $ 40,000 |
| Less non-reimbursed expenses | ( 16,000 ) |
| Net profit | $ 24,000. |

*or*

| | |
|---|---|
| Gross fees | $ 40,000 |
| Other income: Client reimbursements | 11,000 |
| Gross income | $ 51,000 |
| | |
| Less reimbursed + non-reimbursed expenses | ( 27,000 ) |
| Net profit | $24,000 |

Incidentally, if your client sends you a Form 1099 stating the annual income paid to you, will expenses be included on the 1099? Who knows? Some clients will not include expense reimbursements; others will. Since the IRS compares the gross income on your tax return with the income information they receive via Forms 1099, including reimbursements in income by using Method One may avoid a later explanation to the IRS.

### State Sales Tax Or Gross Receipts Tax

Many states have a sales or gross receipts tax that you as the seller of a service or product must charge your clients. These receipts, similar to reimbursements, are not income to you but must be accounted for as inflow. Your income log needs to clearly show your collection of that tax. And depending upon your state, its regulations, and the amount of sales tax that you collect, you may have to tally your income on a frequent basis such as monthly or semiannually.

### Deposit Slips

If you choose not to keep an inflow log because payments to you are straightforward or seldom then be even more careful in denoting every deposit on the paper deposit slip or in the electronic deposit. For instance, if three clients pay you in cash then list each client on the deposit slip and the amount paid by each. Save every deposit slip or deposit transaction. Tally them for your year-end inflow/income record.

If paper, be sure your deposit slips have a duplicate that you can keep for your records since the original goes to your bank. If you deposit via smartphone or other digital device, then keep the check you deposited, and be sure your onscreen or email confirmation from the bank is saved and or backed up for your easy access.

If copying every check that comes in makes your recordkeeping easier for you, then by all means, copy away. Attach the check copies to your copy of the deposit slip.

Get those loose deposit slips out of your pocket and off the car floor and into a folder labeled "2013 Deposit Slips."

Anything that works for you is fine as long as there is a ***tangible, clear record*** of what you received, when you received it and from whom. The less elaborate the better because you will stick with something simple.

---

### ALERT!

Note that I said "tangible." I know that many indies keep digital records. Be aware that the IRS has purchased 1500 to 2000 licenses from Intuit and has IRS agents trained in QuickBooks to assist in tax return examinations. According to a Senior Liaison Specialist at the IRS: "The IRS has found that many taxpayers do not save hard copies of their records or the copies they have are incomplete." When that happens the examiner is authorized to obtain the taxpayer's electronic, QuickBooks, records.

Electronic or digital recordkeeping is further discussed in **Five Easy Steps**.

---

### The Straddle: Be Careful of New Year's Cheer

Be aware that there are some clever business people who will write out a check for you dated December 31. For them it is deductible in the year they wrote the check. For you, a cash basis business, it is income when you receive it. (Cash basis versus accrual method was explained in CHAPTER 14, page 154.) If that check doesn't reach you until January 31 of the next year, well then, that's when you claim it as income. The exception to that rule is when the client paying you includes that December 31 payment in the Form 1099 sent you for that year. In cases like that you should complain to the payer and discuss it with your tax professional. Then decide which year to claim the income. If you do claim the income as reported to you on the 1099, then be careful not to claim it again in the following year.

### Understand Constructive Receipt

If you have an agent and are unclear on when payment is considered income to you re-read about constructive receipt in CHAPTER 17, page 173.

## TO SUM UP THE BASICS OF INCOME RECORDKEEPING

- Not all inflow is income.
- Don't rely on others for a record of your income.
- Clearly identify all inflow on deposit slips.
- Review Forms 1099 as soon as you receive them.

## CHAPTER 22: DILIGENCE GENERATES DEDUCTIONS
## The Basics of Expense Recordkeeping

Let's see: You know if you're self-employed; you know whether or not you're running a business; you know the basics and importance of recording inflow and how to recognize income; you can spot a business deduction hidden under a rug; you know all the benefits of good records. Let's now take a look at the basics of recording expenses.

> ### Reality √ Check
> Syd System helped Hildy Housewife install the genealogy software that she'd just purchased. Hildy paid Syd the $400 fee by check. It was late on Friday; Syd ran to the bank, deposited $100 of the check, and kept $300 cash. Then a quick trip to Office Arsenal to buy a $20 USB cable for which he paid cash; next he picked up a bottle of wine for his neighbor; then he met his friend Stella Sellit for dinner – his treat because she was advising him on his new website campaign. He paid cash for the wine and the dinners. Saturday morning Syd left on a ski trip.

Do you think that when Syd returned from his winter weekend, he remembered any of the hasty financial transactions he'd made on Friday? Or do you expect, as do I, that the memory of it all is buried deep in the snow and when tax time comes around, in spite of the spring thaw, nothing will be revealed?

Syd's hectic pace is characteristic of the business life of many independent professionals.

In CHAPTER 6: INDIE POWER MINDSET, I urged that you adopt an indie power mindset based on the concept that you are an indie business. If you've forgotten the basics in that chapter, re-read it. It's a short chapter and imperative to building a strong foundation on which to build your recordkeeping system whichever bookkeeping routine you choose.

The indie power mindset does call for a different way of thinking. This is not theory: It is a method that you will incorporate into every day of your life. One of its strongest tenets is: ***Whenever you reach into your pocket for money, you may be engaging in a business transaction***.

Whether your freelance venture or sole proprietorship has been up and running for several years or you're planning to open for business the week after Labor Day, this part of the indie power mindset starts now! In the last chapter I talked about inflow. Now you're going to learn the basics of outflow. It's simple, yet very important.

## GET BACKUP FOR EVERY DOLLAR YOU SPEND

This is the cardinal rule, the keystone, the get-go, the core of my **Most Simple System** or any recordkeeping system used by an indie. There is nothing philosophical about it and it doesn't involve debits, credits, trial balances or ledgers. It's just something you do.

From this day forward, pay for absolutely everything by check or credit card, or if you must pay by cash, then get a receipt. No matter what it is – personal expenditures or business expenses.

Do not take money out of your pocket – literally dollars, or their virtual equivalent, a check or credit card, or online purchase – without getting something back for the other pocket: a cancelled check (a photocopy arrives as part of your bank statement), a credit card slip, a computer printed receipt, or a cash receipt. Let's call it backup.

I'll say it again: Get backup for everything! Groceries, a hat, a bottle of wine, a birthday card, a computer, diapers, office supplies, flowers, books, everything!

When paying by check your backup is your cancelled check or the copy of the cancelled check that is part of your bank statement.

When you pay by credit card, your backup is your credit card receipt slip – keep them all.

When paying on line, your backup is your printout of the paid confirmation.

If you must pay by cash get a receipt as your backup. Or handwrite your own receipt.

As long as you pay for everything by check or credit card, or get a receipt, there's little else you need to do all year. The difficult part: Getting into the habit of doing it all the time. Think of the regimen as developing your indie power mindset.

Furthermore, this rule applies not only to everything you spend, but to everything your spouse spends. Yes, even if your husband is not in business for himself and has nothing to do with your business he, too, needs to get backup. Why? Because the chair he purchased at the garage sale may have been intended for the kitchen, but when he brought it home you decided it was perfect for the sunny corner in your office. And, this applies to your children as well – whenever they pay for something for you, get them into requesting a receipt for their purchase. It's good training. Their future professions may be part of the growing self-employed workforce.

Sometimes I have to talk reluctant indies into this new way of thinking. I remind you that this is the cardinal rule of the most simple way of keeping records. It's worked for my clients for more than 25 years.

Sure, it's a bother to ask for a receipt for everything you spend. And Sammy Segar CPA has advised you "just save business receipts" and he handles a couple of big companies and was your father's accountant for years. And your brother never saves receipts and he got a huge refund. So I suppose you've got to be talked into it. Listen up, here are some real indie situations that will convince you.

---

### Reality √ Check

At the Total Foods checkout counter Nyssa Nutritionist decides against the hassle of writing out a check; besides it's just groceries anyway. She puts four twenties on the counter, takes her change and leaves the receipt on the counter.

That evening when the three women from the county senior center meet at her home to discuss the workshop she will present next month on healthy eating, Nyssa serves dessert and coffee that she bought that day at Total Foods.

The expense of that food and drink is a deductible MEALS & ENTERTAINMENT business expense. Poor Nyssa has no receipt. And those organic desserts were quite expensive.

If Nyssa did have backup for the food she purchased that day she would deduct only the cost of the items she served to her business associates; she would not deduct the entire Total Foods amount if it included her weekly groceries.

---

> ### Reality √ Check
>
> Nadine Novella must get her manuscript and Christmas cards mailed before leaving to visit her father in Vintage Village, Florida. Nadine follows the cardinal rule of the indie power mindset: She pays for everything by check. So in her haste, no need to think about the business deductibility of postage – of course she paid for the postage by check. Months later when she goes though her cancelled checks she'll have her proof of the POSTAGE expense for mailing her manuscript, and for the stamps used for that portion of Christmas cards sent to her business associates.
>
> During that stop at the post office resourceful Nadine also mailed a letter confirming her appointments with several board members and oldest residents of Vintage Village. She is planning to write a piece about the disposition and mood change of old folks when the "kids" arrive for the holidays. She had written the co-op board several months ago explaining her idea for the article and requesting interviews. Of course she is paying all her TRAVEL expenses by check or credit card.

Why do you get backup for every dollar you spend? So that you don't have to make decisions on the spot. You have the option of deciding later whether the expense relates to your business, and therefore whether it is deductible. When pushing to meet a deadline or hurrying from a cab to make your next appointment, taxes are the farthest thing from your mind. But if you never miss that first step – backup for every dollar you spend – should you find after re-reading CHAPTER 10: GETTING AROUND, that your Florida trip is a business deduction, or a partial deduction, all your receipts are available. You won't have to reconstruct your expenses after the fact.

So be sure the flashing light goes off – when money, in any form, leaves your pocket, you must get something in return – a cancelled check (eventually), a charge slip, a printout, or a receipt for cash.

Let's examine each of these methods of payment and the pieces of paper or computer record that are your evidence of expenses.

## Checking Accounts
You are not required to have a separate checking account for your business. ***You need only one checking account.***

That piece of information causes Sammy Segar CPA and his like-minded professionals near apoplexy. Not kidding. Just read the checking account posts on my blog at http://junewalkeronline.com/blog/checking-account/. And it's not just Sammy who disagrees. In an IRS publication you are urged to open a business checking account and "although a bank may charge you an extra fee for a business account, the new account will more than pay for itself in accounting efficiency." The very next example from the IRS in the publication is the mixed-use – personal and business – of your automobile. So, let's see how efficient two checking accounts would be in this situation. Hmmm … guess you are expected to pay for each gas purchase with two checks – one for the personal use amount of gas and a business check for the business use portion.

Most accountants have strong disagreement with my position. That's because they don't know you like I know you. My system will save you money and time; their advice will cost you money and time.

---

### Reality √ Check

Let's look again at Nyssa Nutritionist shopping for groceries at Total Foods. If she had both a personal and a business checking account, which one should she have used to pay for her groceries, assuming she knew the three business associates were coming over that evening?

Oh! Says Sammy CPA, she should have divided the groceries into two piles, one for family and one for business guests. And paid with two checks.
And what if Nyssa's three-year-old was tearing at the display case while she was at the checkout and she was late picking up her 10-year-old at soccer practice?

---

Sammy Segar always insists that a business checking account is a must. But Sammy, if Nyssa is just starting out, where does she get the money to put into her business account? Sammy says, transfer it from her personal account. But I thought that you're supposed to keep these accounts separate. Okay, says Sammy, after she has made a little money, transfer the funds back to her personal account. But whoa, wait a minute, Nyssa transferred too much out of the business account; now she'll have to move some back to the business account again. It's beginning to get messy already, and how will she keep a record of those transfers? Well, she won't get any help from Sammy: he hates working with those eccentric indies.

As long as your records are accurate one checking account is perfectly acceptable to the IRS.

I think one big factor in the insistence on a business checking account is that it's supposed to cover up financial shenanigans. Many people like to believe that because something is paid by a business check that makes it a business deduction. Of course, that is not so! The attaché case for your daughter's twentieth birthday, even though purchased with your business check, is not a business expense. But the flowers, paid from your personal account, given to your mother as thanks for typing your business plan, is a business expense.

As I've said before, in the lives of the self-employed the line between personal and business is not clearly drawn; it wiggles around a lot. By the nature of indie businesses and by the structure of a sole proprietorship, personal and business often intertwine – almost always so in the creative fields. You do not want to struggle with business versus personal decisions every time you spend money.

*It is not from which account the money comes that is the determining factor in a business deduction but for what purpose the money is used.*

Besides, a business checking account costs money, while your own checking or savings account is usually free of charge. So who needs the extra expense? Well, sometimes it's unavoidable. For instance, it may be necessary to have a separate account if you do not use your own name as your business name.

---

### Reality √ Check

If graphic designer Victor Visual called his business the "Double V Studio" most folks would pay him with checks made out to his business name. If his bank does not allow both names – Victor Visual and Double V – on his account he'll have to have an account in the name of his business in order to deposit his checks.

The simple (and money-saving) alternative is for Victor to open a savings account in his business name, deposit the checks into it, and then have the bank do an automatic sweep of the funds from his savings to his checking account whenever the funds reach a certain amount specified by Victor.

The bank may require additional documents such as a business license or EIN.

---

Most banks now provide as part of your bank statement photocopies of your cancelled checks rather than the actual cancelled checks. Some indies pay $2 per month to get photocopies.

Whenever possible get a paper invoice or bill for whatever you are paying by check. If you pay by check for an item purchased online, printout the order.

Whenever you pay a bill by check, write the check number and the date paid on the invoice. If you paid your cable bill on March 14 with check number 607, it might look like this:

---

**Costly Cable, Inc.**

**One Month Interrupted Service: You Owe Us $399.48**

**Pay NOW**

✓#607   3/14/13

---

The easiest way to file your check backup – the receipts – is consecutively, by check number, in a folder labeled: "***2013 Check Backup.***" Depending on which recordkeeping method you choose, you will do something with them later.

***Reconciling A Bank Statement:*** Yup, that's what they call making sure you or your bank didn't make a mistake. Think of it as reconciling your differences. You should – yes, I said "should" reconcile your bank statements monthly. If you think that there's no need to look over your bank statement, well, you know that guy you saw at the bar last Friday night, a little tipsy and not too bright? He is the one entering your numbers in the bank's computer system. Whether on paper or online, make sure your transactions match the ones the bank says that you made.

So many indies do not reconcile their bank statements. Think about it, and the tipsy guy at the bar. Then grab hold of your indie power mindset, take it to the bank with you and ask a manager to show you how to reconcile your account. Or if you bank online, go to the tutorial. You will walk away from the bank or push your chair from the computer a much more confident indie.

## Credit Cards

Using one credit card simplifies your financial life. If your finances can handle it, open two credit cards, but use only one. Hide the other for emergencies such as when the first one is lost, stolen or fraudulently used or to take when traveling and keep in a place different than where you keep the one you plan to use. Just in case.

An exception to this dictum is credit card purchases online. I've had a $100 Christmas gift certificate fraudulently charged to my account. The crooks assumed, or hoped, that in the high volume of transactions during the holiday season, a mere hundred dollars wouldn't be noticed. Hah! They didn't know who they were dealing with! On another occasion I had cheaters bill thousands of dollars in computer equipment to my card. You can reduce the hassles of dealing with such fraud by using a separate card for online purchases only and by requesting a low credit limit on it.

---

### ALERT!

You do not need credit card insurance that simply protects from fraudulent purchases or card theft.

You are not responsible for fraudulent purchases made on your credit card. It is the seller who is supposed to check the identity of the purchaser. The seller is the one who loses out if he allows such a purchase.

A credit card also protects you from fraudulent sellers when you use your credit card for the purchase. Not so when you pay by check. I recommend using your credit card whenever possible. When a new gym opened up nearby. I was one of the few who paid my year's membership via credit card. The owners skipped town in the middle of the night. I copied the story from my local paper, sent it to CitiBank with the easy-to-complete required form and the charge was removed from my account.

---

Put all credit card receipts into a folder, envelope, box, container or attach them to the credit card statement. Just as with your check backup, depending on which recordkeeping method you choose, you will do something with them later.

## End-of-year Expenses And Straddle Statements

In your recordkeeping, do not combine or straddle years. Start on January 1 and end on December 31. Stop using your check register on December 31 and put it with that year's records. Start a new one on January 1.

Most bank and credit card monthly statements do not start on the first day of the month nor end on the last. They straddle months, and therefore they straddle years – for instance, the last statement of the year may cover December 14, 2012 through January 13, 2013.

*Any check written or bank credit card purchase made on or before December 31, 2012 is a 2012 expense, regardless of when the check clears or when you pay the credit card.*

### Paying Cash And Getting Receipts

Get receipts for anything that you did not purchase by check or credit card – from shelf brackets at the hardware store to aspirins at the drugstore. Write a $ (a dollar sign) at the top of the receipt. It will help you identify it as a cash expense at recordkeeping time. This is also the time to note a description on any indistinct receipts.

Put your cash receipts into a folder, envelope, box or container. Depending on which recordkeeping method you choose, you will do something with them later.

Without exception all cash receipts go into your container of choice. Although this is the time to note on the receipt a description of the item if it is not evident, there is no need to make a spot decision as to whether or not it is a business expense.

---

### Reality √ Check

You and a friend, Celia Ceramist, do lunch at Diners Delight. While waiting for your food you express dissatisfaction with the work of your print shop. Celia tells you about the new Pronto Press that just opened in her neighborhood, which is offering first time customers big discounts. Your response: "Thanks, Celia. I'll be able to get the postcards out on time. You've saved me a bundle. Lunch is on me."

You both talked so long that you hurried out, paid cash and forgot to get a receipt.

When you get back to your home office later that afternoon don't concern yourself whether the lunch is a business deduction or not (it is) but remember that as an indie power thinker using the Most Simple System you must have backup for all your expenses. So take one of those scraps of paper that you have in small piles ready for just such occasions and write on it – today's date, the name of your business associate, the amount of lunch including tip, and the reason for the lunch.

---

> ### 6/14/13 with Celia Ceramist
>
> lunch --  33.00 w/tip
>
> suggest printer re Pecos Postcards

Victor can throw that handwritten receipt into his cash receipts container. For now he's finished with it.

Just remember: If you forgot to get a receipt, make one. Get a scrap of paper and write down the important information: Date; Description; Amount.

---

### Reality √ Check

Celia Ceramist returned to her studio equally late, with just enough time to get the tiles ready for the kiln. She had taken the bus across town to buy supplies before meeting you for lunch. Now, while cleaning up in the studio, she remembered having no bus fare receipts. So on a scrap of paper she wrote the date, the destination and the fare. She threw the note in the big urn that she keeps conveniently on the floor near the door to the studio.

Celia probably would not have written down this expense if first she had to clean her gummy hands and then get a ledger book from her desk located on the studio second floor; nor enter it into her digital bookkeeping program on her computer, also on the second floor.

---

> ### 6/14/13
>
> **business errands & lunch w/ Victor Visual**
>
> **bus $8.00**

## Online Purchases

I prefer shopping late at night, online. I am sure that many of you do, as well. Whether you make those purchases using your credit card, an eCheck, or your online merchant account, get a receipt. That means print out something that says what you bought and how much you paid and when. An added precaution when ordering online: Put that printout in a "Waiting" bin. Leave it there until you receive the merchandise you ordered. An order of supplies may arrive from Office Arsenal in 5 different deliveries. By checking off items as received you can readily be aware of a shipping department mess-up because of a back-order or sleepy clerk.

If you are a black belt in online recordkeeping then backup, backup, backup. I won't tell you the horror stories of client crashes over the years. They are too upsetting.

## Estimated Expenses

If you lack receipts but can show that you do a 100-customer mailing three times a year may you estimate the POSTAGE cost and deduct the expense? Yes, you may.

Allowing estimated expenses is a concession that was wrung out of the IRS many years ago, and it's called the Cohan rule. It's named after a man well-known not only in Broadway history but tax history as well: George M. Cohan, the famous songwriter-playwright and all-around Yankee Doodle Dandy.

In the 1920s Cohan appealed an IRS ruling disallowing his travel and entertainment expenses because he couldn't document any of them. The appeals court decided in his favor, stating that absolute certainty of expense figures was not necessary. In 1963 a court case ruled that BUSINESS GIFTS and MEALS & ENTERTAINMENT expenses must be backed up (as I noted in PART II) but the Cohan rule still applies in other categories.

If an indie power mindset becomes your habitual perspective, and you use the knowledge you have acquired here, you are well on your way to taking advantage of every deduction available and becoming a confident indie.

## TO SUM UP EXPENSE RECORDKEEPING BASICS

- Use one checking account. A business account is not necessary.
- Get some sort of backup in return for every dollar spent.
- Until you have developed your own recordkeeping system be sure to set up catch-all folders or containers for:
    - o Check backup
    - o Credit card receipts
    - o Cash expense receipts
    - o Online purchase printouts

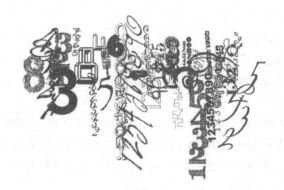

# PART V: TAXES

Real estate tax, payroll tax, sales tax, excise tax, city tax, federal and state income tax, personal property tax, fuel tax, breathing tax, luxury tax – only kidding, there's no tax on breathing. It may be a slight comfort for you as a highly-taxed citizen to know that the self-employed pay the same taxes as everyone else. And just as with W-2 people, an indie's tax liability varies due to amount of income and deductions, and local and state tax laws. In **PART V** we are going to look at taxes from the perspective of the self-employed.

---

**WHATTA CONCEPT!**
**Tax Liability**

Tax liability is the total tax assessed on a tax return for the year – not what is paid in, not what is owed, nor what is refunded. It's the important number: The sum of income tax plus self-employment tax that is paid or will be paid on the year's income.

Other taxes such as payroll tax for a domestic employee (e.g. nanny, housekeeper), penalty on early withdrawal of pension funds, may add to overall tax liability .

---

# CHAPTER 23: YOUR FAIR SHARE
## A Simple Explanation of Taxes

"How do I pay estimated taxes?" is usually the first question on the lips of a self-employed. And it's almost always asked before he has any idea of what estimated taxes are. So before I explain how to calculate the amount of an estimated tax payment and when and where to send it I want to give you a basic orientation on the taxes that a self-employed pays.

**Estimated tax payments** are payments you make to the government. The amount of the payment is based on the tax liability you expect to have for the year. That tax liability is based on your projected, or estimated, income.

Estimated payments to the IRS cover two taxes: Income tax and self-employment tax. You can be liable for one but not the other, because – as you read in previous chapters – each tax is based on different criteria.

- Income tax is based upon taxable income.
- Self-employment tax (SE tax) is based upon net self-employed earnings and is the self-employed's combined Social Security tax and Medicare tax. It corresponds to an employee's FICA and Medicare withholdings.

Which brings us back to the confusion that Woody Awlwood exhibited in CHAPTER 16, page 170. Remember? He didn't get it when his tax preparer informed him that his income tax was zero, but he still had to send $1,239 to the feds.

Woody did not understand the difference between income tax and self-employment tax. He owed taxes because on his net self-employed income of $30,000 his SE tax was $4,239 and he had paid only $3,000 in estimated taxes.

In the next few pages I will explain the difference between income tax and self-employment tax and things like who must file, filing status, tax bracket and marginal tax rate. Don't get hung up on the terms; this is intended solely as a basic, fundamental explanation that will be useful to your general understanding of an indie's taxes.

## UNDERSTANDING INCOME TAX

As you learned in PART III, there are various kinds of income – stock sale gains are one kind, for example, and payment for jury duty another. Most kinds of income are taxable – that is, subject to income tax. Some income, however, is not taxable – like municipal bond interest. And some income is sometimes or partially taxable, for example, Social Security payments received.

Just because income is *subject to tax* doesn't necessarily mean you will end up paying tax on it. You pay income tax on taxable income and many items can reduce it.

Let's take a look at Aunt Ada, the quilter from CHAPTER 3 whose hobby was supported by her investment income:

CHAPTER 23: YOUR FAIR SHARE:

| Investment income | $ 30,000. |
| Deductible medical expenses | ( 10,200. ) |
| Property tax | ( 6,000. ) |
| Charitable contributions | ( 10,000 ) |
| One exemption | ( 3,800 ) |
| Taxable income | -0-. |

Aunt Ada has zero taxable income. She has no income tax liability.

## Who must file a tax return?

Since Aunt Ada had no taxable income did she still have to file a tax return? Yes.

If your gross income – that's all income subject to income tax before taking any deductions – is more than a specified minimum, then you must file a return. However, just because you must file a tax return does not mean that you will have any tax liability. You may have enough deductions – as did Ada – to completely wipe out taxable income.

**Filing status** (for example, single or married-filing-jointly) and **gross income** determine whether you must file a tax return. At this writing the amounts for 2012 were not available. You can expect a slight change from 2011. For instance, in 2011, a single person, under 65, and not self-employed, must file a return if his gross income is at least $9,500. A husband and wife, neither self-employed, both under 65, are not required to file unless gross income reached $19,000. The threshold amount creeps a little higher each year.

Aunt Ada's gross income – subject to tax – was $30,000. Therefore, she had to file a tax return.

In the determination above on when you must file I excluded the self-employed. I'll explain why I did that in just a bit. I also want you to be aware that the gross income in the above explanation is not the gross self-employed income of an indie's business but rather all income of the taxpayer (and his spouse) that is subject to tax.

## What's a tax bracket?

As taxable income increases so does the federal income tax rate. The rate at which you end up is called your **tax bracket**. Another term for tax bracket is **marginal tax rate**. They both mean the percentage at which your next dollar of income is taxed. If you're in a 15% tax bracket, for instance, on the next $100 of taxable income you will pay $15 in income tax. If in a 28% bracket, then $28 of the next $100 taxable income will go to the feds.

Gross income determines if you must file. Then filing status and taxable income determine the rate at which tax is paid. For instance, in 2012, a single person would be taxed at a 10% rate from one dollar taxable income through $8,700. Then the rate increases to 15%.

Advancing to a higher tax bracket does not mean that all your taxable income is taxed at the higher rate. It means that any income from that point on is taxed at that rate. So, if Siegfried Single has $48,400 in taxable income this is how it works:

| The first | $ 8,700 ...... is taxed at 10% | = $   870. |
| Then | $26,650 ...... is taxed at 15% | = $ 3,998. |
| Then | $13,050 ...... is taxed at 25% | = $ 3,263. |
| | | |
| Total Income: | $48,400        Total tax: | = $ 8,131. |

Siegfried is in a 25% tax bracket. That is his marginal tax rate.

---

**ALERT!**
Complex tax rules can alter your marginal tax rate. If you are considering a financial move in which your tax bracket is an important factor, check with your tax pro before making any decision.

---

Here's another term for you: **The effective tax rate**. Think of it as the real tax rate. In the Siegfried Single example above, a total of $8,131 tax was paid on a taxable income of $48,400.00. If we divide the tax by the taxable income we get:

$$\$8,131 \div \$48,400 = 16.8\%,$$

or a little more than 16%.

Although Siegfried was in the 25% tax bracket, his effective tax rate was about 16% of his taxable income. The effective tax rate is somewhere between the tax bracket you are at and the previous lower rate. It is the percentage of your taxable income that goes to the federal government for income tax.

***There's more than one income tax!*** All but a few states, and some cities as well, impose an income tax. Some tax at a flat rate, some at a progressive rate similar to the way the fed does it. If you have self-employed income you may need to pay estimated taxes to your state to cover state income tax and sometimes city income tax. Check with your tax pro and your state.

## UNDERSTANDING SELF-EMPLOYMENT TAX

While income tax is paid on any kind of taxable income, self-employment tax is paid only by people who work for themselves. It is the Social Security and Medicare tax for the self-employed and is paid on an indie's net earnings.

I have already told you about net profit, but not about net earnings. And, as you have been warned before, the IRS is disposed to set up similar-sounding names for similar – but not identical – kinds of income. Net profit is what you have left after subtracting all business expenses from your gross receipts. Net earnings are a portion of net profit and are tabulated according to the following formula:

Net Profit times 92.35% = Net Earnings

The reason for that peculiar percentage is not important. What is important for you to know is that you must pay self-employment tax if net earnings from self-employment are $400 or more. The other way to look at it: You must pay SE tax if your net profit is $433 or more. Here's the arithmetic:

$433 Net Profit times .9235 = $400 Net Earnings

---

### Reality √ Check

In 2011 Agua Fresh, a single guy, grossed $3,532 cleaning pools his first summer in business. He had $3,100 in expenses. Therefore, his net profit was $432. Since $432 is less than $433 he does not have to pay SE tax. And since his gross income is less than $9,500 he does not have to file a tax return.

---

You know that filing status and gross income determine who must file, but now we have another must-file criteria: ***Regardless of income, if you are subject to SE tax then you must file a tax return.***

---

### Reality √ Check

Fred Fixit, who lives with his parents and has no income, decides it's time to earn a living. He starts his repair business on December 28th. He does one repair job for the family across the street. He's paid $450, he has no expenses. Yes, he has to pay SE tax and so he must file a return even though he is single and his only income is from that one repair job.

---

### WHATTA CONCEPT!
### Watch Your Decimal Point

• Just in case your memory about decimals has faded, here's a refresher.

• One dollar is made up of 100 cents. 100 cents is 100% of a dollar

• A dime – 10¢ cents – is 10% of a dollar. We could also write it as .10 or 10/100 or 1/10.

• If you cut a penny in half and have 10 and one–half pennies you'd have 10 ½ ¢ or 10.5% of a dollar or .105 of a dollar.

• When a percent sign ( %) is used, the decimal point is moved two digits to the right: .9235 is the same as 92.35%.

• An inventor who claims to have received a six-figure payout for his car-waxing machine may be running out to buy a Porsche or a Hyundai depending on the placement of the decimal point. Did he receive $900,000.00 or $9,000.00?

---

My own personal decimal story goes like this: When I ventured to buy back my previous book from the publisher, the publisher's attorney said the company had a six-figure payment in mind. I promptly replied: Which side of the decimal point are those figures? He didn't think that was funny. I did.

## The Basics of Self-employment Tax

- SE tax kicks in if net profit from self-employed income is $433 or more. You must file a tax return if your net profit is $433 or more no matter how much or how little all your other income; no matter how young or old you are; no matter if you're collecting Social Security or in grammar school; no matter if married or single.

  - In case you missed it: yes, you must pay SE tax even if you are an elder statesman collecting Social Security and have income from business consulting, You also must pay SE tax if you are a kid burning CDs and selling them to fellow students.

- SE tax is paid on 92.35% of all net profit.

- Typically, the SE tax rate is 15.3% and is made up of two components: 12.4% Social Security tax plus 2.9% Medicare tax. Social Security benefits are available to self-employed persons just as they are to wage earners. Your payments of SE tax contribute to your coverage under the Social Security system which provides you with retirement, disability, and survivor benefits. Medicare coverage provides hospital insurance benefits.

  - There is, however, a small tax break currently – for 2012 – on the books. The SE tax is split so that half is paid by the employer and half is paid by employee. At this writing, the employee's share of Social Security has been reduced from 6.2% to 4.2%.

- Many indies confuse Social Security payments and unemployment compensation. Employees receive coverage for both benefits. If a W-2 person has worked for a certain amount of time and leaves work under certain conditions he can receive payments while not working. This is called **unemployment compensation** and it is taxable income. ***The self-employed do not receive unemployment compensation.***

- Payments toward the Social Security tax portion of SE tax stop when earned income reaches a specified amount, called the **taxable wage base**. In 2012, for employer, employee, or a self-employed, the cutoff is $110,100. That means if ***any combination*** of Social Security wages, tip income, or net earnings from self-employment reach $110,100, no more Social Security tax must be paid. The cutoff point rises a little every year.

- If as a salaried employee you earned $110,100 in 2012 and you had a sole proprietorship as well, you would not have to pay any of the Social Security tax portion of SE tax no matter how high your net earnings from self-employment because you had already paid the maximum..

- If your net earnings from self-employment or your salary or a combination of both were $110,100 *you would pay the same amount of Social Security tax as your neighbor who earned five zillion dollars.*

- All earned income is subject to the 2.9% Medicare tax. There is no limit. You and your high-earner neighbor will pay very different amounts of Medicare tax.

- Typically, an employee pays one half of his Social Security and Medicare tax and his employer pays the other half. As a self-employed you pay both the employer's share and the employee's share of Social Security and Medicare taxes.

- You pay both shares and you get to deduct your share. The deduction is taken as an adjustment to income on the front of your tax return, in the same section as self-employed health insurance premiums and your pension contribution. It reduces only income tax. It is not a deduction against net earnings from self-employment.

- The amount of Social Security you receive in your golden years is based upon your earnings over a lifetime. The Social Security Administration gets its figures on earnings from your tax return. If you've shown little or no income over the years you will receive little or no Social Security when you get old. That's what happens to all the under-the-table housekeepers and nannies. No Social Security when the arthritis sets in and they can't work anymore.

## INCOME TAX PLUS SE TAX EQUALS A LOT OF TAX!

Here's an eye-opener on a solo's tax liabilities:

A $10,000 net profit for a self-employed at a 15% tax bracket means that $1,500 would go for federal income tax and another approximately $1,500 for SE tax. Add them up: 15% + 15% = 30%. Depending upon state and city, the indie may owe another 5% to 15% or $500 to $1,500 for state and city income taxes. That could bring the total up to 45% of net profit going toward taxes, or approximately $4,500 of every $10,000 net income. And remember, 15% is one of the lower tax brackets. For some the government takes a bigger bite – how about at a 35% federal rate! That would change the above total income going for taxes to 65% (35% + 15% + 15%).

## Reality √ Check

Kristin Knockoff received a $12,000 fee for her design work. With expenses of $2,000, she came out with a profit of $10,000. Whoopdeedoo! But Kristin shouldn't start partying just yet. Other income on her return brings her to the 28% federal tax bracket, and she lives in New York with a state income tax of 7%. Kristin also has a pension plan that allows her to put away 20% of her net profit. With all these considerations, see below for just how much she has left for partying.

| | |
|---|---|
| Consultation fee (gross SE income) | $ 12,000. |
| Business expenses | ( 2,000 ) |
| Net profit | $ 10,000 |
| 28% Income tax | ( 2,800 ) |
| 15% SE tax | ( 1,500 ) |
| 7% NY state income tax | ( 700 ) |
| 20% of net for pension contribution | ( 2,000 ) |
| Remainder for other spending | $ 3,000. |

Kristin gets to spend only $3,000 of her $10,000 net profit. That's just 30% left after 70% is allotted for taxes and pension contribution.

It is important for indies to understand the relationship of gross income to what they really have on hand for household expenses, vacations, new cars, and kids' shoes.

## THE FLIP SIDE: DEDUCTIONS REDUCE HIGH TAXES

High taxes emphasize the importance of deductions. As I just showed you, being in the 15% tax bracket can result in 30% of your profits going to the feds for taxes. The flip side, a $1,000 business expense decreases your taxes by $300; expenses of $10,000 drop your taxes by $3,000.

A deductible business expense of $10,000 that saves $3,000 in taxes means that a $10,000 purchase reduces your cash flow by only $7,000. Yes, $10,000 is going out for the expense, but $3,000 is **not** going out for taxes. A business trip that costs $5,000 will save $1,500 in taxes, bringing the real cost of the trip to $3,500 ($5,000 minus $1,500).

---

### Reality √ Check

A few days after Christmas, with New Year staring him in the face. What could Ivan Inventor do to save some tax money? Luisa Lifecoach told him to go out and buy that $1,000 scanner he needed. But Ivan had no money until the end of January when he is to receive the big royalty check for his latest Digital Gizmo. Luisa told him to charge the scanner to his BigBank VISA. He could write it off this year. He'd save three hundred tax dollars (30% times $1,000) and he needn't pay anything toward the $1,000 expense until the following year when the January credit card bill arrives.

---

### ALERT!

Even though a business expense can save you 30% to 65% in taxes – depending upon your tax bracket and state and city tax rates – never spend just to save taxes. It is not a dollar-for-dollar write-off. In other words: A $1,000 business deduction does not save you $1,000 in taxes. It saves you less than that. How much less depends on your combined federal, state and city taxes.

---

## OTHER TYPES OF TAXES

Federal, state and some city income taxes and self-employment tax are paid via estimated tax payments (to be explained in the next chapter). There are other taxes of special importance to the self-employed.

---

### ALERT!

If your city or state requires you to charge sales or gross receipts tax you must collect the tax from your customers and forward it to the appropriate government agency. That collected tax was never your money. You collected the tax for the government. Therefore if you don't send it in on time, you're in big trouble. The same holds for employment taxes that you have withheld from your employees. It's the government's money, not yours. Think of holding on to it beyond the deadline as stealing money from the government. Not good.

---

As I noted in CHAPTER 5, federal excise taxes are imposed on items such as guns, tobacco and alcohol or their ingredients, fishing rods and arrows of a certain length or their components, as well as fuel and certain vehicles. If, in your self-employed business, you sell or lease products you need to check with your tax professional as to whether you need to pay excise taxes.

Every state, county, and municipality has its own tax requirements. Get to know the local requirements. Messing up can be costly. Ask questions. Then ask the same questions again in a different way. Compare the answers. Do they make sense? If not get more information.

# 24

## CHAPTER 24: ESTIMATED TAX PAYMENTS
### Who Must Pay. How Much to Pay. When and How to Pay.

Federal income tax, Social Security tax and Medicare tax are pay-as-you-go taxes; that is, the tax must be paid as income is earned. Dennis Dubya-two, shipping clerk for Toys 'n' Things, receives a paycheck every week. Each week Toys 'n' Things withholds all applicable taxes from Dennis' pay and forwards them to various government agencies. At the end of the year Dennis receives a W-2 which shows income earned and taxes paid.

The self-employed must follow the same pay-as-you-go method as do wage earners like Dennis. As an entrepreneur brings in income he withholds taxes from himself – that is, he puts money aside – and then sends his taxes to the government via estimated tax payments.

***Not every self-employed has to make estimated tax payments.*** Your indie cousin brags that he never has to make estimated payments. Why is that? Because it is the overall tax liability of a self-employed that determines whether estimated tax payments are required and there's a good chance that Cuz is not required to make any payments because of his other financial circumstances.

An indie's total tax liability is made up of SE tax on his net earnings and income tax on all his and his spouse's income as well as any other taxes due with his federal tax return. SE tax and income tax on net profit or loss are not necessarily the only factors in calculating estimated tax payments. If, for instance, you had self-employed business income of $10,000 and also had investment dividends of $30,000, both these sources of income (totaling $40,000) would be elements in your estimated tax calculation. And if your wife earned $90,000 at her W-2 job, the taxes withheld from her income would also be a factor in those calculations.

Because someone is self-employed doesn't necessarily mean that he must make estimated tax payments. Consider the following situations:
- When all income and deductions are combined, there is no tax liability.

- Enough tax may be withheld via a W-2 job to cover the entire tax liability. (In order to avoid making estimated tax payments you may choose to increase tax withholdings at yours or your spouse's W-2 job. To do this, request an additional sum be withheld every paycheck. You may have to complete a Form W-4[18] for the employer.)
- Enough taxes may be withheld from pension withdrawals to cover the entire tax liability.
- The previous year's tax refund may be carried forward in a sufficient amount to eliminate the need for estimated payments.

## WHO MUST MAKE ESTIMATED TAX PAYMENTS

Although there are exceptions, here's the safe and simple rule: **You must make estimated tax payments to the federal government if you had a tax liability for the previous year and you expect to owe tax of $1,000 or more when you file your tax return.**

You may want to read that again. It says "owe" $1,000 when you file your tax return; it does not say have a "tax liability" of $1,000. For a refresher, check page 219 on the meaning of tax liability.

The IRS says it doesn't want anyone to pay more than his fair share of taxes. And you want to make sure that when you pay your fair share you do so at the last possible moment, keeping your hands on your money for as long as possible while at the same time avoiding any interest or penalty fees.

There are three approaches to paying estimated taxes. At tax filing time, you can:
- Break even.
- Owe something to the government.
- Get a refund from the government.

Breaking even is smart. Owing something to the government is even smarter, if it can be done without paying interest or penalties. The third approach, paying so that you get a refund, is dumb, dumb, dumb.

# FOUR METHODS OF CALCULATING ESTIMATED TAX PAYMENTS

## 1. Prior Year Method
*Pay this year what your tax liability was last year.*

This is the easiest calculation and the safest if your income increases every year. Whatever your total tax was last year, divide that amount by four and make four payments to the United States Treasury.

For instance, if last year's tax was $8,000 then make sure you pay at least $8,000 this year. If neither you nor your spouse have federal income tax withheld from jobs or pension payments, you should make four payments of $2,000 each. If you had a part-time job and $1,000 federal income tax was withheld (do not include FICA or Medicare taxes withheld), and $500 of the previous year's refund was carried forward to this year, your calculation would be as follows:

| | |
|---|---|
| Payment required for this year | $ 8,000. |
| Less withheld | ( 1,000.) |
| | ———— |
| Balance to pay | $ 7,000. |
| Divided by four | $ 1,750.  Per payment |
| Less carry forward subtracted from 1st payment | (   500. ) |
| | ———— |
| Payment 1: | $ 1,250. |
| Payments 2, 3 and 4 | $ 1,750.  Each |

If your federal tax for this year came in higher than $8,000, using the prior year method, you do not owe any interest or penalty on the balance owed as long as it is paid by April 15!

High rollers beware! The above method applies to an adjusted gross income (AGI) of up to $150,000. If your AGI exceeds $150,000 instead of paying 100% of last year's tax you must pay 110%. If married filing separately, the 110% applies to those with an AGI over $75,000.

---

**WHATTA CONCEPT!**
**Adjusted Gross Income – AGI**

**Adjusted Gross Income** (AGI) is the amount of total income subject to tax, minus various deductions called **Adjustments to Income.**

**Adjustments to Income** include deductions such as IRA or self-employed pension contributions, one-half of self-employment tax, and alimony payments.

Your **AGI** is the amount on the last line of the first page of the tax return, Form 1040.

It is from Adjusted Gross Income that personal itemized deductions and exemption amounts are subtracted in order to arrive at taxable income.

---

The prior year method – called a "safe harbor" by the IRS – is easy and avoids interest and penalties for an indie with a rising annual income. The IRS uses the term **safe harbor** – a place where harm cannot befall a vessel – to mean that although a taxpayer can choose several alternatives, no penalty will ensue if the safe harbor alternative is followed.

Once again, to be clear: If you use Method 1, Prior Year Calculation, no matter how much tax you owe come April 15 you will not have to pay any penalty or interest.

## 2. Current Year Method
*Pay 90% of this year's tax.*

If you expect this year's income to be less than last year's, your tax will probably be less. (I say probably because factors other than income play into the calculation. Be careful.) In this method you pay the feds 90% of this year's tax in four equal installments.

Typically, your tax preparer will set up estimated payments for you at the time she prepares your previous year's return. If your crystal ball tells you that your income will decrease this year, let her know so that she can calculate your payments.

The drawback of this method: Your income projections for the remainder of the year have to be accurate. For many solo operators that's a hard trick. If you send in less than 90% of your taxes and you owe $1,000 or more you are liable for interest and penalty.

### 3. Annualization Method
*Pay according to taxable income earned each quarter.*

This is the most complicated method and the most time-consuming – for both you and your preparer. It requires several tax reviews over the course of the year.

In this method your taxable income is calculated to determine the amount of tax liability for each quarter of this year. It's like doing your tax return four times a year.

If you plan to use this method to calculate your estimated payments, discuss the procedure with your tax pro.

So why would you even consider Method 3? Because in rare instances, if your income is very high or very irregular, it could work to your cash flow advantage. I'm talking about the computer games developer who had a really good previous year – net income of almost $300,000. Didn't know what this year would bring. Made no money right through the summer then on Halloween he sold his patent for a payment of $190,000. That was his only business income all year. Since he is not required to pay taxes on income before it's received, putting off the tax payment on this income was to his advantage.

### 4. Government As Savings Bank Method
*The least savvy – aka dumbest – method.*

The next time Friend Freddy tells you that Sammy Segar is a great accountant because every year he gets Freddy a big refund, ask him this: "Are you sure CPA Segar doesn't work for Uncle Sam part-time? Why else would he set you up so that you loan your money to the IRS for a whole year – interest-free?"

How so? If you get a $1,000 refund from the government at the end of the year that means that your money was sitting in the IRS bank earning interest for Uncle Sam. If it earned 5% that's $50 in the fed's pocket not yours. And, to rub salt in the wound, let's say you had a $1,000 balance on your credit card all year that you didn't pay off because the IRS had your $1,000. At 18% that cost you $180 in finance charges. The IRS made $50 on your money, while you lost $180. So much for Sammy Segar's big refund.

I know, lots of folks like getting a tax refund, saying it's the only way they can save money. I say, get it together and quit throwing money away. Whether through withholding or estimated taxes, if you are paying so much to the government that you get a sizeable refund, then change your ways. If you or your spouse have a W-2 job then reduce your withholding at work and have the difference automatically deposited into your own special savings account. Or, cut back on your estimated tax payment and when writing out the estimated checks to the government, write one to your savings account.

> ### ALERT!
> There is now additional incentive to avoid a refund situation. With the rise of eFiling there is more and more identity theft. The IRS is holding up refunds, typically for 75 days, if there is any question about the taxpayer's legitimate identity.
> Therefore if Gary Geekery filed and requested his $2,000 refund, and another Gary Geekery (yes, there are two guys with that name) made the same request and there were some confusion, then the refund is on hold until identity can be verified. So much for Gary's summer vacation plans. No refund means he heads to the beach in the fall.

## All Methods

The smartest way to pay estimated taxes is to send the government as little as possible as late as possible, using one of the above methods.

No matter what the method, remember to look at total tax liability – not just self-employed income. And be sure to take into consideration any tax paid through withholding at a job or via other payments to you.

> ### ALERT!
> If you must make estimated tax payments and you have a household employee, you need to include any employment taxes for your domestic employee when figuring your estimated tax.

# WHEN TO PAY ESTIMATED TAXES

Under most circumstances you will make four estimated tax payments to the IRS and also possibly to your resident state and, if you earn self-employed income elsewhere, to a non-resident state as well. The methods used to calculate the IRS estimated payment amount usually apply in the same way to the states – but to be sure you ought to confirm this with your tax preparer or state tax office.

The following chart shows the dates for making estimated payments.

| WHEN TO PAY:  ESTIMATED TAX PAYMENT DUE DATES | |
|---|---|
| **For The Period** | **Due Date** |
| January 1 through March 31 | April 15 |
| April 1 through May 31 | June 15 |
| June 1 through August 31 | September 15 |
| September 1 through December 31 | January 15 the following year |

It is not a crisis if you're late on a payment due date. Depending on the amount of tax payment, an interest and/or penalty amount will be calculated at the time your tax return is prepared. The IRS rate is lower than most credit card finance charge rates. There's more information on penalties and interest in the next chapter.

## HOW TO PAY

There are several ways to pay estimated taxes.

### Carry Forward A Previous Year Overpayment

When you file your tax return, if you have an overpayment of tax you can choose to have the refund returned to you or you can apply part or all of it to your estimated tax for the following year.

The amount you have carried forward as payment toward the following year should be taken into account when figuring your estimated payments. You can use all the carry-forward amount toward your first payment, or you can spread it out in any way you choose among any or all of your payments. If you find the January 15 payment difficult because of holiday spending then use your carry-forward to ease your cash flow and have it applied to the fourth payment.

## Pay by Check

Use Form 1040-ES, Payment Voucher, to pay federal estimated tax. There are four numbered vouchers. Include one with each payment by check.

Be sure the voucher is filled in accurately. If you are married then put the names and Social Security numbers in the same order as they appear on your tax return.

Make the check or money order payable to the "United States Treasury." On the check or money order write your Social Security number and, if payment is for 2013, "2013 Form 1040-ES." Don't staple or clip the check to the voucher.

Most indies have their estimated tax payments set up for the next year when they have their tax returns prepared. If not, find estimated vouchers at www.irs.gov/. Search for Form 1040-ES.

---

### ALERT!
Never send a payment to the IRS (or any government agency) without the correct document, properly filled out, accompanying it.

---

## Pay by Credit Card, Electronic Payment, Or Withdrawal

Be careful if you pay your estimateds, or any other tax, by credit card. To pay by this method you must use a service provider who charges a fee. And your credit card company will treat it as a cash advance. WOW! That'll be a huge finance charge. The options for credit card and electronic tax payments or funds withdrawal are changing rapidly. You can get the most current information on electronic payments at the IRS website, www.irs.gov/uac/Electronic-Payment-Options-Home-Page.

# 25

## CHAPTER 25: WHAT DADDY'S ACCOUNTANT FORGOT TO TELL YOU ABOUT TAXES
### Hiding Behind The Tax Code

Let's look at why paying penalties to the IRS should be avoided, but paying interest – well, that's not the end of the world. And if you need or want some extra time to file your tax return, an extension is not only easy, it may be to your advantage.

## PENALTIES AND INTEREST

If you do something wrong, the IRS can't flog or pummel you, but it can hit you with penalties and interest. Unless you've done something fraudulent or have not paid a lot of owed tax for a very long time, the penalty and interest charges, although they can add up, are not going to send you into shock.

For instance, late payment penalty is ½ of 1% per month (.005). That's 6% per year. If you were 3 months late with a $2,000 estimated payment the penalty would be a little more than $30 ($2,000 times .005 times 3 months) .

If you do not file your tax return it can be costly. A failure-to-file penalty is higher than a failure-to-pay penalty, usually 5% per month of the unpaid tax, up to 25%. If you didn't file, and you owed $2,000 in taxes your failure-to-file penalty could be $500.

More on penalties and interest:
- Interest on balance due: Rate changes every three months.
- If you file your return more than 60 days after the due date or extended due date, the minimum penalty is the smaller of $135 or 100% of your unpaid taxes.
- Penalty for a frivolous return: $500
- Accuracy-related penalty: 20% of the underpayment.
- Fraud? We're not even going there. For starters you're looking at 75% of the unpaid tax added as penalty to the tax owed.
- And the list goes on …

In this chapter I'll cover only those few penalties and interest assessments that would most likely affect a solo entrepreneur.

## Beg or borrow?

With the seemingly never-ending list of penalty and interest that can be imposed upon you, deciding whether you should beg or borrow the money to pay the government rather than make some other arrangement depends on what kind of tax you owe to which government.

State or city sales or gross receipts tax that you collect – as I've said before – is not your money. It is the government's money that you are holding. The same is true if you have employees. Any payroll tax that you withhold from their pay is not your money. It belongs to the government. You are the government's collecting instrument and you must pass the collected tax on to the government on specific due dates. If you don't hand it over you have in effect stolen the government's money. On these taxes, yes, you beg or borrow to get them paid. If you have employees, there is no out for not paying payroll taxes. You must pay them. If you haven't paid them then hire a tax attorney. Pronto.

On the other hand, tax that is paid via estimated payments – income tax and SE tax – is your money that you owe to the government. If you can't make a timely payment you will be charged some interest and some penalty. No need to go to pieces. You'll see below how the costs are calculated. But first, let's look at the most reliable and least stressful way to prepare for estimated payments.

You saw in CHAPTER 23 on page 226 that for an indie a combination of federal income tax, SE tax, and state income tax can typically add up to about 40% of net income. That means when you get a check from a client 40% of the after-expense amount is not yours to spend. It must be earmarked for taxes. A simple method is to ballpark an expense amount against that income, then sock away 40% of what's left. If you think it's hard to do when you get the check that's nothing compared to how difficult it will be three months later when your estimated tax payment is due.

The 40% figure is of course an estimate. You may be in a higher tax bracket or have so many personal deductions that you have no income tax liability, or you may live in a state with no state income tax. However, 40% is a good starting point.

And just how do you sock away 40%? That depends on you. Some of us are so disciplined about money that just telling ourselves not to spend it is enough, while others must actually remove the money from sight. There is no good or bad way. There is only a way that works or a way that doesn't work – for you. If you want to open a separate bank account and call it the "not-my-money" account, or the "TAX" account, that's fine. When you get a check from a client deposit the entire check into your checking account, then immediately write a check to yourself and deposit it into the TAX account. Or if you get lots of small payments from customers deposit them all and then at the end of the week, or end of the month, make your TAX account deposit. Your TAX account could be a checking account, savings, money market – doesn't matter. But don't put it into an account in someone else's name. One indie thought the safest course was putting his tax money into his domestic partner's account. Safe maybe but not good in the eyes of the IRS. No straight audit trail there.

As you read in CHAPTER 24 there are different ways to calculate estimated tax payments. The money you have put aside most likely will not match the amount of estimated tax payment due. If you find you are putting aside a lot less or a lot more than is required for your estimated payment discuss it with your tax preparer. Keep in mind that if you're using Method 1, Prior Year Calculation then your payments reflect last year's income not the current year income. Even if you do not need to send as an estimated payment all the money you have put aside for taxes, don't spend it, it may be due come April 15.

As I said at the beginning of this chapter, the when and why of IRS interest and penalty charges can be very complicated so I'm going to give you only the basics.

### Interest on Balance Due: Rate Changes Every Three Months
If all taxes due are not paid by April 15, then in addition to the 6% per year late payment penalty, there is interest charged on the tax owed and on the late payment penalty that is owed.

The interest rate changes every three months. Figure it to be pretty close to a typical home equity loan rate.

What if you just don't have the money to pay your taxes on time?

You will see from the numbers below that being late or missing an estimated payment is not the end of the world. It costs you money. Depending upon how much you owe and how late you are it could cost you a lot of money. Plan ahead so that you don't get bogged in a financial quagmire – paying last year's tax this year, and then this year's gets paid next year. However if you need a month or two because of cash flow problems it doesn't mean the swamp monster is around the corner.

---

**Reality √ Check**

Stella Sellit received payment from Cool Cooking magazine in May. However, because she had to pay for brochure printing for another client, Total Foods, she could not pay her second estimated tax payment due June 15. She paid for the printing and then when Total Foods paid her in July she paid her second estimated one month late. If her payment were $5,000 the penalty would be $5,000 times .005, which equals $25. The interest charged, if at a 4% rate would be $5,000 times 1/12 of 4%, which equals about $17. Her total penalty and interest for the one month late payment would be about $42.

---

**ALERT!**

Don't file your return late. If you do, in addition to any other penalties and interest, you could also be hit with a late filing penalty: (See below for how to file for an extension.)

---

**Death or Destruction in Your Life:** The IRS will waive penalties for failure to file tax returns and for failure to pay tax if the failure is due to reasonable cause and not willful neglect. Death, illness, divorce, fire, theft are reasonable causes. Talk to your tax pro if any of these kinds of events prevented your paying or filing on time.

## TAX RETURN EXTENSIONS

Tax returns are due April 15. There's an automatic extension that gives you until October 15 to file.

An extension of time to file your return is just that – more time to file your return, **not more time to pay your taxes**. Taxes are due by April 15. To get an extension you must file Form 4868: Application for Automatic Extension[19] of Time by April 15. You may paper file or electronically file. You will then have until October 15 to file your return. On the extension you need to write your total tax liability for the year, then subtract how much you've paid already. If there is a balance due, pay it if you can. If you can't, you are now aware of the penalties and interest that could be assessed.

Yes, I said write in your total tax liability. Well, what if the midnight hour of April 15 fast approaches and your tax preparer is not returning your calls? How do you figure out your total tax? Do this:

Use last year as your guide. If your income is higher than last year your tax will most likely be higher. If expenses are less – didn't buy another $5,000 computer – then your net income will be higher and so will your taxes. Be conservative in your calculations. Estimate your income higher than you think and your expenses lower. Come up with a net income. Compare it to last year and use a simple proportion to figure your tax. Income 25% bigger, means your tax will be at least 25% higher than last year.

***Here comes a homemade safe harbor***. Both your extension for last year and this year's first estimated payment are due on April 15. Instead of sending to the government two separate payments designated for different years, combine the amounts and send one payment designated for last year with your extension voucher. The amount would include whatever you expect to owe for last year plus the amount of the first estimated payment due this year.

Just in case you miscalculated last year's tax, part of what you had allocated to this year's estimated may be used for last year's tax due. Your tax pro can make adjustments in your estimateds when she completes your tax return. This way you won't be hit with penalties for last year.

You may need to file a state extension. Ignore the old husbands' tale that filing an extension sets you up for an audit. It just isn't so. If it gives you more time to collect your material, review your return, or make sure everything is as it should be, all the more reason to give yourself more time.

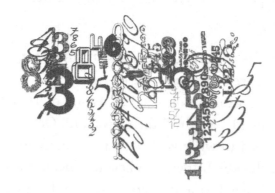

# BEYOND THE BASICS

My aim throughout this book has been to guide you through the tax and recordkeeping basics of an indie business. You will find that **THE CONFIDENT INDIE**, because it is a book of basics, does not cover all indie business financial circumstances. It does, however, provide a firm foundation for the more complex situations that will arise as your business grows and changes.

A look beyond the basics, includes topics such as: Payroll; hiring subcontractors; the often-missed opportunity that could save you a bundle of tax money by putting your helpful and competent spouse on your payroll; saving some money by employing your child while teaching him or her the ropes of your indie business; the many and varied pension plans available for an indie; and, of course, recordkeeping.

Recordkeeping is a necessity. It must be on your agenda. You need a recordkeeping system. Well, I've got one for you – actually it is a two-part system – and it's available in my companion book, **Five Easy Steps**. My method is quick, simple, money-saving, audit-proof and includes worksheets. You'll learn how to manually keep the most simple, yet accurate, records. And the twist: If you need and are ready, you can also learn how to adapt one of the many recordkeeping software programs – written for the world of employees – to the unique needs of your indie business. The system detailed in **Five Easy Steps** works whether you keep records manually, digitally, or a combination of both.

For additional resources to guide and inform you on beyond-the-basics topics and to learn more about the business side of indie life visit my website and blog and subscribe to or check out the archives of my eLetter, **Ways Through the Maze**.

And, finally...

---

**ALERT!**

I've said this earlier, but it's important enough to say again: Choose your tax professional as carefully as you would any other pro in your life. How many solos does she have as clients? Do you understand what she says? Does she treat you with respect and have an understanding of your solo business? If not, does she appear interested in learning more about it?

---

## ALERT!

I've warned you to watch out for Sammy Segar and others telling you to incorporate. Well, in the old days (Sammy's going to be 103 on his next birthday) a big reason for incorporating was that it provided the only way someone working for himself could sock away a lot of money into a pension. Sammy's still working with the old rules but those old pension laws are gone. A wide choice of pensions with tax savings opportunities are now available to the indie. If you find that you are bringing in more money than you currently need to live on be sure to talk with a savvy tax pro who can explain all the pension possibilities to you – including giving your employee-spouse a generous retirement plan.

## ALERT!

Never ignore a letter from the IRS.

Some years ago a woman who cleaned house for me showed up at my door in tears. The IRS had put a lien on her checking account. When I asked her if the IRS had contacted her earlier, she cried harder and sobbed, "under the sofa." After some coffee she explained that all the unopened letters from the feds were under her sofa. However daunting it may be you must deal with the IRS if they contact you. The longer you wait the greater will be the impact on your life.

## ALERT!

All through this book I've encouraged you to do the recordkeeping and information-gathering and let your tax professional prepare your return. But if you choose to prepare your own tax return using one of the available software tax programs, be careful! Just as the tax laws and computer bookkeeping programs are written for the W-2 world – for employees or for "small businesses"[20] (which by the way are defined as those with a gross income of millions or a good many, maybe 50, employees) – so are the tax preparation programs. I have seen them mess up office-in-the home, auto use, SE tax and a lot more. A new client, with fine-tuned solo business skills, came to me having prepared his own return using a tax preparation program. He did everything right. The program did not. After I corrected the errors made by the program he saved an additional $3,973 in federal taxes on an income of $150,012.

Tax laws change; some of the specifics in this book may change – who knows, the $25 per person per year limit on gift deductions may soar to $30 – but the general concept and your grasp of the indie power mindset as presented in this book will not change. You can use **THE CONFIDENT INDIE** as a reference book for as long as you work for yourself.

May your quest for and attainment of knowledge guide you to walk with sure-footedness and confidence through the tangled tax maze that trips up so many indie endeavors.

To each of you I wish success in your unique independent pursuit.

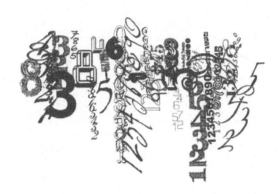

# ACKNOWLEDGEMENTS

To my clients and all fellow indies go my greatest thanks. They make me think, laugh and mutter profanities. Some are wealthy enough to be one-percenters. Others are barely making it. All of them, however, are talented, resourceful, accommodating, intelligent, and fun. An indie musician, composer, music professor, and band leader best summed up the financial situation of many artists: What's the difference between a large pizza and a musician? Answer: A large pizza can feed a family of four.

Some clients have brightened what could be a dull tax time with notes like the following (sometimes addressed to The Tax Goddess or The Tax Ayatollah). From a **New York Times** reporter: "Here is my tax material, late, naturally. I am poised between Pakistan (nuclear bombs) and Kosovo (impending genocide), business as usual … Hope all is well with you." From an artist in New York: "Once again and forever, I offer my deepest thanks to you. In a world where, as Dylan has it – even the swap-meets are pretty corrupt – you assist those in need. In need of yer bitchin advice that is! Let's rock even harder next year." Responding to a seminar I was about to give, a New Jersey psychologist suggested the following ad: "Bring me your tired, your disorganized, your jumbled indies yearning to live free. The wretched refuse of the IRS. Send them … the self-employed, to June." From an award-winning writer after tax prep turned his brains to mush and his prose to doggerel: "June, June – It's tax time soon. So what do I owe? I don't want to be slow. Try to limit the blow. I just need to know…"

That Big Brother agency IRS will not allow me to utter client names so let me say that many of mine have helped me. Some by suggesting changes to make my examples accurate to their professions, for instance, a psychologist, advised when I used psychologically inappropriate examples. Another, after reading an early draft of the chapter "How Long To Keep Records" supplied my favorite editorial comment: "You told me more about penguins than I really wanted to know." Writers walked me through several editorial quandaries. Literary agents were generous with their time and sage advice. Tech people help me wend my way through the digital maze. To all go my sincere thank you.

This book would not be in your hands or on your digital device were it not for Damian Taggart and his Mindshare Studios, http://mind.sh/are/, and his sterling information architect, Bryce Corkins. Together we forged this new path in publishing my first electronic / print-on-demand book. It was a fun hop, skip and jump along the trail and I would not have made it without them. Frances White, designer, http://franceswhitedesign.com/, who has been there for me for decades, deserves high praise. She is equally nimble with color, line, and phrase. She designed my cover and was there for me whenever I got stuck. Tim O'Brien, www.obrienillustration.com/, gets a hug for giving the confident indie the perfect look that says: I'm an indie. I'm confident. I am you.

A thank you to that indispensable friend of writers, **The Authors Guild**, www.authorsguild.org/.

Gratitude to my son, Shane Keats, whose encouragement is unflagging and whose ideas and business advice are abundant. To my son Thatcher Keats, www.thatcherkeats.com/, a much needed helpmate in this visually digital world, kudos and wonder that mother-son could work together so smoothly.

Of course, cheers to my grandchildren, Luisa Del Prete, Miles Del Prete, Lily Keats, Charlotte Keats, and Clement Keats. Perhaps each is a future indie. Clem has already advised on technical matters and helped me place my references in the 21st Century – totally.

And a flourish of trumpets and drum-roll for my husband, Warren Sloat, a writer who taught me how to write.

June Walker
Santa Fe, New Mexico
January 2013

# LINKS TO SOME SOURCES USED IN THE CONFIDENT INDIE

### June's Website
junewalkeronline.com/

### June's Blog
junewalkeronline.com/blog/

### June's eLetter Ways Through The Maze
archive.constantcontact.com/fs010/1102176382380/archive/1102256039587.html

### Five Easy Steps: How-to Guide for Manual And Digital Recordkeeping
junewalkeronline.com/learning-tools/five-easy-steps/

### For questions and commenting on The Confident Indie
junewalkeronline.com/learning-tools/confidence-comments/

1 ix **according to Technology Review**
www.technologyreview.com/news/427787/are-smart-phones-spreading-faster-than-any-technology-in-human-history/

2 ix **Small Business and Self-employed Operating Division of the IRS**
www.irs.gov/uac/Small-Business-Self-Employed-Division-At-a-Glance

3 ix **survey of 900 self-employed people by Kelly Services, Inc.**
www.crainsdetroit.com/article/20090128/FREE/901289979/25-of-u-s-workers-self-employed-kelly-services-reports#

4 3 **Form W-2**
www.irs.gov/pub/irs-pdf/fw2.pdf

5 4 **Form 1099-MISC**
http://www.irs.gov/pub/irs-pdf/f1099msc.pdf

6 8 **IRS decision followed a lawsuit which ended in a $97 million settlement**
archive.washtech.org/news/industry/display.php?ID_Content=5016

7 8 **"For those companies who haven't changed their policies, this settlement sends a message that it could be very expensive not to change."**
www.nytimes.com/2000/12/13/business/technology-temp-workers-at-microsoft-win-lawsuit.html

8 23 **on-line bag-of-tricks will fool the gullible folks at the IRS**
www.freerepublic.com/focus/f-news/604664/posts

9 23 **"you can magically turn personal expenses into tax deductions"**
www.google.com/search?q=magically+turn+personal+expenses+ into+tax+

deductions&rls=com.microsoft:en-us:IE-SearchBox&ie=UTF-8&oe=UTF-8&sourceid=ie7&rlz=1I7ADFA_enUS445

10  36  **Obtain a Federal Identification Number**
www.irs.gov/Businesses/Small-Businesses-&-Self-Employed/Apply-for-an-Employer-Identification-Number-(EIN)-Online

11  97  **(GSA) Domestic Per Diem Rates**
www. gsa.gov/portal/category/21287

12  97  **get a per diem app at the GSA website**
/www.gsa.gov/portal/category/102091

13  97  **U.S. Department of State Foreign Per Diem site**
aoprals.state.gov/web920/per_diem.asp

14 139  **The United States tax court ruled that a taxpayer running two business from one home office may deduct the expenses of that home office**
www.ustaxcourt.gov/InOpHistoric/howard-crowley.sum.WPD.pdf

15 151  **IRS Small Business and Self-employed Center**
/www.irs.gov/Businesses/Small-Businesses-&-Self-Employed

16 185  **$20,000 fine or prison or both**
www.collegemadesimple.com/false-info-fafsa/

17 201  **Form 1099-K**
www.irs.gov/pub/irs-pdf/f1099k.pdf

18 231  **Form W-4**
http://www.irs.gov/pub/irs-pdf/fw4.pdf

19 241  **Form 4868: Application for Automatic Extension**
www.irs.gov/pub/irs-pdf/f4868.pdf

20 244  **"small businesses"**
junewalkeronline.com/blog/taxes/whats-a-small-business/

# INDEX